8/29/22

1. —

Doctrine and Theology in The United Methodist Church

DOCTRINE AND THEOLOGY IN THE UNITED METHODIST CHURCH

Edited by

Thomas A. Langford

KINGSWOOD BOOKS
An Imprint of Abingdon Press
Nashville, Tennessee

DOCTRINE AND THEOLOGY
IN THE UNITED METHODIST CHURCH

Copyright © 1991 by Abingdon Press

Library of Congress Cataloging-in-Publication Data

Doctrine and Theology in The United Methodist Church / edited by Thomas A. Langford
    p.   cm.
    Includes index.
    ISBN 0-687-11019-X (alk. paper)
    I. United Methodist Church (U.S.)—doctrines.   2. United Methodist Church (U.S.)—
Theology.   3. United Methodist Church (U.S.), Doctrinal Standards and our theological
task.   1. Langford, Thomas A.
BX8382.2. Z5D63 1990   230'.76—dc20   90-44914

99 00 01 02 03 04 — 10 9 8 7 6 5

Contents

Preface

The statement on "Doctrinal Standards and Our Theological Task" adopted by the 1988 General Conference of The United Methodist Church (and now included as Part II of the 1988 Book of Discipline) represents an important moment in the life of this church. The statement stands as a conciliar agreement on the doctrinal and theological self-understanding of United Methodism. As such it is both an important marker in the life of the denomination and a provocative impetus to further theological activity within the church. The fundamental beliefs of United Methodism have been set forth.

This statement challenges the church to ongoing theological activity. Because the disciplinary paragraphs are so full of content, because they describe our history and tradition, and because they set forth central themes about what United Methodists believe, they deserve close study within the denomination. Because no expression of the Christian faith is final, the statement calls for continuing consideration, reappraisal, and potential restatement.

The study of that document could help produce a new theological seriousness in United Methodism. It is a rare opportunity in our church to be at a moment when self-definition is taking place in such a conscious and intentional manner, and it is an unusual opportunity for a wide range of persons within the denomination to be engaged in such a study.

The materials gathered in this set of resources represent some of the background documents and new commentary on the 1988 statement and should enhance study of the disciplinary paragraphs. Two additional resources are essential: first, the 1972 Discipline, which contains the statement that represented the theological agreement of the newly formed United Methodist Church. That statement should be read with care to understand the background of the 1988 document, the second essential resource. The present statement is published in the 1988 Book of Discipline (and is available separately in reprint form); it is the primary document to which reference is made in this collection. Because these two statements are readily available they are not reproduced in this book.

The opportunity to study the new theological statement is significant for The United Methodist Church. We are challenged to study our doctrinal self-understanding and to engage in critical and creative theological reflection. There is, with this study, the possibility for spiritual and intellectual renewal and an invitation to venture in new ways as congregations and as a denomination. To encourage such possibility these resources have been gathered together.

Thomas A. Langford

Introduction

A WESLEYAN/METHODIST THEOLOGICAL TRADITION

by Thomas A. Langford[1]

In what sense is there a Wesleyan/Methodist theological tradition? What is our debt to John Wesley? What connections remain between our beginnings and the ongoing theological life of United Methodism? What debt is owed? What new developments represent and enrich this tradition? It is with these questions that we begin our study.

The Progenitor

John Wesley is the father of Methodism. He is the inaugurator of the revival movement which issued in international Methodism. He was also the theologian whose teachings underwrote the revival. Since we are concentrating on the Methodist theological tradition, let me comment on this statement. John Wesley was a theologian; this must be said clearly. Professor Gordon Rupp always wanted to say this, but say it softly. Wesley, he claimed, was not a "Doctor of the Church"; he was not a peer of Martin Luther, for instance, though he was suggestive, especially about the formation of Christian life. Professor Albert C. Outler has been stronger in statement. Wesley was a theologian and a significant one, especially if one recognized Wesley as a theologian for common people, a "folk theologian," who spoke clearly about complex issues and who conveyed the practical import of Christian doctrine. Professor Martin Schmidt speaks even more affirmatively of Wesley as a seminal theologian. Wesley's contribution to understanding the church as mission and his arrangement of priorities in constructive theology are taken to be of basic importance. Wesley was a theologian, this is clear. His stature and contribution as a theologian remain subject to various interpretations.

Whatever Wesley's standing in some pantheon of theological leaders of the Christian church, we are concentrating on his role as a theologian in the Methodist tradition and on the relation which this tradition has to Wesley. Both overt and tacit relationships are important so we shall be looking not only at acknowledged interdependencies but also at assumed and quietly accepted presuppositions. To do this, let us return to the question of the type of theologian John Wesley was and what sort of influence we should expect to find.

John Wesley was a practical theologian; his theology was "Practical Divinity." But what is practical theology as Wesley employed it? Practical divinity, for Wesley, treats theology as intrinsically related to life; conversely, theological themes cannot be separated out and interpreted independently as an intellectual enterprise. Practical divinity is intentionally transformative, it underwrites proclamation and the nurturing of Christian life; on the contrary, practical theology is neither a distanced reflection upon life nor an intellectual interpretation of life. Practical divinity is pragmatic in the sense that it operates on the conviction that knowledge is only gained through engagement; contrariwise, knowledge is not found through spectatorship as an abstract observer. Practical divinity holds text (biblical) and context (social and cultural) in tight tension; each requires the other for insight and interpretation. Conversely, practical theology never allows an ahistorical text or an independent social order to function as a matrix of interpretation. Practical divinity, as I see Wesley practicing it, is a mode of life-thought which is engaged in revival and reform, in confrontation and challenge, in service and sanctification. It could be no other.

Another critical characteristic must be noted: Wesley—in spite of his sometimes imperious nature and autocratic manner (strong leaders are seldom easy companions)— did not call for imitation. Rather, he consistently pointed beyond himself to that which was more important, namely Jesus Christ as Lord, the scriptures as the Word of God, and participation in the means of grace. Wesley intended that participants in his revival movement should say about him what Karl Barth said about John Calvin. "Of course I stand in the Reformed tradition, but I believe, as Calvin did, that there is only one Master in the church and in the world. Consequently, I try to be obedient to Christ and not to Calvin."[2]

We have claimed that John Wesley is a theologian and certainly a significant one for the Methodist tradition. But now we must ask: in what relation does he stand to that tradition? and in what relation does that tradition stand to him? What sort of theological tradition does a practical theologian set in motion and how may an ongoing tradition perpetuate such a practical character?

Tradition

For two decades the question of what constitutes a tradition has been a matter of debate among historians, literary critics and philosophers, as well as natural and social scientists. There is no present consensus; consequently I want to indicate how I shall use the term. Traditions (whether we are discussing chemistry, English literature, or Kantian philosophy) may not be neatly traced as flowing through sharply marked channels. Consequently, a tradition is a fluid, changing, malleable reality which is not static or set; tradition is a process, a shaping, forming ongoing strain of experience. A tradition is defined by communal themes, and the corporate character of a tradition is primary and persistent. This means that a tradition is a rich and complex set of relationships which can never be fully explicated but which conveys formative power through a corporate sphere.

To possess a name, to have common experiences, hymns, and mission is to have a tradition. Cannot one, however, have all of these things without any theology? On the surface it may seem so. But traditions are also shaped by convictions and beliefs which are indispensable ingredients in a larger whole. To say that there is a Wesleyan theological tradition is to recognize a common fountainhead and a reciprocal relation among the various aspects of Methodist life, thought, ritual, and action.

The Wesleyan tradition is not primarily theological, and this is a part of its character. But it is also theological, and this is a part of its distinctive character. The flow of the historical movement of Wesleyanism has stressed the wholeness of embodied values and bequeathed a particular set of historical specificities. To be in the Wesleyan tradition is to live, as Wesley did, at the intersection of multiple influences: Anglicanism, Protestantism, Roman Catholicism, early Christianity. It is also, as was Wesley, to be a part of post-Enlightenment western culture and to face the challenge of interpreting the Christian gospel to a secular age. More, to be in the Wesleyan tradition is to have been nurtured by rituals, styles of preaching, concern about social challenges, and establishment of friendships which make those in the Wesleyan tradition closer to one another—even with all of their obvious differences—than they are to any other confessional family.

Tradition should be recognized as an ongoing process which is always interrelating with its particular environment in such a manner that new configurations are formed. John Wesley has been responded to but not slavishly followed. Each historically specific time in the continuum of the tradition possesses its own integrity of character, both in reference to its originative points and as evident in its particular interpretations. So, for instance, early nineteenth century Methodism had its own setting and character. We ask of that period (and of any period) not, how did it mimic its past? or how is it a precursor of our own era? Rather, we ask, how were those Methodists, in their variety of ways, attempting to be faithful to their inheritance and to their own situation?

Martin Heidegger speaks of the worse traditions as those which attempt to restrict the development from the past by overexplicit rules and rigidly controlling tactics. A cultural heritage is not a static accumulation of anachronisms, but is a dynamic process whereby what is handed down and preserved is necessarily reinterpreted in light of the interests and concerns of the present. Hans-Georg Gadamer has added the insistence that tradition is never complete; it is ongoing, newly being formed and forming, provocative not conclusive, and that each new interpretation constitutes a fresh recreation of a tradition.

Traditioning

The relation of a founder to a living tradition is dialogical. It is an ongoing conversation, argument, interplay of a community with its received history and its struggle with that inheritance. There is a persistent point of reference—John Wesley for Methodism—with whom succeeding generations are interactive. A tradition supplies language, symbols, rituals, tasks, sensibilities, friends, and antagonists. A religious tradition is a received way of viewing and living in the world. A way which, at its best, invites both conformity and critique.

Methodism is unusually difficult to identify as a tradition because it has changed rapidly and it remains open to further change. Methodism lives its continuities through tacit and affective modalities more basically than through rational construction or explicit doctrinal formulations. The difficulties this presents for reconstruction does not mean that Methodism possesses no tradition; rather, it points to the type of tradition Methodism represents.

The traditioning context of Wesleyan theology is the historical process of Methodist bodies as they have worshipped and lived and taught, as they have developed institutions, assumed missional tasks, found common symbols, rituals, and styles of life. As a part, and only as a part, of this total complex can Wesleyan theology be adequately appreciated. John Wesley projected these possibilities. He has not controlled the development. He has functioned as a point of reference rather than as an establisher of structural boundaries.

Methodism has a distinctive character. Interpretation is related to action; intellectual love of God is intrinsically bound to service of God; understanding, interpretation, and praxis are inextricably interfaced. Thought, affection, and action are inseparably bound together. Methodist theology is radically historical; that is, it is set within specific historical contexts and is affected by these settings. Consequently, we look to John Wesley and our ancestors not to understand them better than they understood themselves, but to understand them differently. The cultivation of a tradition continually opens up new possibilities of meaning.

Let me illustrate this from one of the theological expressions of our Methodist tradition. In the "Advertisement" to his *Theological Institutes*, Richard Watson notes, "It is hoped also that it may supply the *desideratum* of a Body of Divinity, adapted to the present state of theological literature, neither Calvinistic on the one hand, nor Pelagian on the other." The point is, Watson is especially sensitive to his own historic situation and writes his theology—which he places in a Wesleyan position—in relation to that situation.

What is Watson's situation? It is revealed in his conviction that it is necessary to begin his theological construction with a statement on the evidences of the Divine authority of Holy Scripture, and to open that discussion with the "presumptive evidence" of direct revelation from God, and initiate that discussion with affirmation of human moral agency. Each of these steps is intentionally made, each reflects Watson's understanding of himself as being in the Wesleyan tradition, each is related to his specific historic setting. It is clear, however, that Watson accepts an independent freedom. He seldom quotes Wesley and never uses Wesley's position to close an argument. Yet his own work is built against a Wesleyan background. He authors a biography of Wesley, he actively participates in the work of the church, he dedicates *Theological Institutes* to Jabez Bunting. Watson is a Methodist theologian not in a creedal sense but through his participation in the Methodist ethos. That ethos helps shape the themes, the approach, and the emphases of his constructive effort. The theological tradition does not dictate either the exact form or content which must be utilized. Watson's character as a Wesleyan theologian is prototypical of this tradition.

One can get a sense of Watson's contextual awareness through those he quotes both positively and negatively. He is contending with and against the Deists (the "Theists") and he is contending for biblical authority, for direct relation of God with creatures, and for moral responsibility. Religious sensibility and moral conscience are assumed by all parties. The debated questions are God's direct revelation (as opposed to indirect, natural revelation) and the biblical transmission of that revelation. This was Watson's setting, differently shaped from Wesley's and different from succeeding generations.

Illustrations of this character of the tradition could continue. Indeed developments in North American Episcopal Methodism from D. D. Whedon through Borden Parker Bowne to Albert C. Knudson to Umphrey Lee to Harris Franklin Rall represent theological interpretations which, while in the Wesleyan tradition, are independent of Wesley and reflect their inheritance through creative reinterpretation. Through this era and through these people the relation of the theological tradition with Wesley became more tenuous, or, at least, the reading of Wesley was done through eyes firmly set by the contemporary situation.

In the 1940s a new reading of Wesley developed, in part occasioned by the general search for theological roots in Protestantism (such as in neo-Calvinism and neo-Lutheranism) and in part by a desire to return to primary texts for interpretation. George C. Cell was a background figure to this movement (*The Rediscovery of John Wesley*, 1935, which was a reassertion of Calvinist elements in Wesley's thought), but it came to fruition in the publication of William R. Cannon's *The Theology of John Wesley* and Harald Lindström's *John Wesley and Sanctification*, both published in 1946. Other scholars such as David C. Shipley, Albert C. Outler, and Robert E. Cushman came along at that time to reinforce the fresh reading of Wesley, with the particular outcome being the publication of a definitive edition of John Wesley's works.

In my book, *Practical Divinity: Theology in the Wesleyan Tradition*, I draw a synoptic conclusion about theological emphases in the Wesleyan tradition. I placed the chief stress upon the theme of grace.

> Around this point—the grace of God in Jesus Christ—several attendant commitments form a tight nexus: biblical witness to Jesus Christ, vital experience of God in Christ as Savior and Sanctifier, commitment to human freedom and ethical discipleship, and the shaping of church life around missional responsibility. Together these themes constitute the nucleus of the Wesleyan tradition, and around these determinate marks of character the more extended life of the tradition has taken shape and has been contoured into its distinctive forms.[3]

This synopsis represents an effort to denote continuity. If there are no cohering points of reference then there is no tradition. I believe the characteristics of grace listed above are present in Methodism in various modes of expression. And these sinews of continuity need to be emphasized. But perhaps our images of these emphases need new conceptualization. I do not think that we can look beneath, within, or above for abiding essences, in the midst of change. Rather, we should think of a continuum with various overlaps, of extended and multi-dynamic interchanges, and of change which continues by reordering what has been received. Methodism, as other traditions, represents a process; it is constituted by those whom we read, with whom we worship, and from whom we take our inspiration, as well as by those with and about whom we argue. Tradition is not mimicry and it is not idolatry; to be in a tradition is to possess a context out of which we think and act, feel and respond.

What we have shown is the difficulty of explicitly denoting the inheritance from our founder or the sharp boundaries of a tradition. We have argued for a continuum of overlaps and historical change which connects at diverse times and in various ways different intellectual content and themes, different symbols and sensitivities, different rituals and activities. The image is complex and the identifying of an historical stream cannot be easily achieved. But to stop here is not satisfactory. To argue that one cannot easily identify a particular stream is not to say that there is no stream. To argue difficulty is not to argue impossibility. So now we come to the point: how can we speak of a Wesleyan tradition in theology that is vitally connected to John Wesley?

Our answer draws together some of our previous comments. First, we as a tradition are derived from a dominant source. John Wesley stands as the inaugurator of this tradition. Second, Wesley bequeathed a spirit, he engendered an ethos which has been evident in his progeny. Third, Methodist theology must be viewed as a part of total Methodist life. In the development (with much change) from a common source of worship and mission, of hymns and service, of struggle over changing spirituality, of arguments over inheritance, etc., there is a part of the total character of this movement which is theological. Fourth, the theology of Methodism has undergone great alteration, yet there continue themes and issues from Wesley which persist. Hence, variations on themes of grace are continually present.

Fifth, Methodist theology is not insular. To be Methodist is to be open to and responsive to other theological traditions, and to be shaped by interaction with those traditions. Indeed, Methodism which is spread thinly around the world tends to take on the coloration of dominant religious traditions in particular settings. This ecumenical interaction is characteristic even though it comes in multiple guises. Finally, the Methodist tradition with its theological ligament has not ended. Biblical, historical and theological work continues. There are bilateral conversations, Oxford Institutes of Methodist Theological Studies, reconsiderations of doctrinal statements at World Methodist Councils and for disciplinary inclusion (among United Methodists), a strong theological commission in Europe, and debate as to the relevance of John Wesley and of nineteenth century developments. What Wesley inaugurated continues.

Traditions never come nicely packaged. Rather, the dynamic of historical change requires continually fresh interpretation and new creation of a movement's internal history. Methodists are advantaged by having a tradition which recognizes itself as open and freshly formative.

The theological statements of 1972 and 1988 are a part of this tradition. These statements are attentive both to their inheritance and to their own situation. Study of these documents and commentary upon them draws one into the ongoing life of this tradition and propels the tradition forward. It is to this engagement that these selections stand as an invitation.

SECTION I

The 1972 Disciplinary Statement

Introduction

In 1968 The United Methodist Church was formed. At the uniting General Conference, a study commission was formed to consider the problem represented by the presence of two separate statements of doctrinal standards, the "Articles of Religion" of the former Methodist Church and the "Confession of Faith" of the Evangelical United Brethren Church. Professor Albert C. Outler chaired the commission and brought their report to the 1972 General Conference. Their report became Part II in the 1972 Book of Discipline of The United Methodist Church. The committee determined that both previous statements of doctrinal standards could remain; what the church really needed was an additional statement that explained The United Methodist Church's doctrinal stance and expressed its mode of being theological. The first article in this section is the introduction of that report to the General Conference.

The next four articles are responses to the 1972 disciplinary statement. Frederick Herzog is ordained in the United Church of Christ and has contributed to United Methodist theology through active interest and teaching in the United Methodist-related Divinity School of Duke University. Schubert M. Ogden and Leroy T. Howe are United Methodist theologians at Perkins School of Theology, Southern Methodist University, and have been contributors to ecumenical theology as well as to United Methodist theological work. Robert E. Cushman has long been a leader among United Methodist theologians and brings his perspective to bear upon the statement.

One of the major innovations of the 1972 statement was the outlining of the "quadrilateral"—that is, the fourfold frame of reference: Scripture, tradition, experience, and reason—and making it an important part of United Methodist theological discussion. Because of the functional significance of the fourfold scheme, the article by Albert C. Outler is included to explain his view of the source and use of this concept.

These articles are understood as commentary upon the statement found in Part II of the 1972 Book of Discipline. The statement itself should be used as the primary source for understanding these commentaries.

Chapter 1

INTRODUCTION TO THE REPORT OF THE 1968–72 THEOLOGICAL STUDY COMMISSION

Albert C. Outler[1]

The most obvious feature of this Report is what it is not. It is not a new creed, nor a new set of Articles of Religion, nor a Confession of Faith, nor a new set of General Rules. The old ones are still retained, in the middle of our text, in their original versions. This is by design, of course—for the next most obvious thing about the Report is that it is not a simple reaffirmation of the old Part II, either. The old Articles, and Confession and Rules have been set in a new context of interpretation, and this means a decisive change in their role in the theological enterprise in The United Methodist Church.

Now this calls for an explanation and any such explanation would have to begin with a reference to our mandate from the General Conference of 1968:

> ... to bring to the General Conference of 1972 a progress report concerning "Doctrine and Doctrinal Standards" in The United Methodist Church. If the Commission deems it advisable [said that mandate] it may undertake the preparation of a contemporary formulation of doctrine and belief, in supplementation to all antecedent formulations. ...[2]

To many in that Conference and throughout the church, this meant a new "creed," or something like that. In the beginning, we were sometimes referred to as "the new Creedal Commission." And, of course, we did consider that possibility: a new creed, a new confession of faith, a new doctrinal summary and affirmation. In fact, one of the general work-assignments for the Commission as a whole was the production of experimental forms of creeds and liturgical affirmation and doctrinal summary—not one but many—and this turned up three or four texts of truly high quality that deserve to be published and used throughout the church.

We are certainly, therefore, not against creed-making. Our concern however is not with a single creed but with the guidelines that should be followed in any given case of creed-making and the claims that any given creed or summary might be able to make to have authority in The United Methodist Church or among United Methodist people. But one of the earliest decisions that emerged in our exploratory discussions was that a single creed, displacing the two that we have now, whatever its form or quality that claimed any sort of official monopoly in the church, would not really serve the cause of theological renewal, or for that matter, of theological clarity.

Doctrinal confusion cannot be overcome by official dogmatic pronouncement. There is something profoundly self-deceiving in the assumption that valid authority in disputed questions can ever flow from the majority vote in the General Conferences. Such majorities weaken rather than strengthen a church's real authority. A better way, we came to realize, was to strike for a new understanding of the problems of the norms and the normative in theology and ethics and then to seek for a clearer vision of our doctrinal heritage as a resource for solving these problems of norms and the normative. This is not a cop out. It is instead the acknowledgement of three decisive factors affecting our current situation in The United Methodist Church and in the Christian world everywhere. . . .

Somewhere in The United Methodist Church there is somebody urging every kind of theology still alive and not a few that are dead, but your commission came to realize that this apparent bedlam is, at least in part, the perversion of an older, profounder principle of positive importance, that is to say, of doctrinal pluralism, doctrinal diversity-in-Christological-unity. Far from being a license to doctrinal recklessness or indifferentism, the Wesleyan principle of pluralism holds in dynamic balance both the biblical focus of all Christian doctrine and also the responsible freedom that all Christians must have in their theological reflections and public teaching.

"We Methodists think and let think," and there was never any doubt for [Wesley that] the taproot of Christianity was the Scriptural mystery of God in Christ and not much else, really. It is simply a fact that United Methodist doctrinal standards have always had a pluralistic cast to them. Wesley's *Sermons* and *Notes* and behind them the Book of Common Prayer, the Anglican Homilies and Articles, and the Evangelical and United Brethren Articles and Confessions never were understood as merely judicial statutes. Rather, they were so many varied witnesses to the truth of Scripture and then to the negative limits of allowable public teaching. What then happened of course, was that all too many

Methodists found it all too easy to slide off the high plane of doctrinal pluralism as a positive virtue into the slough of doctrinal indifferentism and chaos.

In my own judgment, the most important single achievement of this report by its intention at least, is our attempted reversal of this trend toward indifferentism, by pointing, especially in Part III, to the central core of common Christian teaching that we share with other Christians, and yet also to our own distinctive guidelines for responsible theologizing in the Wesley, Albright, Otterbein tradition. How well we have succeeded is, of course, for this Conference and the wider theological forum outside this church to judge.

In any case, to have come to you with a doctrinal creed or summary that would have pretended to monopolize the doctrinal enterprise would have been profoundly unwise, and misleading to boot! Moreover in the second place, we were very soon and very deeply impressed by the vitality and the relevance of the various new protestant theologies, protesting theologies, emerging in this epoch of radical change: "black theology," "women's liberation theology," "third-world theology," etc.

While rejecting their exclusivistic claims—as we have also rejected all doctrinal monopolies, on principle—we are still very eager for all Christians to hear what the Spirit is saying to the churches through them: their protests against injustice and indignity to any of God's children, their protests for the paramount rights of the human person at every level of interpersonal and social relationships, regardless of race, sex, nationality, or life-style.

We are also prepared to take seriously and urge you to take seriously all the various emergent theological viewpoints that are bidding for dominance, or at least a hearing, nowadays: "process theology," "development theology," "linguistic analysis," "existentialism," the "new transcendentalisms" of various sorts—as well as the veritable kaleidoscope of special-interest theologies of "hope," "ecology," (and, over on the other side, the new "pentecostalisms," the "Jesus Movement," "the Children of God," etc.).

Taken all together, these various "protestant" and "special-interest" theologies point to the rich diversity that the Christian mind can, and ought to, make room for. But by the very same token, they also suggest that the official sponsorship of any one of these theologies by The United Methodist Church, to the derogation of any of the others, would be wildly imprudent in practice and wrong in principle. Besides, we must never forget that the question of doctrinal standards in The United Methodist Church is closely related to our long-standing commitment to the larger cause of Christian unity.

The prime imperative in all serious ecumenical dialogue is that each tradition be prepared to interpret itself to all the others, honestly and openly, without triumphalism or apology, without misleading claims and fruitless polemics. For United Methodists this plainly means, not only to confess, but to expose our doctrinal pluralism. Our concern for pluralism as a positive theological virtue has been reinforced by a third distinctive feature of our epoch and this may be the most important one of all: the rise and spread of what John Courtney Murray (and Wilhelm Dilthey before him) spoke of as "the historical consciousness," by contrast with the older "classical consciousness" that dominated the Christian understanding of doctrine and dogma since Constantine.

In the European State Churches, and even in America up to our own time, there has been a tendency to regard creeds and confessions much in the same way that the secular states construe their legislative statutes: that is, as juridical enactments, enforceable by punitive sanctions against all violators, or else let simply slide into the oblivion of the dead letter, which in fact happens to our Articles in our Discipline. But whereas positive law has gone on changing, dogmatic formularies tend to resist change—and in one sense rightly so, since Christian truth, if it ever could be fully stated in propositional form, would then be the creed to end all creeds, the doctrine to end all doctrinal formulations and only have to be repeated thereafter till people understood it properly.

In the past, the appearance of new creeds has always meant displacement of the last one you had with the normal implication that the last one had some sort of insufficiency (or maybe error!). But once you confess the past creed had an error, that your forefathers and some others could not see . . . what may be lurking in our creed that our children may see? This juridical mindset was as typical of "classical Protestantism" as of Roman Catholicism up till Vatican II.

Now, our emerging historical consciousness that all of us in this room share, one way or another, has altered this static view of dogma beyond all recognition and control. Nowadays we ask, as if by instinct, about the historical context of any document or pronouncement.

This sense of context and perspective has made modern history possible, and modern biblical study, too, as one of its byproducts. It allows us to appreciate the ancient creeds and confessions afresh and then to repossess their living truth in the light of radically new experience. This holds true for the Apostle's Creed, the Augsburg Confession, the Westminster Catechism. It holds for Wesley's *Sermons*. It holds for his *Notes*, and especially it holds for our Articles and Confession.

Time was when these landmark documents were "contemporary" and the interesting thing is that the most "contemporary" thing about them when they were first formulated is the things that are now most clearly "dated" about them in our own eyes. But each one of them also enshrines perennial Christian truth; and in that sense they are still "contemporary"! Old articles don't have to be discarded. They don't have to be reiterated, either. Thus, we have felt ourselves quite free to retain our historical landmarks without embarrassment or apology. But, then, quite deliberately, to set them in a new twin perspective of inter- pretation—of our heritage, on the one hand, and that's part one, and our contemporary crisis on the other. And that's what part two is talking about.

We hope that you have noticed that we have tried to clarify the contextual relationships between the Articles, the Confession, and Wes- ley's *Sermons* and *Notes* and *Rules*—in order to clarify the reference in the First Restrictive Rule about "our present existing and established standards of doctrines." We have not altered these standards, as such, but we have proposed a genuinely new principle for doctrinal self-un- derstanding in The United Methodist Church. Thus, we have tried to reaffirm our share in the Christian tradition, as a whole, even as we have also tried to accent, once again, the distinctive Wesleyan guidelines (Scripture, tradition, experience, reason); and it is these guidelines that we propose to you as our best safeguard against doctrinal indifferentism!

Now, Mr. Chairman, we would not wish to claim too much for this report. It bears the blemishes of haste and the inelegancies of committee- English. There is at least one misspelling that I apologize for, and one split infinitive that proves that the Committee got the best of the Chair- man more than once. It is, as some of you say, "too long." To this, one might respond, without any disrespect and with all-loving friendship, that in a Discipline that has 268 pages devoted to "Administrative Order" and 53 pages to "Property," less than 40 pages for "Doctrinal Statements and the General Rules" is not wildly disproportionate, (applause) espe- cially when you look at our early Doctrines, where they, so to say, had gotten the "hang of it."

If this Report could be put to fruitful use in promoting theological reflection amongst United Methodists and if it could also serve the urgent cause of helping our theological identity in the eyes of other Christians, the extra print and paper would be as well justified as most of the wood pulp we use up daily.

And yet, for all its faults, there are three bold claims I make for the report, without any personal immodesty or misgiving. The first is that it is a truly corporate product of this Commission as a whole—an un- stinted, cumulative, cooperative effort by a wonderfully representative (which is also "hard-headed" and difficult) group of United Methodists, all working on marginal time and within a very frugal budget! . . .

Now, my second claim is that minimally, at least, the report faithfully represents the best in the traditions of the Wesleys, of Albright, and Otterbein, not by replication but by re-presentation and re-interpretation. As such, it is offered as a useful guide for those who wish to repossess those traditions and to renew them for further service in Christian mission. This is crucially important if The United Methodist Church is to have any sustainable revival of the Gospel in a contemporary version of John Wesley's catholic spirit.

My third claim is that, however crudely, this report lays the foundations for the still further development of a stable theory of doctrinal interpretation in The United Methodist Church. It is offered less as a legislative statute than as an act of encouragement and enablement. We have tried to open the way for the widest possible participation of United Methodists in the mutual task of the teaching church. Instead of presuming to tell our people what to think, theologically, we have tried to offer basic guidance as to how we may all do theology together, faithful to our rich and yet very diverse heritage, and yet also relevant to our present ideological confusion. If it is adopted and taken seriously enough, which would also mean critically enough, it could quite conceivably become something of a landmark in itself. It could also, of course, serve this Conference and the church to a barely stifled yawn and go down as yet another of our high-minded but largely wasted efforts. Our fears go one way; our hopes and prayers go the other. . . .

Chapter 2

United Methodism in Agony

Frederick Herzog[1]

> You will work for them but not with them. Your heart will bleed for them but not your head or your hands. You will be their advocate but not their friend. You will sponsor them and their causes, but their cause is not your cause anymore because you are middle class.[2]

In "Doctrine and Doctrinal Statements" in Part II of the Book of Discipline (1972), occasional reference is made to agony, "the world's agonies"[3] or "the agonies of history."[4] Could it be that besides the agonies of the world and of history there are also the agonies of the church? There is need to raise this question in the present struggles of Methodism. Otherwise the church might seem an isle of bliss in an ocean of turmoil. Discussion of the doctrinal statements affords an opportunity to focus on United Methodism as a "microcosm" of the woes of American Protestantism today. Here we might be able to discern what is going on in a large segment of American Protestantism as a whole. Thus the question: United Methodism in agony? We need to zero in on at least three concerns. On the one hand, there is the attempt to revive the doctrinal mandate of the church.[5] On the other hand, there is the struggle to see the church as agent of liberation.[6] And finally, there is the lonely battle of the black community[7] and other minorities to come to grips with the mandate of the separate constituencies. It is difficult to see how these three concerns are *effectively related*. If not anything else, the obvious compartmentalization of the Christian witness makes for agony.

Back to God and Adam Smith?

Most theologians by now have realized that a great shift in perspective has taken place from the sixties to the seventies in this country. No one as yet has been able to articulate fully all the implications of the shift. What is clear to all is that social concerns have given way to more religious efforts. "Those who talk about adventure or change and those who take actions designed to bring about drastic change, have largely if momentarily disappeared."[8] Some hope that the lessons of the sixties have not been lost on us and that the shift is not an indication of a "return to God and Adam Smith."[9] But the stark facts are that in some ways most people in the sixties were not where most of the activist theologians were. And in the seventies they are even less there:

> Equality is . . . an expensive luxury for that white man who knows that bringing blacks up to his status in the factory assembly line may mean a threat to his own job, or that moving the Chicano into his neighborhood may downgrade property values there. So he will be resentful of people who use the resources of his religious group to jostle the system.[10]

Problems appear when theological or pastoral work does not take into account the peculiarities determinative of our situation. One cannot say that what the average person wants is strong religious certainty. In fact, there is just the opposite tendency toward what Martin E. Marty calls "boundarylessness,"[11] especially among young people. And as far as sheer human existence is concerned, "What the average man wants . . . is security."[12] It is a far cry from liberation and social change. It may be that what the churches are still offering are wares no one really wants. In any case, a denominational programming in which doctrinal certainty, ethical challenge, and minority critique are offered *separately* contributes to agony in the church. The holistic grasp of the present Christian task goes begging.

Immunized Doctrine

On first sight, reading Part II seems to bring together the different pieces rather well, also taking into account the struggles of the minority groups:

> Of crucial current importance is the surfacing of new theological emphases focusing on the struggle for human liberation and fulfillment. Notable among them are black theology, female liberation theology, political and ethnic theologies, third-world theology, and theologies of human rights. . . . They reflect the consequences of tragic victimization and deep natural yearnings for human fulfillment. . . . Since these aspirations are inherent elements in God's original design for his highest creation, we cannot resent or deny the positive objectives these theologies espouse nor withhold support from their practical implementation. Indeed The United Methodist Church encourages such developments so long as they are congruent with the gospel and its contemporary application. However, no special-interest theology can be allowed to set itself in invidious judgment

over against any or all of the others, or claim exemption from being critically assessed in the general theological forum.[13]

As one ponders the implication of these sentences a question arises. Is there such a thing in the Christian community as special-interest theology? The acknowledgement of new developments in theology is admirable. But can we regard them as simply *outside* the mainstream (the general theological forum), so that we would have done our job after having "critically assessed" them? Could it not be that the so-called special-interest theologies are actually *common*-interest theologies, so that we would rather need to ask in what way they are also critically *addressed* to us? What if in the crucible of the special-interest theologies also the true interest of theology itself were *re*-born? "From our response in faith to the wondrous mystery of God's love in Jesus Christ as recorded in Scripture, all valid Christian doctrine is born."[14] What if today God's love were communicated in a new form in the special-interest theologies, so that all valid Christian doctrine would need to be *re*-born? "We hold common faith in the mystery of salvation in and through Jesus Christ."[15] What if today the very phrase "the mystery of salvation" would no longer communicate the real power of God's love? "Salvation" might no longer encompass what crucially needs to be said about the Gospel today. "At the heart of the gospel of salvation is God's self-presentation in Jesus of Nazareth."[16] Could it not be that "the gospel of salvation" today is appropriated more in terms of a *mystery religion*, a religious cult primarily dealing in soul salvation?[17]

> By grace we mean God's loving action in human existence through the ever-present agency of the Holy Spirit. Grace, so understood, is the spiritual climate and environment surrounding all human life at all times and in all places. In Christian experience, it is self-conscious and personal.[18]

What if grace were more concrete, the new corporate selfhood of man *in the person of Jesus Christ*, wrenching us free from privatism and atomistic selfhood for solidarity with the outcast and downtrodden? "The Word became flesh . . . full of grace" (John. 1:14). Jesus Christ *is* grace. He is not just the mediator of a climate of grace. As the true man, the new humanity, he is grace. And the question he confronts us with is in what sense we will find a new selfhood in him, i.e., in what way grace will become constitutive of our selfhood. Grace in him is much more than "the spiritual climate and environment surrounding all human life." Grace in him as corporate selfhood liberates us from the contrast between special interest and common interest, especially from the special interest we have in determining "the general theological forum."[19] "The theological substance of [common Christian history] begins with the biblical witness to God's reality as Creator and his gracious self-involvement in the dramas of history."[20]

Need not the insight of God's gracious self-involvement in the dramas of history permeate especially our grasp of God's involvement in the life of Jesus of Nazareth? He was more than the "mystery of salvation" in the broad sense in which this phrase is being used. He brought a new manhood through his identification with the lost. It is this particular drama of history that needs careful retelling lest Christian doctrine becomes immunized, i.e., lest the pain and hurt of God's involvement in this history get lost, and we no longer see the *common* interest in this hurt and the hurts of the Christian brotherhood as well. We can by theologizing so immunize Jesus Christ that the "tragic victimization" which has produced several theologies apart from "the current mainstream options"[21] is seen primarily as object for critical assessment and not as subject-agent for making all theology begin with tragic victimization of which God's grace in the Cross of Christ is the center.

Activist Ethics?

> There will be no peace with justice unless *liberation* is gained by those who have been manipulated and victimized by interests that have been willing to profit from the continued deprivation of the weak and powerless. But, the oppressor needs to be liberated as truly as the oppressed. Liberation affects the whole man. It is salvation; it is humanization. It is social, economic, political and spiritual.[22]

In *The Bishops' Call for Peace and the Self-Development of Peoples* we find several of the emphases that we seem to be missing in the statement on "Our Theological Task" in Part II (pp. 29–42). The more one ponders the *Bishops' Call*, the more one regrets that the two statements could not have been written somewhat more in concert. For they could have fructified each other. It is *in the actual process of liberation* that one learns the need for utmost doctrinal clarity: one needs Jesus Christ as grace. The *Bishops' Call* speaks of the need for "literal *conversion* of persons; of attitudes and values."[23] If we read these words in the light of Part II, it is nowhere clear that conversion for liberation is through identification with the new corporate selfhood of Christ. It all seems more like reorientation *within* our own selfhood. Radical conversion *to* a completely new selfhood— where is it mentioned? So the *Bishops' Call* easily gives the impression of an invitation to further activism, however little intended. That is, it suggests activity without much doctrinal underpinning. It is at this point that we need to come clean theologically in our day. New radical Christological reflection will help us here. *The kind of men we are today* proves *us* unable to carry out the hopes and expectations expressed in the *Bishops' Call. We* simply are *not ready for it.* That is, we have a fairly smoothly running society of competition. By no stretch of the imagination could it be called a brotherly society. We are educated to act towards each other not as brothers, but as atomistic individuals pitted against each other. The other is always first the competitor, not the friend—as far as the principle of the thing is concerned. However, this is never explicitly acknowledged as a hermeneutical presupposition of church and theology or even understood.

Part II of the 1972 Book of Discipline views the principle of the interlocking of doctrine and ethics quite adequately: "The purpose of Christian theologizing is to aid people who seek understanding of their faith . . . infusion of that faith in life and work, and courageous ministries in support of justice and love."[24] Or, in different words: "United Methodists have stressed that personal salvation leads always to involvement in Christian mission in the world. Thus we assert that personal religion, evangelical witness, and Christian social action are reciprocal and mutually reinforcing."[25] It is also fully understood that this mission hinges on a transformation called forth by Jesus Christ: "Those who even now find in him their clue to God's redeeming love also find their hearts and wills transformed."[26] This understanding is later amplified:

> We hold that a decisive change in the human heart can and does occur under the promptings of grace and the guidance of the Holy Spirit. Such a change may be sudden, dramatic, gradual, cumulative. Always it is a new beginning in a process. Christian experience as personal transformation expresses itself in many different thought-forms and life-styles. All of these have a common feature: faith working by love.[27]

But, then, one begins to wonder whether or not a particular thought-form or life-style might be called for today. Part II offers direction in this regard when it declares:

> Christian experience is not only deeply private and inward; it is also corporate and active. The Bible knows nothing of solitary religion. God's gift of liberating love must be shared if it is to survive. The range of reconciliation must continually be widened to embrace the world and all who are alienated and who suffer. "Christian experience" carries with it the imperative of ministries of liberation and healing in the world.[28]

Here the problem emerges, however, how one is to put all this together, so that personal religion, evangelical witness, and Christian social action really *are* mutually reinforcing.

The agony of United Methodism seems to lie exactly as this point. There is the really exciting challenge to action in the *Bishops' Call.* But on what doctrinal grounds does it arise? And there is Part II on doctrine and doctrinal statements. Yet what action will it produce? There seems a Christological vacuum in it all. Today it is not just a matter of saying that Christian experience is not only private and inward, but also corporate and active. Our dilemmas today cry out for clarifying in greater detail what this means as "new life in Christ."[29] For in Christ we find that there is *no* principally "private" Christian experience whatsoever, nothing "deeply private." At stake is how we understand the constitution of Christian selfhood. In Christ all men are one. His selfhood is corporate. The prisoner is part of his selfhood, the outcast, the hungry, the naked, the lost (Mt. 25:31–46). When the *Bishops' Call* speaks of the conversion of persons this needs to be taken into account. For much preaching and teaching Christ today is still done on the model of the private and the corporate juxtaposed, forgetting that in Christ there is no private self. So first a man is still converted "privately." And only then is he supposed to act corporately. But is conversion to Christ ever anything less than conversion to the corporate Christ? "God's gift of liberating love *must* continually be widened?" Why *must*? If Jesus Christ is grace in corporate selfhood, liberating love is already being shared, the circle of reconciliation is already being widened. If this is not kept in mind the call to action can easily issue in sheer activism, spurts of activity that do not change much in society, since the person who acts in this mood is not really *in* his action, but somewhere else, i.e., in his private shell. When the chips are really down it is difficult to see how the "ministries of liberation" are really possible in this kind of setup.

Ideology Critique?

Both in Part II and the *Bishops' Call*, the core difficulty is that neither document asks very radically who the man is who is supposed to do the liberating. What does "the imperative to engage in ministries of liberation" really mean? The *Bishops' Call* realizes that "the oppressor needs to be liberated as truly as the oppressed."[30] But who is the oppressor? What if all the good people called Methodists—and the rest of us church people as well—were themselves the oppressors? What does this language—and I am sure it was not lightly used—really mean? C. Eric Lincoln's words to the black United Methodists assembled at Atlanta, December 12, 1973, cited at the beginning of this essay, bear repeating.[31] It is not our business as whites to interfere with black business. The blacks will have to settle that one for themselves, at least for the time being. But one observation might be in order: if all this is true of black

31

Methodists how much more might it be true of white Methodists! There is no easy way out of the dilemma.

One thing is for sure: we do not very carefully examine the inter-locking of our economic and our Christian commitments, if at all. The point has to be made loud and clear that probably most of us Americans are primarily economic animals and Christians only in a subsidiary way. As an economic animal, man will not voluntarily surrender his power advantage to the oppressed. He will fight tooth and nail to keep it. There can be no question that between Christ's corporate self and the American economic self a head-on collision takes place, once the question of liberation arises. So we need to examine the relationship between money and Christianity, economics and faith—as much as the relationship be-tween personal religion and society. There is simply the fact of the amalgam between religion and striving for pecuniary success, religion "setting the final seal of approval on pecuniary success."[32] Max Weber suggested that the Protestant work ethic looked upon the acquisitive impulse as willed by God, quoting John Wesley as august example: "We ought not to prevent people from being diligent and frugal, we must exhort all Christians to gain all they can, and save all they can; that is, in effect to grow rich."[33]

Today we face the consequences of this kind of theologizing in the black/white confrontation. Is it entirely out of order to wonder whether the implications of using the language of liberation and appealing to the imperative of ministries of liberation are fully understood? *Does The United Methodist Church realize the sacrifices that kind of talk implies?* The frightening aspect of both documents, Part II and the *Bishops' Call*, is the seemingly self-confident posture that nothing could be wrong at least in principle with the Methodist faith-stance itself. That is, it couldn't pos-sibly be an ideology, a legitimation of secular culture. I myself do not see how the Methodist church—as any other large American denomina-tion—in its present state could possibly engage in ministries of liberation to the world unless its own economic stance were changed. That is, I fear that all doctrine today which is not explicitly also a critique of the present economic system *eo ipso* also becomes a justification of the system, and opium for the people.

What is religion? Worship, yes. But it is first of all in our society the legitimation of our way of life, the ideological underpinning sanctioning everything we do economically and politically (to wit, the flag in many of our churches). It belongs to the agony of present-day Protestantism that this insight breaks through only at the boundary of the painful confrontation between the races and in the clash between the majority and the minorities. Christ can become so imprisoned in doctrine that he cannot break through as liberator. In the present state of affairs, he remains the Savior mainly of the soul. Ministries of liberation by the church as a whole are impossible today. It's truly "Mission Impossible." The oppressor himself needs to be liberated. In the church, that means first of all theology and the theologian.

Common-Interest Theology?

I doubt that it is possible to indicate within a brief conspectus how one might get beyond the agony. The first step probably is to realize that there is agony at all. That might lead one to attempt to merge the special-interest theologies and the mainstream. "The theological spectrum in The United Methodist Church ranges over all the current mainstream options and a variety of special-interest theologies as well."[34] It is exactly this kind of compartmentalization that keeps us from tackling the Christological vacuum. What is more, has no one noticed what kind of capitalist language one is using when one speaks of "special interest?" The fact of special-interest theologies is not a sign of order in the church, but of disorder. There is no reason why we should congratulate ourselves upon the division between the mainstream and the special-interest theologies as a sign of healthy pluralism. Did not St. Paul say, "If one member suffers, all suffer together" (I Cor. 12:26)? As long as the special-interest theologies cannot transform the mainstream because they are dammed off from it, and the mainstream does not change its course in a radical metanoia, we'll remain in a fix. Does not our predicament today call for hard work on a common-interest theology, a theology of the Christian "common-wealth," wealth here being God's very own treasures? All this does not mean that the minorities again have to bend to our will, but that finally we find solidarity with them.

My query arises at the point where I am completely uncertain as to whether or not so-called special-interest theologies play any formative role in Methodist doctrine. From the formulations of the documents before us it seems not. In the *Leaders' Guide* these theologies appear as worthwhile mentioning only near the end of the six suggested instruction sessions. I am not prepared to argue that the tail should wag the dog. But I do believe that these theologies belong much more organically to the dog than the document allows. The document suggests asking only in what way special-interest theologies incorporate "the values of the common Christian heritage."[35] It does not intimate that they might also *transvaluate* that heritage. Throughout the *Leaders' Guide* there is reference to traditional terminology only. Appeal is made to the diversity

33

of theological positions (p. 2), doctrinal pluralism (p. 7), the fundamentalist, liberal, existentialist, conservative, and so on, positions (p. 12), confessionalism (p. 6), indifferentism (p. 7), the catholic spirit (p. 7), historical relativism (p. 9), and tradition as norm (p. 14)—to select a few of the technical terms used. At one point it is said that the leader should help the group "recognize that the creedal statements themselves inevitably reflect a definite and temporary cultural perspective and situation" (p. 9). But that theology as a whole could reflect a definite temporary cultural perspective and situation—this problem is not envisaged. It seems that only a common-interest theology could bring about the desired change, since it would mean that Methodist tradition itself would be radically questioned. Could it not be that Methodism meanwhile has become as ossified as Anglicanism in Wesley's day? So that we would need a radical conversion away from what appears as Methodism today in order to be truly Methodist?

From Christology to Praxiology?

It will be important to stay with the original genius of Methodism in unravelling the issues. In reference to the common Christian tradition, Part II states that Methodism has distinguished itself by "a typically practical attitude toward theological reflection. Generally, we have been more interested in relating doctrine to life than in speculative analysis. The ethical fruits of faith concern us more than systems of doctrine."[36] The practical theological stance can be only to the good in the present American climate in theology. It might well be the "saving factor" in the whole picture. But we need to know the *terminus a quo* as to relating doctrine to life. Our analysis up to this point has made it clear that we need an explicit Christology at the base of our doctrinal formulations. Only Christ as the corporate self can bring forth the ethical fruits of faith, effectively changing our culture. What is more, it is he who qualifies our practical attitude in terms of a definite praxiology, a framework for effective action, so that there is rhyme and reason for what we are doing and so that we are not just trying hectically to catch up with a floating crap-game. The "function of critical reason"[37] in church and theology depends especially on the activity of our living Lord. Effective action depends on critically understanding our involvement in ideologies to which faith often lends its support.

Even the best doctrine is undermined by ideologized faith. The work of H. Richard Niebuhr on *The Social Sources of Denominationalism* is still pertinent to this point. Some forty years ago his observations for many people probably seemed interesting finds. But one seldom knew how to functionalize them as praxiology, i.e., as a framework for effective action. Meanwhile—in the agony of the church in which we find ourselves —the ideological dilemmas have become less tolerable. There is not a single doctrine we could think through apart from them. We realize much more how with every doctrine we also tend to legitimate our way of life, glorifying it with a religious halo. We discover the burden of being middle class.

> The sanction of religion is invoked upon the peculiar virtues of the group itself; honesty, industry, sobriety, thrift, and prudence, in which the economic structure of business as well as the economic and social status of the individual depend, receive high veneration while the virtues of solidarity, sympathy, and fraternity are correspondingly ignored.[38]

As is well known, Methodism was not immediately a religion of the middle-class. It was a matter of gradual development, illustrating "the manner in which a church sloughs off its original endowment and accepts a type of religious life more in conformity with its new economic interest and status."[39] The John Wesley quote Max Weber referred to has to be seen in its full context and in regard to its full implications. Wesley goes on to say that those who gain all they can should "likewise give all they can."[40] Wesley himself was certainly exemplary in this regard. But with the passing of time, the poor were left behind, as it were, and no longer influenced theological reflection at its core. So Niebuhr continues:

> The passage well describes the rise of Methodism in the Old World and later in the New from a church of the poor to a middle-class church, which, with its new outlook, abandoned the approach to religion which made it an effective agency of salvation to the lower classes in the century of its founding.[41]

It is impossible in this limited essay to do full justice to the origins of Methodist social doctrine. The point here is to indicate that there is a long tradition of social attitudes to be reckoned with in Methodism. A study of Methodist doctrine has to take them into account, if it wants to do justice to the full doctrinal dynamics operative today. "Methodism was far removed in its moral temper from the churches of the disinherited in the sixteenth and seventeenth centuries. Briefly, the difference lay in the substitution of individual ethics and millenarianism."[42] This does not mean that it was callous toward human need:

> It had some interest in the economic fortunes of its constituency and in the social inequities from which they suffered, but it was much more interested

in the correction of their vices, from the point of view of their religious fortunes.[43]

What interests Niebuhr, however, is the outcome of the process in the middle-class outlook:

> Thus Methodism was adapted from its beginnings to become a church of the respectable middle class, even though the emotionalism of its religion continued to make a strong appeal to the untutored. . . . More than Presbyterianism or Congregationalism Methodism came to be the religion of business classes.[44]

Obviously there are also other ways of interpreting this history. If Methodism, however, wants to come to grips with the special-interest theologies, must it not also take into account Niebuhr's type of interpretation? What of the status of theology itself as middle-class, taking its cue for the hermeneutical presuppositions of theology from the reinforcing legitimation of middle-class theology? Does it become understandable that the doubts about the "ministries of liberation" creep in, in view of the middle-class climate? And how would the liberation of the church itself from middle-class captivity be initiated? Christology offers some cogent reasons for a praxiology not oriented in middle-class values.

Theology as Praxiology?

The *Leaders' Guide* indicates quite clearly the intention of Part II: "It is an outline of a *theological methodology*."[45] One may ask whether for history—in which Christianity has its matrix of existence—*methodology* is an adequate approach. Some would prefer to speak of a hermeneutic.[46] But this is not the crucial point that needs to be made now. The issue is the inescapable interdependence of doctrine and life in Christian origins—holistic truth. Here soul and body are one, deed and act, so that word is deed (worddeed) and deed is word (deedword). As a consequence, every doctrinal utterance is also a statement about a particular action, not in terms of the detail of decision-making, but in regard to the framework in which it takes place. So it is not just a matter of "relating doctrine to life," but of doctrine itself being that life. There are no ethical fruits of faith without understanding that faith itself is an ethical fruit—in fact, *the* ethical fruit. Under the impact of the "special-interest theologies" a making whole of the faith could take place in dimensions not dreamt of before. "How can a church of ten million members achieve theological depth and relevance?"[47] Let it be understood, the special-interest theologies are not *eo ipso* inclusive. But they point to the importance of concrete suffering and pain. If a church of ten million members takes one suffering member of humankind utterly seriously, might this not be the first step toward theological depth and relevance? The inclusiveness begins where the millions identify with the lot of *one* lost human, *one* oppressed neighbor, *one* prisoner.[48] But are not our theologies—the mainstream theologies—thus far more geared to the millions who are not really "lost" than to the one shut out from their privilege? Theology as praxiology is intent on facilitating the radical identification with the *one* lost: "What do you think? If a man has a hundred sheep, and one of them has gone astray, does he not leave the ninety-nine on the hills and go in search of the one that went astray" (Mt. 18:12)?

Critical Self-understanding?

One of our avowed ecumenical commitments is that our own distinctive emphases shall not simply disappear, but be gathered into the larger Christian unity, there to be made meaningful in a richer whole. But this requires a deliberate effort on our part to engage in critical self-understanding. . . .[49]

This essay is an attempt to share in the critical self-understanding. Is Methodism, a church of ten million members, a giant in agony? If so, for what reasons? How will critical self-understanding come to be?

(1) Will it not depend on a limitlessly inclusive mainstream doctrine making special interests in the church its very own?

(2) Will it not depend on an ethic grounded in inclusive doctrine, so that every action can body forth the wholeness of truth?

(3) Will it not depend on outsmarting the trick played by religion on men in its legitimating their privilege and status?

(4) Will it not require putting the common interest above promotion of religious pluralism, and liberation of the church above liberation of society and culture?[50]

(5) Will it not require discovering our own special-interest histories *in* the mainstream of the church which keep us from the larger Christian unity grounded in the solidarity of humankind?

(6) Will it not require abandoning the methodology of treating the Christian faith as an *object* of analysis and arriving at a praxiology in which the outcast is the *subject* of receiving and sharing Jesus Christ as grace?[51]

The point of the essay: what would happen if these questions were put to the study material on doctrine and doctrinal statements? Would the fact of the agony of Methodism be better understood? Would radical *metanoia* in the footsteps of John Wesley become possible?

Conclusion

The Reformed maverick who wrote these lines never felt exactly out of place among the Methodist princes. But he knows his place. Just for that reason he wants to express his appreciation to the *Perkins Journal* for letting him appear among them as though he, too, were an heir to the throne. Three Methodist friends at Duke have helped him "spruce up" for the occasion: Dean Thomas A. Langford, Professor McMurry S. Richey, and Professor Charles K. Robinson. Usually the word in such a bind is: they are of course not responsible for any errors, false judgments, heresies, etc. Well, in this case I can't let them off the hook that easily. They administered too many blood transfusions of Methodism into my Calvinist bloodstream all along. And they weren't all from the Methodist mainstream either!

Chapter 3

DOCTRINAL STANDARDS
IN THE UNITED METHODIST CHURCH

Schubert M. Ogden[1]

At least three reasons seem to me sufficient to make discussion of this topic timely, if not, in fact, imperative. First, the question of doctrinal standards is a basic question for any church that is serious about its mission, and this is all the more so, given the peculiar history of The United Methodist Church, which, for a variety of reasons, has long made this also an urgent question. Second, recent developments culminating in the action of the 1972 General Conference have led to a new formulation of the Church's official position on this question, which, just because it is new, still needs to be assimilated by the Church generally at the local, district, and annual conference levels. Third, despite such success as this new formulation may rightly claim in dealing with the question, it can be properly assimilated by the Church only through the kind of critical appropriation which also becomes aware of its limitations.

But I myself must go on to add that the limitations of the new position are serious enough to make me feel a special responsibility for critically discussing it. I am well aware, of course, that the Report of the Theological Study Commission on Doctrine and Doctrinal Standards, which now appears as Part II of the 1972 Book of Discipline, was all but unanimously approved by the General Conference. Furthermore, I am not in the least disposed to question the assurances I have received from members of the commission who bore the responsibility for conducting its study that its final report is almost certainly as adequate a report as could have been made at this time by any comparably representative body in our church. But, far from in any way lessening my sense of responsibility, these considerations serve only to heighten it. For if, as certainly seems to be true, the position our church has now officially taken on doctrinal standards is the position that we as United Methodists deserve, the reasons for the limitations of this position must be sought finally not in conditions peculiar to the Theological Study Commission or to the General Conference but in conditions pervasive in the life of our church at large. Since I do indeed believe this to be the case, I feel not only justified but in fact constrained to share some of my own reflections on these conditions of our life generally as an ecclesial community. My sole purpose, however, is to challenge all of us to think more carefully and critically about the life of our church, for which all of us bear responsibility and for whose most basic failings each of us must in his own way accept the blame.

Needless to say, I have no intention of essaying an exhaustive analysis of the conditions in our church today that may be reflected in its official position on doctrinal standards. Moreover, I will not be able to say very much about the larger question of church discipline in general, of which the question of doctrinal discipline is, after all, but a part. If I am right, much that I shall say is also relevant to this larger issue. But, for our purpose here, it will be sufficient if we can get a somewhat clearer idea of some of the conditions in our church's life that finally account for what I take to be the serious limitations of its position on doctrinal standards.

As I see it, there are two such conditions that repay closer attention—the first of which is rather prominently reflected in what is now Part II of the Book of Discipline, the second of which is only marginally reflected there, even though it is arguable that it is a far more basic, as well as a more disturbing, condition in our life as an ecclesial community.

In turning now to the first of these conditions, I begin by recalling the main motives, positive and negative, behind the position on doctrinal standards now incorporated in the Discipline. Negatively put, these motives are expressly said to chart a course between "doctrinal dogmatism" on the one hand, and "doctrinal indifferentism" on the other (p. 70). More positively, the position is motivated by a concern both for some kind or measure of doctrinal discipline in the church and for the freedom to carry on its theological task in the way mandated both by the witness of faith itself and by the new opportunities and limitations of an ever-changing historical situation.

Now, simply on the basis of this express statement, I suspect few of us would be moved to dissent from the position, and I, at any rate, find myself entirely sympathetic with it. As a matter of fact, I should think that the most basic reason for such soundness as may be rightly claimed for it is that it officially commits our Church to avoiding dogmatism and indifferentism alike by expressly endorsing our historic concern both for theological freedom and for doctrinal responsibility. The question I find myself impelled to raise, however, is whether the position as actually developed in Part II of the Discipline does not, in fact, show more worry about the dangers of "doctrinal dogmatism" in our church than about the opposite but hardly less serious dangers of "doctrinal indifferentism."

The reason I am led to ask this, of course, is that my own sense of the real dangers in our church today causes me to have the opposite kind of worry. For a long time now, I have had the distinct impression that the body of Christians who boast of a Discipline are among the most undisciplined persons in Christendom, especially when it comes to matters of doctrine. It is notorious that, at every level in the Church, from the local congregation to the General Conference, it is possible to disseminate the widest range of doctrines, both theological and ethical, regardless of the extent of their contrariety to the doctrinal standards we have officially acknowledged. In fact, one measure of the situation that has long prevailed in our church is that the vast majority of its members, ministerial as well as lay, would still be hard pressed simply to name the standards of doctrine of The United Methodist Church—to say nothing of having any operational understanding of their contents in relation to the church's continuing witness.

This is where it seems to me we in fact are, even though, for whatever reasons, our official position reflects a rather different assessment of the dangers that confront us. As balanced as it may appear to be in the express statement of its basic motives, it is in fact excessively preoccupied with avoiding doctrinal rigidity, literalness, and inflexibility, with the result that, for all of its concern to avoid the opposite dangers of indifferentism, it does rather less to that end than I, for one, take to be both possible and necessary.

But enough now about the basic motives of the position and the one-sided way in which, as it seems to me, they are expressed in its formulation in the Discipline. Judging simply from the structure and contents of the formulation (and thus prescinding from its motives, as well as the pressures and counterpressures under which it was finally worked out in the Study Commission), one can only conclude that it is concerned to clarify two important questions, both of which it addresses against an appropriate, if briefly developed, historical background (pp. 39–52). These questions are: (1) What are the doctrinal standards of The United Methodist Church, and what role should they play in its life? and (2) What is the theological task that United Methodists, as well as other Christians, are called to carry on?

With respect to the first part of the first question—as to the identity of our doctrinal standards—I judge the formulation to be entirely successful, and I am personally profoundly grateful for the clarification it now provides. If all of us who are members of the Church will make such use of Part II of the Discipline as we are supposed to make of it, it should at last serve to rectify the scandalous ignorance even as to the identity of our doctrinal standards that has so long prevailed among us. But, for the rest—i.e., as to the proper role of our doctrinal standards and as to our theological task—the present position of the Discipline does not seem to me to be anything like so successful.

My first difficulty with the answers I understand it to give to what remains of its two questions is this: Because of what I take to be its failure clearly to grasp the difference between the role of doctrinal standards in the church and the task of theology, its fully justified concern for theological freedom entails an obscuring of the proper role of doctrinal standards; while, conversely, its no less fully justified concern for doctrinal responsibility entails an obscuring of the theological task. In short, as our position is now formulated, theological freedom and doctrinal responsibility are so understood that they can only be played off against one another, with the result that justice is done to neither—though, as I have indicated, rather less injustice is done to theological freedom than to doctrinal discipline. Let me now try to explain in more detail why I say this.

Unless I am mistaken, the role finally assigned to what have now at last been identified as our doctrinal standards is far from the role of being standards of doctrine in the proper sense of the words. One telltale symptom of this important change is the use of the phrase "landmark documents" in place of the phrase "standards of doctrine" which has appeared in the First Restrictive Rule of our Constitution without alteration since 1808. The formulation as a whole makes clear, I think, that the built-in ambiguity of referring to our historic standards as "landmark documents" exactly answers to the ambiguous role that is in fact assigned to them in the new Discipline—allowing, of course, that to speak of them so is definitely to say something rather weaker than that they are and remain standards wherewith to measure the doctrinal adequacy of the witness of the contemporary church. But a particularly revealing passage in this connection occurs under the subheading, "Doctrinal Guidelines in The United Methodist Church":

> Since "our present existing and established standards of doctrine" cited in the first two Restrictive Rules of the constitution of The United Methodist Church are not to be construed literally and juridically, then by what methods can our doctrinal reflection and construction be most fruitful and fulfilling? The answer comes in terms of our free inquiry within the boundaries defined by four main sources and guidelines for Christian theology: Scripture, tradition, experience, reason.

What is implied by this passage if not that our historic standards of doctrine are not really to play that role at all?

To be sure, later in the formulation reference is made not only, as here, to the four "guidelines" of Scripture, tradition, experience, and reason, but also to "our doctrinal heritage," and we are told that all theologizing and all productions in the arts (hymns, poems, multimedia presentations, etc.) should meet "two conditions" if they are to be taken seriously: "careful regard for our heritage and fourfold guidelines, and the double test of acceptability and edification in corporate worship and common life" (pp. 80f.). But, surely, the question is whether "careful regard" for our heritage or "loyalty" to it entails any role for our doctrinal standards, other than that which belongs to *any* element of this tradition. So far as I can see, the position now taken in the Discipline certainly does not want to deny a special role to our historic standards, only, in its excessive concern that they not be construed "literally or juridically," lest theological freedom be imperiled, in effect to deny them any such special role—or, at best, to fail to provide a clear and coherent account of what that role is.

Which returns us to the suggestion I have made as to the reason for this apparent difficulty. If I am correct, the reason, finally, why the role of doctrinal standards is left quite obscure or ambiguous is that the Discipline also displays a certain confusion as to the nature and task of theology. On the one hand, theology is said to be a matter of "free inquiry" within the boundaries defined by the four main guidelines (sources or norms) of Scripture, tradition, experience, and reason. On the other hand, theology is apparently assigned the task of United Methodist "doctrinal reflection and construction" (p. 75) and, in this connection, is expected to develop also within "the framework of our doctrinal heritage" (p. 79). But, so far as I can see, these are two quite different, in fact, incompatible, understandings of what theology is and is supposed to do. If theology is expected to remain within the framework of our United Methodist heritage, I do not see how it can at the same time be said to be a free inquiry bounded only by the general Christian theological guidelines of Scripture, tradition, experience, and reason. In other words, I do not see how theology can be defined both as *United Methodist* theology and as *Christian* theology, since these are on the face of it quite different things—or, at least, can be said not to be different only as the result of theological reflection, not as its presupposition.

The point I wish to insist on is that the only theology The United Methodist Church or any other Christian church has any reason to promote is a theology which is not itself subject to the discipline of any church's doctrinal standards. Theology is not subject to such standards,

43

namely, because, properly understood, its task is precisely the critical understanding, and, as may be, correction, of these very standards by reference to the basic norms of Scripture and tradition, on the one hand, and experience and reason, on the other. In short, my view is that theology is called to play a very different role in the total economy of the church's life from that quite properly played by the doctrinal standards of a particular church or churches. As I see it, both of these roles are necessary and important—if not to the being of the church, then certainly to its well-being. Even so, everything turns on recognizing that the roles are different and that neither is likely to be played well unless this is clearly understood.

But, in all fairness, I must admit that the point on which I am insisting has not been clearly recognized throughout much, if not most, of Christian history. If our Discipline exhibits confusion as to the nature and task of theology, it is essentially the same confusion that can be traced down through the Christian tradition, Protestant as well as Catholic. Until the emergence of Protestant liberal theology at the beginning of the nineteenth century, theology has usually been understood as, in effect, the ideology of the Christian community, the rationalization of its witness, and hence its intellectual weapon in the militant struggle for the sake of the Kingdom and against the powers of this world to which it knows itself to be called. Thus, so far from being sufficiently independent of the church to be critical of its continuing witness, theology has been expected to be of service to the church by simply formulating this witness in conceptual terms. There is, of course, the difference which derives from the fact that on the traditional Protestant understanding, as distinct from the Roman Catholic, something different has been understood by "church" from any particular human institution. Thus, whereas, in the traditional Catholic understanding, theology is, in effect, the ideology of a particular *institutional* church, in the Protestant view, the church whose witness theology serves to rationalize is rather that *visible* church, which, as the Westminster Confession classically puts it, has been sometimes more, sometimes less visible. As such, therefore, the church cannot be simply identified with any of the institutional churches, either individually or collectively—from which it follows that, in the Protestant understanding, theology is only indirectly in the service of any institutional church, being directly service of the divine Word itself, by which the preaching and teaching of all churches are continually judged. Despite this important difference, however, the tradition of the church prior to the emergence of theological liberalism has uniformly failed to recognize the independence of theology, and hence the freedom that must be guaranteed to it if it is to do its proper work. There is no question, then, that the position I am challenging can claim an impressive amount of support in the theological tradition.

Yet, having admitted this, I want to press my challenge, insisting that the proper role of theology in the church is to seek a fully reflective understanding of its witness with a view to answering the question as to its meaning and truth.[2] So far from being anything like the church's ideology, theology properly functions in the church to vindicate the claim of the Christian witness to be decisive for human existence solely and simply because it is true. In other words, theology is the process of continual self-criticism whereby the church ever and again proves to be vastly more than a mere human sect or party, whose witness could be nothing more than an ideology. From this standpoint, the existence of radical theological freedom in the church is the clearest evidence it can give of its deep conviction in the abiding truth of its witness. Just because or insofar as it is convinced that the witness it is called to bear is true, not only for Christians but for every human being, it sees to it that the whole of its life is accompanied by theological reflection—which is to say, by the kind of critical reflection that continually tests its confidence in its witness against the normative forms of that witness in Scripture and tradition and against the only universal norms of meaning and truth in the cumulative experience and reason of mankind.

In an indirect way, then, the process of theological reflection does indeed contribute to the church's "doctrinal reflection and construction." But the task of theology as such is not to construct United Methodist doctrine, or any other church's doctrine; and much less is theology called merely to interpret and to help to enforce such doctrine. Theology's task, rather, is continually to test the Church's doctrine, along with all other Christian doctrine, against what The United Methodist Church itself, along with other Christian churches, acknowledges as the only final norms for its witness—namely, the incarnate Word of God attested in Scripture and tradition and that unincarnate Word of God which, being the light that enlightens every man, is universally attested by human experience and reason simply as such.

When theology is thus understood, however, the entirely legitimate concern for theological freedom not only *need* not, but also logically *can* not, be played off against the equally legitimate concern for doctrinal responsibility. Because the role of theology in the church is distinctively different from that of its doctrinal standards, a concern for theological freedom cannot excuse one from being equally concerned that the church have explicit standards of doctrine as an essential component of the standard or rule by which it disciplines its life and witness.

45

This becomes clear as soon as one recognizes the proper role of such standards, which, quite simply, is to provide a norm or measure by which the continuing witness of a particular church can be tested for its adequacy. Of course, to bear witness is the whole meaning of the outward or public life of every Christian, and each baptized person who is confirmed in the calling of his baptism accepts the responsibility of bearing such witness. Both explicitly, through all the forms of specifically religious belief, rite, and church organization, and implicitly, through all the other forms of culture—moral, political, scientific, aesthetic, etc.— each Christian simply as such is called to share in the constitutive witness of the visible church. But among the other responsibilities this includes is to help to determine and then enforce what the particular Christian community to which he belongs is to accept as its proper witness. If this responsibility is fully carried out, it inevitably leads to the formulation and enforcement of something like doctrinal standards, to which each individual in the community is accountable in bearing his own individual witness and in co-operating with his fellow churchmen in bearing theirs.

To be sure, no such standard of doctrine can be formulated or acknowledged which is in principle different from the doctrines expressed or implied in the continuing witness of the church, whether gathered or dispersed. On a Protestant understanding, at any rate, even the doctrinal standards which a church establishes to discipline its witness are and must be simply results of the ongoing process of theological reflection, which by its very nature is always pointed beyond its results to that of which they are at best only inadequate expressions. This means, among other things, that doctrinal standards, quite as much as all the other doctrinal statements constituting the church's tradition of witness, always are and must be subject to critical interpretation—to interpretation of what they *say* on the basis of what they *mean*. Thus the only way in which Wesley's standard sermons, for instance, can be properly invoked as doctrinal standards is by way of just such critical interpretation. What is binding in the sermons is not what they say but what they mean, or, better, perhaps, what they say *is* binding, but only by virtue of the meaning the terms and concepts express, not by virtue of the terms and concepts themselves. It could not be otherwise, since it is entirely possible to accept everything Wesley says without accepting thereby what he means, just as it is also entirely possible to accept what Wesley means without accepting thereby everything he says —at least in the terms in which he says it. Nevertheless, as the Discipline itself stresses, to claim the support of The United Methodist Church, as each United Methodist does and must, is also to become accountable to the witness which that church has in all responsibility determined to be *its* Christian witness. In this connection, then, the role of our doctrinal standards is simply to give concrete content to this accountability: to make clear both our rights and our responsibilities as members of *our* witnessing community. But this they can do, obviously, only if we who are members of the church understand them as precisely *doctrinal standards*; and this means, at the very least, only if we do not take the Discipline's designation of them as "landmark documents" as an excuse for consigning them to a past with which we no longer have to do because it no longer has to do with us.

In summary, then, my first point is that an adequate position on the question of doctrinal standards in The United Methodist Church waits on all of us achieving a rather different understanding of theology from that which is present in the Discipline just because it is also pervasively present throughout the church. Only when theology is understood in its proper independence of the church's witness can we break out of the dilemma in which we now are caught of securing theological freedom only at the risk of doctrinal irresponsibility—by obscuring the equally proper role of doctrinal standards and the discipline of our continuing witness that they alone make possible.

The second condition in the Church that seems to me reflected in its presently inadequate position on the role of doctrinal standards is both more basic and less prominent in the new formulation now incorporated in the Discipline. Indeed, I must be frank to say that I am sufficiently uncertain that I am entirely justified in discerning its presence to put my criticism more in the form of a question than as a confident claim. Could it be, I want to ask, that the deepest reason for our dangerous drift toward doctrinal indifferentism is an understanding of ourselves as church that, however widely represented in the Christian tradition, can no longer claim the support of the witness of Holy Scripture?

I have been strongly encouraged in pressing this question by the reflection of the Roman Catholic theologian, Juan Luis Segundo, in his recent book, *The Community Called Church*.[3] According to Segundo, the conception of the church which alone is warranted by the New Testament, as well as early Christian tradition, is very different from the conception that has prevailed throughout most of Christian history right up to the present. On this prevalent conception, the church is understood to be the exclusive, or, in any case, privileged, locus of God's salvation of mankind in Christ Jesus. Backing up this conception are such basic theological assumptions as the following. Although all men were originally created by God and presented with the gift and demand of faith in his love, men have in fact universally declined their divine calling and have lived instead in sinful estrangement from God, as well as from their neighbors and themselves. But, since God was unwilling that his original plan in creation utterly come to naught, he has since taken it upon himself to redeem at least some of mankind by first calling Israel and then, finally, by sending his Son, whose life, death, and resurrection are the foundation of the new Israel which is the church. All, then, who are incorporated into this visible Christian church are vouchsafed the possibility of salvation from sin and of a new life of faith working through love—though, as the prevalent conception has maintained, *only* those who are thus taken into the church have any share, or, at any rate, fully share in this possibility.

But now, on Segundo's view—and here he but speaks for an ever-growing number of Catholic theologians—this whole conception of the church, together with its supporting assumptions, is inadequate and lacking in scriptural warrant. For, according to Scripture, the God who is decisively revealed in Christ is "the living God, who is the Savior of *all* men," who "desires *all* men to be saved and to come to the knowledge of the truth" (1 Tim. 4:10, 2:4; italics added). Consequently, God's purpose in sending Christ and establishing the church is not to effect the salvation of some men but to disclose once-for-all and decisively that he in fact wills the salvation of *all* men, and hence is, ever was, and ever will be present in every human life as the grace necessary and sufficient to that end. In other words, the church is not the privileged locus of salvation itself, which has no privileged locus, since, by God's grace, it is a strictly universal possibility of every human life; rather, the church is the privileged locus of the *knowledge* of salvation, the place where the deep mystery of saving grace in the existence of every man and of all men is expressly revealed and continually attested by thought, word, and deed. Accordingly, Segundo argues, the whole purpose of the church is to be a "sign-bearing community," the community whose preaching and sacraments and style of life are supposed to be the decisive sign in the world of God's universal plan for salvation. "The Church is, essentially and primarily, a *sign*. It has been placed here precisely and exclusively to pass on to men a certain signification, i.e., a message, something that is to be grasped, comprehended, and incorporated to a greater or lesser degree into the fashioning of history and the world." Hence, "the primary preoccupation of the Church is not directed toward her own inner life but toward people outside. Unlike other organizations founded for the benefit of [their] own members, the Church is a community sent to those who live, act, and work outside her own narrow limits."[4] Because this is so, however, because the church "must always keep her attention focused on the rest of humanity," "the first interior concern of the Church . . . is the clarity and transparency of her sign-function."[5]

Now this is the point at which Segundo's argument becomes immediately relevant to our concern here. For, if the church's first interior concern is that she be a fitting sign of the universal mystery of salvation that she is called to bear witness to, the task of disciplining her life and witness, and hence also her doctrine, becomes a primary obligation. Since in reality every Christian is a representative of the church, it is imperative that every Christian be so equipped and disciplined that he can in truth represent the church to the world—so that he can himself be a fit witness to God's universal will to salvation, and hence to his redemption not merely of Christians or of the church but of mankind. Conversely, however, Segundo argues, if the church neglects its obligation to discipline itself by so opening its membership as to include even those who do not accept or assist in enforcing this essential self-discipline, it but makes clear that it is, in fact, determined by that other prevalent, but radically unscriptural, understanding of itself as the privileged community of the saved. As he sharply puts it, "if we are driven by a desire to expand the boundaries of the ecclesial community by eliminating this responsibility of self-giving, we are actually living as if membership in it were a *privilege* that *always* betters the situation of those who possess it [whereas the truth is that] 'membership in the ecclesial community saves people [only] when it is shouldered as a new and more profound responsibility.' Cherishing a shameful aristocratic outlook, we seek to excuse our seeming prerogatives by sharing them as widely as possible."[6]

The question I wish to press should now be clear. My own belief is that at the bottom of our failure fully to assume the responsibility of discipline in The United Methodist Church, including most especially the discipline of its doctrine, is the very conception of ourselves as church which Segundo argues, to my mind convincingly, is not at all the conception of the New Testament. Thus, by us, too, the church is most commonly regarded not merely as the divinely authorized witness to God's salvation of mankind in Christ but as itself the only locus, or, in any case, the privileged locus of that salvation. Given this self-understanding, then, together with a serious acceptance of our mission to all mankind, we are naturally reluctant to exclude anyone from its membership, since such exclusion is tantamount to being excluded from the effective reach of God's saving love itself. And this reluctance inevitably becomes all the greater when we recognize, as we now must in our pluralistic world, that the visible Christian church has up to now comprised but a very small minority of the human community. Thus there are the strongest pressures against maintaining any kind of church discipline; and, considering the peculiarities of Methodist history on the North American continent, no one should be surprised that doctrinal discipline in particular virtually ceases to exist, if not in theory, then certainly in fact.

Of course, I should not wish to claim that this misunderstanding of the church is the only self-understanding evident in Part II of the Discipline. But I do find it ominous that the utter universality of God's salvation as attested by the New Testament is, at most, of marginal importance in that formulation and that, again and again, what it stresses is the oneness of *Christians* in Christ instead of the oneness in him of *all mankind*. Thus, even though we read at one point that grace is "the spiritual climate and environment surrounding all human life at all times and in all places" (p. 73), the only other explicit reference to "that environment of grace" identifies it as that "in and by which all *Christians* live" (p. 77; italics added). In keeping with the same restriction, then, the affirmation in which we United Methodists are said to join our fellow Christians is not the oneness of *all* men in Christ, but "*our* oneness in Christ"; we affirm not that the forgiveness of sins and life eternal are the birthright of *every* man, claimed for him by Christ and attested by his baptism, but that they are "*ours* through the power of God's invincible love," etc., (p. 72; italics added). True, there is an acknowledgement at the end of the formulation that "the ecumenical process has expanded across the boundaries of Christian unity, to include serious interfaith encounters and exploration between Christianity and other living religions of the world"; and we are advised that "we must also be conscious that God has been and is now working among all people" (p. 81). But, in view of what is otherwise said or implied throughout the formulation, this acknowledgement and this advice are scarcely more than qualifications of a conception of the church that Segundo and many others are seriously challenging.

My second main point, then, is simply to raise the question whether this belief of mine about our church is as well-founded as I am inclined to think. Could the deepest reason for our failure to discipline our ecclesial life, and hence for the limitations of our present position on doctrinal standards, be this basic misunderstanding of ourselves as a Christian church?

Whatever the answer to this question, of one thing I am quite certain: the mission to which the Christian church is called ineluctably implies the obligation of self-discipline in all aspects of its life and witness, including the doctrine disseminated by its preaching and teaching. A sign in the world of God's universal salvation which is not as clear and

50

transparent as human frailty allows is not the visible church of Jesus Christ—just as salt which has lost its savor is "no longer good for anything except to be thrown out and trodden under foot by men" (Matt. 5:13). Contrary to what one might assume from the prevalent conception of the church, the point of putting a pinch of salt in a dish is not to turn the whole dish into salt, but so to permeate the dish with its savor as to make the dish itself tasty to eat. But, then, the salt is of no use without its saltiness—any more than the church is of any use to the world it is sent to serve without that sound doctrine which the establishment of doctrinal standards and their responsible enforcement throughout the church alone make possible. "You are the salt of the earth; but if salt has lost its savor, how shall its saltiness be restored?"

Chapter 4

United Methodism in Search of Theology

Leroy T. Howe[1]

At its 1972 General Conference, The United Methodist Church approved a normative statement on doctrine and doctrinal standards by which its theological reflection henceforth is to be guided. Scrupulously avoiding any hint that preaching and teaching ought to be tested by reference to a comprehensive system of beliefs, Part II of the new Discipline seeks instead to articulate clearly the nature of theology as a *task* in which every believer must engage. Though the document outlines a style of reflection which is both ecumenical in spirit and decidedly Methodist in emphasis, it remains to be seen whether a distinctive "Methodist theology" can ensue in the decades to come, granting for the moment that there is something to be said for "denominational" theology in this sense. But it is possible now to discern many of the features such a theology would display, were there to emerge such, as well as what some of its most pressing difficulties would be like. Both subjects comprise the concern of this present essay, whose underlying conviction is that between the extremes of system-building and essaying which lack universality, and ecumenical theologies which lack concreteness, there still is a place for theological reflection rooted self-consciously from the outset within the traditions of a particular believing community.

Major Emphases in United Methodist Theologizing

The 1972 statement on doctrine and doctrinal standards (hereafter referred to by the abbreviation DSS) clearly affirms the purpose of doctrinal standards to be that of guiding faithful preaching and teaching within the church. Insofar as it is rooted in the church's life, *theology* must include among its many tasks that of seeking to identify that body of doctrine which is to be the basis for the church's critical self-reflection in the present age. More importantly, however, DSS recognizes that every such body of doctrine now functions only for extremely varied constituencies; hence, theology's more crucial task is to expound church doctrine according to diverse interpretations of its import for contemporary living. It must steer a middle course between "dogmatism," which views adherence to doctrines as a test of faith, and "indifferentism," which precludes from the outset any assessment of preaching and teaching by supposing that *any* belief is acceptable if piety remains firm. It is interesting that, though the American Methodist experience clearly has been indifferentist theologically, DSS nevertheless refrains from the obvious corrective, a new creed: "The effort to substitute new creeds for old has a long history of partisanship and schism." It will be argued subsequently that such a stance tends to affirm rather than correct indifferentism.

An important indicator that this is indeed the case can be seen in DSS's penchant for contrasting theology as a process of thinking with theology as a doctrinal corpus. It is most especially concerned to specify doctrinal standards in terms of a *style* of theological reflection: e.g., "The viability of all doctrinal opinion demands that the processes of theological development must be kept open-ended, both on principle and in fact." Though every act of theologizing must possess some form and structure, theology is itself most definitely an ongoing process. And it is the kind of enterprise in which every Christian both can and must participate. In the strictest possible sense, United Methodist theology is to be *lay* theology, produced continuously by all who call themselves Christians. Rather than specialized inquiry conducted only by a small coterie of specially trained professionals, theology is an enterprise germane to *every* Christian's growth in faith.

The major purpose of DSS is to provide aids to theologizing in this very broad sense of the term. It seeks to accomplish this purpose in three distinct ways. The first section of the document is a brief but insightful essay on the historical backgrounds of Methodism and the Evangelical and United Brethren traditions, respectively. The second section collects documents from both traditions which are definitive of their historic theological perspectives: "landmarks." Finally, an attempt is made to define the theological task in the present, specifically, how the essential historic heritages can continue to mediate the Gospel's challenge to men and women living in a time "of catastrophic perils and soaring hopes." Here, the principle of *doctrinal pluralism* is enunciated uncompromisingly, along with that which is to govern responsible theological reflection within a pluralistic milieu: "free inquiry within the boundaries defined by four main sources and guidelines for Christian theology: Scripture, tradition, experience, reason."

The body of doctrine which is to be the touchstone of United Methodist theological reflection is specified by a cataloguing of materials deemed the indispensable starting point for theologizing. These landmarks are: Wesley's *Sermons* and *Explanatory Notes*, his revision of the thirty-nine *Articles of Religion* of the Church of England, and the *General Rules*, along with the *Confession of Faith* of the former EUB churches. With the list of documents is given also the principles by which they are to be interpreted: the guidelines of Scripture, tradition, experience, and reason. Whether as "source" or as "norm," the guidelines are to aid in thinking about the landmarks, within the broad historical context both of the landmarks' relevance for contemporary experience and of the "common Christian history" out of which they have arisen as one individual expression. The insistence upon the landmark documents as indispensable seems to call United Methodists to see that they do indeed have a significant history with which they must come to terms in their life and thought; this is the intended corrective to American Methodism's a-historical (and even anti-historical) perspective.

It is in the discussion of the guidelines, however, in Section II, that DSS's really distinctive contribution is to be found. For it is here that the intention and tonality of the entire document, with its stress upon theology as process, becomes evident. Most especially, upon close examination of the guidelines in particular, one discovers how strongly the emphasis in DSS falls upon *tradition*, in several senses of the term. About the other three guidelines (Scripture, experience, and reason), little is said which is distinctive except the explicit denial of *sola scriptura* and the concomitant assertion of Scripture's primary rather than exclusive authority. The key to DSS lies in the way tradition is expounded in the guidelines section. United Methodists are to reflect upon their tradition, and to be led through that tradition to a "common heritage" out of which their history arises and in the light of which alone their distinctive heritage can mediate a contemporary witness to the Gospel. Common Christian tradition, with a recognizable core of doctrine, is at all times and everywhere the judge of any particular Christian history. It is *the* theological norm, and not merely one among four guidelines, as becomes clear in the way that it is alleged to control the functioning of historical consciousness itself.

DSS refers repeatedly to historical consciousness as the indispensable condition for present-day theologizing: unless one thinks historically, it is alleged, he cannot think theologically at all. Theological judgment always proceeds for reevaluations, themselves conditioned by history, of the church's more inclusive history, for the sake of faithfulness to God's presence in present and future history. But Christian historical consciousness, it is also maintained, is normed by something other than itself, by the truth of God revealed in and through THE CHRISTIAN TRADITION, "the history of that environment of grace in and by which all Christians live, which is the continuance through time and space of God's self-giving love in Christ." Clearly, by so speaking, DSS aims to facilitate United Methodism's coming of age in ecumenical dialogue. Its views of the normativity of "the Christian tradition," in the *various* senses of this term, is precisely the direction in which serious ecumenical discussions in Christendom now are pointing. That the Study Commission which produced the statement was chaired by one of Protestantism's greatest ecumenists, Albert Outler, might have made the outcome foregone, but surely happy.

Some Internal Criticisms

One overall effect experienced in reading closely this document is the sense of being tantalized by the imprecision in so many of its governing images and metaphors. Deliberately choosing the language of suggestion in order to elicit a process of continuing reflection, DSS falls short of articulating a helpful definition even of the process for theologizing itself. For instance, it is quite puzzling that the terms "source" and "guideline" are used interchangeably. Certainly it is a net gain to substitute "guideline" for "norm" (except at one point, apparently: in the discussion of the guidelines in interaction, the reference is to four *norms* for doctrinal formulations). Both classical and contemporary theology tend to construe "norm" frequently in a wholly transcendent sense which precludes human beings' employing it for critical purposes. But because "source" often appears to be a synonym for "guideline," and because "source" is not itself clearly defined, the normative question remains unclear. At times, "source" seems to mean "origin," while at other times it is used as a synonym for "criterion." The argument would have been better served had the term been reserved to refer only to revelation itself, namely, God's self-disclosure, toward which all the guidelines guide Christians in their reflection. For surely it is God himself who is the "source" both of faith and understanding; in this light, the guidelines would aid believers' discerning more adequately those events of divine self-presentation from which alone faith and understanding originate. Not even the guideline of Scripture, alleged to be primary, can be the source of faith. It *can* be a source of judgments made *about* faith, in the sense of a criterion by which such judgments constantly are scrutinized.

This same kind of consideration is germane to the use of the term "wellspring," when it refers to *biblical* wellsprings: e.g., Scripture "as the constitutive witness to biblical wellsprings of our faith." Now if "wellspring" means something like an ever-present and adequate supply of something, as dictionaries tend to suggest, it is quite bibl*icist* to look to the Bible as the wellspring for faith rather than to the power and grace of God, *to which* the Bible witnesses. Finally, there is considerable imprecision about the fourfoldedness of the guidelines. The document says only that all four must be appealed to in every doctrinal discussion. All that is added by way of elaboration is that Scripture has a primary place, and that in one's theologizing, one may begin with any one of the four guidelines.

Intriguing as these latter recommendations may be in their permissiveness, they leave at least three serious questions unresolved. The first is that in those situations in which one of the guidelines might appear to have more than equal weight, no principle for adjudicating relative weight is given. It simply cannot be the case that all four would be equally cogent in diverse discussions such as: universal vs. limited election, whether a zygote is a human life, or the meaning of Christ's real presence in the Buddhist experience of emptiness. Secondly, there is always the possibility that contradictory doctrinal proposals might proceed from the guidelines taken together. For instance, some have held that the doctrine of original guilt, though powerful in tradition, is unscriptural. What is one to do upon such a discovery? How could one follow the Bible's primary lead without giving it exclusive authority, since to follow it at all would seem to entail a negating altogether the normative tradition since Augustine? Finally, though not indifferentist by intent, in practice the quadrilateral seems to be infinitely permissive. It is difficult to conceive of even a single serious theological proposal which, upon application of the four guidelines, one could exclude unambiguously from consideration as beyond the range of permissible utterance within the Christian community. By arbitrarily defining the degree of force one or another guideline is to have in a particular discussion, one could establish almost any belief as Christian.

A further difficulty has to do with the definition of "experience" in the highly restricted sense as the "new life in Christ" made possible by the work of the Holy Spirit. While there is evident precedent for construing the term in such manner within the Wesleyan tradition, by doing so in such an exclusive sense DSS precludes considering the important contemporary issue of whether it is possible any longer to experience the world according to the interpretive canon of biblical religion. Is it not possible that contemporary experience makes *less* recoverable United

Methodism's rich heritage, or at least less recoverable that heritage in its richness? DSS as a whole is far too confident about the authoritativeness of the past, although its confidence surely reflects the mind of the church at this moment in its history, a church not yet impressed with how very strange this new land may be within which Christians now dwell. The point is not that present experience *does* annul the authoritativeness of the past; it is simply that adequate theological reflection requires a concept of "experience" inclusive enough to allow the question to be *asked.* By defining the term wholly in Wesleyan language of the "assurance of the Spirit," this crucial question has no legitimate status, to the detriment of serious contemporary theologizing.

Finally, more extended comment is in order upon the relationship DSS asserts between historical consciousness, Scripture, and tradition. At the outset, the position is stated unambiguously that

> the principle of the historical interpretation of all doctrinal statements — past and present—is crucial. Such statements never have been and ought not to be legal tests for membership. We should interpret them, appreciatively, in their historic contexts.

But the principle clearly needs to be applied more extensively than it is applied throughout the document as a whole. There is no good reason why only *doctrinal statements* should be subsumed under the dynamic of historical reason, and not the whole range of human experience, which as a whole constitutes that of which doctrinal statements presumably are illuminative. Most specifically, by narrowing the field of inquiry within which the principle of historical interpretation is to function normatively, DSS cannot do justice to an obvious feature of Scripture: *its* "doctrinal pluralism." By speaking of tradition as *biblical* interpretation and avoiding confronting directly the possibility that the Bible, even and especially as a whole, is itself a variety of interpretations which must be understood historically if they are to be understood at all, DSS can achieve an adequate historical interpretation *only* of the limited United Methodist heritage and not of Christian history as a whole, especially that attested to by Scripture.

There are further ambiguities about how the relationship between Scripture and tradition is to be conceived. One crucial statement is that "Scripture is the primary source and guideline for doctrine . . . the constitutive witness to God's self-revelation." It would seem, then, that tradition is clearly made derivative from Scripture, insofar as it is the interpretation of biblical revelation. And yet, it is also maintained that it is a *common conviction* of all Christians that Scripture is primary. Here, tradition becomes the warrant for the primary place accorded the Bible;

57

Scripture is the *church's* book. Everything seems so to point until it is noted that Scripture *uniquely* witnesses to that divine revelation which is given in tradition and which creates the "transcendent history" which is God's own. Most especially, paragraphs 2, 3, and 4 of the discussion on "United Methodists and the Christian Tradition" are intended, Professor Outler has pointed out in conversation, as a "non-juridical *regula fidei*" grounded in Scripture! But if Scripture is doctrinally plural in *essence*, it cannot be appealed to in this fashion, as the warrant for other claims themselves advanced from within a pluralistic context.

The most pressing difficulties of all arise when one asks about the extent to which the principle of historical interpretation does and does not apply to *tradition*. Of the four uses of this term in DSS, only two appear to be governed by the principle: tradition as the historical process of interpreting biblical revelation, and tradition as the concrete histories of particular communities within Christendom. But the term is used also to refer to THE CHRISTIAN TRADITION, the *Heilsgeschichte* in which all Christians live, whose source is divine grace alone. According to DSS, participating in *this* tradition is what enables Christians to recognize one another as Christians, even as each group represents different traditions in the two previous senses of this term. If THE CHRISTIAN TRADITION is *transcendent* history, then it cannot be subject to the dynamics of historical consciousness. Since, however, historical consciousness is *the* way of appropriating an historic heritage in *any* sense, as DSS strongly affirms, then such transcendent history cannot be appropriated by anyone at all. The fourth use of "tradition" refers to a "common heritage," a "core of doctrine" which is the "touchstone" by which all Christian teaching is to be tested. This is the crucial referent; as has been pointed out previously, it is this sense of "tradition" which articulates *the* theological norm in DSS, its many statements to the contrary notwithstanding. Tradition in *this* sense clearly is what possesses the *primary* status among the four guidelines. For DSS finally maintains that the "common heritage," with its common "core of doctrine" (specifically the non-juridical *regula fidei* referred to above), is what transcends doctrinal pluralism, and by so doing, becomes normative *for* historical consciousness. But how can this be so? If one is truly to take historical consciousness seriously, must he not subsume *every* kind of tradition under it, even the "common core," leaving open the possibility that even that very common history may have to assume a radically new form in new worlds of meaning yet to emerge? While a "common tradition" is a presupposition of theological reflection, it cannot become the norm for such reflection except as statements about it are themselves governed by the principle of historical interpretation.

(A brief addendum on this same subject: DSS refers to *two* ways in which Christians come to acknowledge one another as Christians, in and through their diverse and rich heritages—through *catholic belief*, and through *transcendent* TRADITION. Its concluding statement speaks of United Methodists' "shared tradition": "Our shared tradition, with other Christians, as well as the distinctive United Methodist emphases, is the context in which we work." In this locution no attempt is made to clarify *which* of these two meanings for "shared tradition" is implied. Is there, inadvertently to be sure, in this document a *decretum horribile* which *identifies* the two?)

A Personal Critique

If the foregoing appraisal is sound, then much the more important emphasis in United Methodist teaching for the foreseeable future likely will be the recovery of catholic tradition. In the following pages reasons will be offered for this writer's growing conviction that catholic tradition cannot be normative for theological reflection, his own especially.

Christian belief in a "common Christian tradition" which is normative for theological judgment rests upon two convictions: (a) that God has intervened directly in human history to sustain the life of a particular community, and (b) that he himself insures that community's witness to his gracious work against consummate error: hence, later generations are assured access to his original disclosures in their saving power. For almost three centuries now, however, there has loomed over these convictions the spirit of Enlightenment humanism, whose own critical convictions are (a) that the enhancement of human experience constitutes the legitimate end of every endeavor and the norm by which every determining influence upon human life is to be evaluated; and (b) that history is a humanly contrived ordering of experience, whose authoritativeness for any generation derives from its contribution to the fulfillment of human possibilities in that generation.

The essential legacy of the Enlightenment is the affirmation that human beings are the measure of history; the authoritativeness of the past always must be subject to their confirmation in the light of their present circumstances. Thus, every achievement of a culture is subject to continuing reassessment by its inheritors, in the light of *their* needs, hopes, and ideals. This is not all to reaffirm the purely polemical side of Enlightenment thinking, which employed critical philosophy and positivistic historiography to undermine *all* claims about transcendent reality and its impingement upon the natural and historical order. The

59

most serious implication of Enlightenment thinking, which ought now to be beyond serious question, is simply and less polemically that Christian history, whether explicitly denominational or truly ecumenical, is *one* way of organizing experience. Christian faith includes belief that God ordains its development, but it cannot establish that belief by reference to universally accepted criteria. The significance of Christian history is its power to illumine the human struggle to cope creatively with situatedness in a world; its very liveliness is as a *human contrivance*. With every heritage, then, Christian history is open to transvaluation if present experience should demand dismantling its cultural forms and institutional embodiments for the sake of a richer present and future.

Enlightenment criticism continues to call into question the authoritativeness of the Christian past through its humanistic approach to the materials of Scripture and tradition. By subjecting the revered documents of Christianity to the criteria by which all historical data are to be assessed, it substitutes, for the belief that Scripture and tradition are divinely transmitted, the hypothesis (which does not *deny* the former, but only brackets it from further consideration) that they are part of the whole body of literature by which human beings express themselves and their responses to the world creatively. The new insights into the materials which such an approach yields clearly is at the expense of their authoritativeness in the traditional sense. From an Enlightenment perspective, the authority of the Bible could derive only from the proximity of its witnesses to the events recounted, not from inspiration, however this latter may be defined.

Once the critical process was begun in earnest, tradition soon was regarded as a corruption of biblical faith. But by the late nineteenth century, the Bible *itself* became questionable as the mediator of an authoritative past. Now, for example, it is known that the earliest copies available of the entire New Testament date from the 4th century A.D., and that there are several; though in substantial agreement as to their content, they permit significant variations, as new translations show. And even if it is supposed that the fourth century texts are accurate copies, one still cannot presume naively that they mediate the witness of Jesus' contemporaries. The manuscripts compile a tradition which developed by word of mouth before any of it seems to have been set down in writing. Did the oral tradition embellish the testimony? Since it was in the interest of Jesus' followers to be as accurate as possible in handing on the message entrusted to them, the risk of error might be said to be minimal. However, those who transmitted the tradition also had the most to gain by presenting it in a positive light; as is well known, those personally involved in events often are the least reliable in reporting them. Finally, the manuscripts represent, especially in the case of the gospels, the gathering of diverse traditions according to principles of organization which cannot be demonstrated to be intrinsic even to the oral tradition, much less to Jesus' contemporaries. Redaction criticism especially makes plain that Christian faith is an *interpretation* of the human situation, by human beings. It is a superlative interpretation. But the original events interpreted seem to be accessible, if at all, only through corporate memory within which interpretation and embellishment have functioned in wholly human senses. Invocation of the divine grounding of Christian history is indispensable to Christian faith; but as a necessary component *within* an interpretation of the human condition, it is difficult to defend convincingly to anyone who has chosen not to enter into the life which so witnesses. (Although it is precisely the task of apologetics to achieve this difficult task, and in ways which do not merely presuppose the interpretation in question.)

This kind of critical reflection frequently and wrongly has been viewed as an attempt to relativize the claims of the Christian faith, with "relativizing" understood as a weakening of their force. Such a view overlooks the profound and paradoxical influence which any interpretation of existence actually can have upon the development of human history and the ordering of human experience. On the one hand, the perspectives by which one lives are eminently changeable, especially when they come to be understood *as* perspectives. On the other hand, however, perspectives also condition human experience inescapably. They do not derive from careful observation and inference; they are "world-views" which provide the very rules for determining whether any appearance is to be accorded the status of significant datum at all. What shall be noticed is defined *by* and not *for* a perspective; the perspective which one inherits to a large extent governs how he will see things. To illustrate: primitive man's perspective apparently included the belief that nothing has definite location in space and time. Thus, he was constantly haunted by the spectre of being overtaken by an enemy, whether living or dead, even those who resided too far away to be a genuine threat. By contrast, moderns perceive things as necessarily locatable at some point in space and time. In both cases, however, the perspective determines *how* things will be seen; it is not itself determined by what is seen. Though human beings have "conversion" experiences, in the sense that sometimes they seem to "leap" from one perspective to another, such experiences are rare.

It is this kind of determining power which enables "perspectivalism" to counter the accusation that its relativizing of Christian history is at the expense of faith's persuasiveness. For while it is true that human beings' histories are culturally contrived rather than divinely bestowed, the authority with which one's history dominates his consciousness is profound. Learning that one's governing standpoint is a humanly conceived perspective does not liberate one immediately to take up another. For instance: one crucial presupposition of the Christian perspective is that faith is a response to revelation; within the perspective it is illegitimate even to *ask* the question whether there *is* any such thing as revelation. Though believers frequently ask whether some specific event is revelatory, if they were to question revelation as such, they would no longer stand within faith. But to know that believing in revelation is conditioned by a perspective which is dependent upon the belief for its very integrity does not itself reduce the force of such believing. Or: the presupposition of the scientific perspective is that nature is uniform. But no proof is ever advanced for this claim; indeed, within science one cannot even *ask* whether nature is uniform. The question is significant only from some perspective other than the scientific one. Knowing all of this, however, does not itself reduce the force of the perspectives in question. It does, however, humanize them. And therein lies the distinctive break with tradition-oriented theologies.

These implications might be avoided through appealing to the transcendent work of the Holy Spirit as the ground of Christendom's authoritative past. But "orthodoxy" affirms also that the work of the Holy Spirit is primarily to attest the truth of *past testimony*. The Holy Spirit is not a new source of insight about God: it enlivens the witness to God already revealed in Jesus Christ. Whatever else the Holy Spirit effects in human experience, he activates faith in *that* God and no *other* God. The Holy Spirit arouses in believers a sense of the presence of God whenever testimony to God's revelation in the *past* is offered again. Clearly, then, the intelligibility of this doctrine depends upon one's already knowing to what that past testimony is testimony, decisively and authoritatively, precisely the kind of knowing which Enlightenment criticism so impressively calls into question. If believers cannot be certain of what those events were like in which God decisively revealed himself, they cannot know what it is which the Holy Spirit is to confirm in their lives.

Conclusion

Unless the church is to theologize as if the Enlightenment had never dawned at all, she now must affirm that the God who always has been loyal to his chosen people is recognized in history because he also and especially makes himself known in *present* power. Theology which aims to articulate such an affirmation comprehensively must seek (a) to illumine those regions of experience, potentially available to all, in which that reality appears *now* whose name is God, (b) to show how participation in a history contributes to the interpretation of those present experiences, and (c) to show how experience of God's presence, occasioned by one's involvement in a community of faith with a history, uniquely energizes human resources for creating the future.

The crucial observation to be made, however, is that to address (b) in such wise is already to subordinate radically the authoritativeness of the past in its own right to the status of a *condition* for the faithful life, whose configurations may move far beyond what that past either could permit or envision. As they presently stand, in this writer's judgment, United Methodist doctrinal standards do not provide an assured standpoint from which to carry out such a project.

Chapter 5

CHURCH DOCTRINAL STANDARDS TODAY

Robert E. Cushman[1]

In Methodism the concept of doctrinal standards is as old as John Wesley himself and, in the church organized in America in 1784, has as old an official status as the First Restrictive Rule of *The Doctrines and Discipline* of 1808: "The General Conference shall not revoke, alter or change our Articles of Religion or establish any new standards or rules of doctrine contrary to our present existing and established standards of doctrine."

Coincident with unification of The Methodist Church with the Evangelical United Brethren, the General Conference of 1968 established a Commission on Doctrine and Doctrinal Standards for study and report. The Commission undertook a quadrennial task and in 1972 submitted its unanimous findings for legislative action to the General Conference, with the stipulation of the chairman that "we do not regard it [the document moved for adoption] as in violation of the First, Second, or Fifth restrictive rules." In accord with the motion, the report was adopted in place of its disciplinary antecedent (1968) and was published as Part II of the Book of Discipline, 1972. The stipulation, on presentation to the General Conference, that the legislation before the supreme law-making body did not invoke or infringe upon the Restrictive Rules was sustained by Decision No. 358 of the church's Judicial Council.

Of Part II of the Book of Discipline there are three sections: (1) Historical Background, (2) Landmark Documents, and (3) Our Theological Task. In principle and fact, Section 2 republishes undoubted historic doctrinal standards of the former churches, now The United Methodist Church. These include the Twenty-five Articles of Religion (1784), the Confession of Faith of the former EUB Church (1962), and the General Rules (1784).

When, in these times, a major Protestant church not only aspires but ventures to risk reexamination of its doctrinal heritage with a view to assessing where indeed it stands with reference to historic norms, present internal uncertainties, and relentless worldly metamorphosis, the result should command the attention of serious churchmen almost anywhere. Not only what is essayed but also what is accomplished may be revealing, or at least symptomatic, of what mainline Protestant Christianity in general may undergo in attempting to give an account of itself doctrinally in an era almost incomparably secularized and markedly pluralized. Nor can we deny that the climate of the age so invades some Protestant communions as that an intramural *consensus fidelium* is hardly to be looked for.

It is primarily the want of this consensus, however, which constitutes, at one and the same time, both the risk of such an undertaking and also its imperative. Herewith the churches confront an agonizing dilemma not unlike that of Pope John XXIII in proclaiming *aggiornamento*. Moreover, derivative of this situation is an inherent, attendant twofold problem: (1) On the one hand, how can a secularized church arrive at a *consensus fidelium*, i.e., viable doctrinal unanimity faithful to the tradition? (2) And conversely, how can practicing theologians function if the churches are doctrinally incoherent or unable for want of consensus to clarify doctrinal standards, either by reaffirmation or by reformulation? With whom or what lies the norm?

United Methodist Conciliarism and Process Theology

As I study Part II, one feature fully merits our attention. It is everywhere implicit and recurrently explicit that doctrinal standards and, indeed, Christian theologizing are taken to be a proper task and responsibility of the whole church, and there is conspicuous absence of any mention of theologians. Thus, a frankly conciliar conception of the source of doctrinal standards is affirmed while, at the same time and somewhat shockingly, it is also affirmed that "in this task of reappraising and applying the gospel, theological pluralism should be recognized as a principle."

In Section 3 this conciliar stress is emphatic in such words as: "The United Methodist Church expects all its members to accept the challenge of responsible theological reflection." If this expectancy is exorbitant, the risk is somewhat curtailed by the definition of "doctrinal guidelines" (i.e., the norms of Scripture, tradition, experience, and reason) and by explicit delimitation of theological initiatives according to a twofold rule, *viz.*, "careful regard to our heritage and fourfold guidelines, and the double test of acceptability and edification in corporate worship and common life."

In sum, Part II, Section 3 commits itself to something very close to corporate ecclesial responsibility for the authorization and development of doctrinal standards. The move seems to be in the direction of a kind of collegial *magisterium*, of which there are no elders or bishops as guardians of the faith once delivered to the saints. Indeed, it is denied that doctrinal statements are the special province of "any single body, board, or agency," and none others are dignified by so much as a mention.

We have, then, I would think, a most emphatic commitment to a species of intramural conciliarism as the source and authorization of doctrinal standards. Procedurally this may not entirely accord with the tradition of historic Methodism, which, in fact, early made the Conference the prime judicatory for both faith and order. To this, Section 1, "Historical Background," itself gives prominence without, however, noting that Wesley's Conference was composed of preachers and was itself something of a catechetical school. Yet it is now daringly proposed that the whole church become, as it were, a catechetical school writ large for the crossing of what are called "theological frontiers" and in "new directions." Then, rather distinguishing the church from its pilgrim people, it is declared: "The Church's role in this tenuous process is to provide a stable and sustaining environment in which theological conflict can be constructive and productive."

From such a statement a question emerges as to what stability may be expected of a church possessed, for doctrinal standards, of little more than "landmark documents" and for whose pilgrim people doctrine is spoken of most nearly as a continuing process of "informed theological experimentation" and "our never-ending tasks of theologizing." This conception of doctrine as process is to be sure not unchecked by the already noted twofold condition: "careful regard for our heritage and fourfold guidelines." We shall, then, have to examine more closely what is allowed respecting the normativeness of our acknowledged doctrinal heritage.

Our Doctrinal Heritage: Status and Function

The authors of Part II are aware that they are faced with the question "as to the status and function of 'doctrinal standards' in The United Methodist Church" as an inherited issue. Both Sections 1 and 3 manifest conspicuous effort to attain firm dialectical balance between the norm of tradition with loyalty to our heritage on the one side and to make way for timely doctrinal restatement on the other. I would wish to acknowledge the earnestness with which our document faces the treacherous task of attempting to balance the reciprocal counterclaims of loyalty and freedom. We can consider only briefly these contraries in tension, the principle of freedom first.

One has the impression that operative in favor of the principle of freedom are certain prepossessions of thought as various as: Wesley's important sermon, "Catholic Spirit"; John Henry Newman's theory of the development of dogma; the *aggiornamento* of Vatican II; American process theology; and a wee bit of existential openness for the future. All these leave their mark, but preeminently does Wesley's denigration of what he called "opinion" in matters religious—a concept popularly misunderstood but not, I think, misused in our document.

Disregarding these presumed prepossessions, certain working principles favoring flexibility in doctrinal standards and hospitable to "yet further unfoldings of history" in continuing doctrinal developments are worth noting. They fall into the following groups: (1) judgments of historical fact as interpreted, (2) principles of historical interpretation, (3) axiomatical theological postulates, and (4) pragmatic-prudential considerations.

Among a dozen historical judgments precedential for the principle of freedom and development are such debatable assertions as: that among the fathers of Methodism "doctrinal pluralism" already was acknowledged; that they declined to adopt the "classical forms of the confessional principle"; that a conciliar principle in "collegial formula" was manifest in the Model Deed; that the role of the Articles was ambiguous early in nineteenth-century Methodism. It is judged that the collegial formula "committed the Methodist people to the biblical revelation as primary without proposing a literal summary of that revelation in any propositional form." This last seems right-headed enough save for the objectionable confusion of creedal symbol with a literal proposition.

Finally, and of large import, is the dubious historical judgment rendered upon the longstanding Articles and the Confession that they "are not to be regarded as positive, juridical norms of doctrine," although it is not clear whether this is meant to characterize their past status by alleged longstanding consensus or their future standing. In response to this judgment, one is disposed to inquire earnestly by what rationale the First Restrictive Rule was first instituted in 1808 and with what purpose it has survived in the intervening wisdom of the church. What was the function of such a rule if indeed the confessional principle was as much a matter of indifference to the mind of the church as is represented?

As to principles of historical interpretation there is space to mention but two or three: emphatically conciliar in import is the hermeneutical principle that "Scripture is rightly read and understood *within* the believing community." This also is anticipated and affirmed in Wesley's way of interpreting biblical language—another question of fact. Secondly, the "new historical consciousness" justifies the historical interpretation of all historical documents and thus also the Methodist Articles or Confession—meaning that they are relative to their given context and so without finality. On this ground, there emerges the third and decisive principle, that all doctrinal standards of the past, present, or future are "landmark documents." They may be pointers to the truth, never finalities. And, finally, the infinite qualitative difference between time and eternity is illustrated in the self-evident proposition that "God's eternal Word never has been, nor can be exhaustively expressed in any single form of words." In consequence, it is perhaps in order to be informed, as historical *fact*, that the founding fathers did not invest "summaries of Christian truth . . . with final authority or set them apart as absolute standards for doctrinal truth and error."

One outcome of this hermeneutic is surely expressed in the following summation: "But, since they are not accorded any status of finality, either in content or rhetoric, there is no objection in principle to the continued development of still other doctrinal summaries and liturgical creeds that may gain acceptance and use in the Church—without displacing those we already have. This principle of the historical interpretation of all doctrinal statements, past and present, is crucial."

The express denial of any status of finality, of course, imperils the very conception of doctrinal standards and would seem to require positive attention to the question of such surviving normativeness they might yet command. The final quoted sentence strikes me as a remarkable understatement. Depending on how it is hereafter to be used, it is momentous in implication for all doctrinal standards whatsoever (i.e., norms)—and not only those past or present, but, on the same principle of historical interpretation, *those of any conceivable future*. Accordingly, it is not out of keeping that Section 3, whether intentionally or not, tends to replace *all* past, present, or future doctrine or dogma with an unlimited *process* of "theologizing."

In this perspective, is it something like the case that the church is now to live perpetually on theological credit? In reflection one is inclined to wonder whether the authors of this document either did not fully understand their own logic as a committee, or that some did, and because they had relinquished any possibility of standards had resort to collective "theologizing" as a permanent substitute for doctrine. Yet this seems to be the outcome of the logic employed, however awkward the new day in which the church is obliged to rely mainly for truths to live by upon the ever-receding promise of the future.

Primary Theological Postulates and the Core of Doctrine

By examining some theological postulates of our document—mainly set forth in Section 3, "Our Theological Task"—we may be better informed respecting the unanswered question as to what normativeness the "landmark documents" may yet possess, deprived, as they are said to be, of any status of finality. At the same time, we may be better positioned to judge the success of our document in achieving a balance between loyalty and freedom toward the heritage of doctrinal standards. That Part II aspires to such a balance is a note variously sounded, as, for example, with reference to emerging ecumenical theology which seeks to "provide a constructive alternative" to the confessional tradition or in the expressed view in retrospect that Part II has been seeking to chart "a course between doctrinal dogmatism on the one hand and doctrinal indifferentism on the other."

Methodologically speaking, this disavowal of indifferentism in doctrine does operate as a theological postulate whether vindicated or not. It has explicit antecedence in Wesley's pervasive teaching on "the catholic spirit," which rejects speculative or practical latitudinarianism and excludes, therefore, indifferentism in either doctrine or ecclesiology. Whether the contrasting phrase "doctrinal dogmatism" is unduly denigrative of "doctrinal standards" we leave unattended. It suffices here to note that on its face our document allies itself with Wesley in rejecting indifferentism and sets aside as erroneous "the notion that there are no essential doctrines and that differences in theology, when sincerely held, need no further discussion." To this extent, then, we must acknowledge that theological pluralism considered as a principle suffers some modification.

A second primary postulate prefaces Section 3: "Both our heritage in doctrine and our present theological task share common aims: The continuously renewed grasp of the gospel of God's love in Christ and its application in the ceaseless crises of human existence." Herewith, it is plainly indicated that the doctrinal process proceeds both with a core inheritance and is undertaken in context. Our theological task, then, is always contextual and, for that reason, must appropriately take the form of an answering process if it is to be living or relevant. This undergirds the postulate of theological development as an inescapable requirement, which is yet a third.

But let us consider the postulate of the "core" of Christian truth as a fourth postulate, although it deserves to be regarded, and does function, as primary in Section 3. I think it is not misleading to say that the core of any surviving doctrinal standard is intended to be encapsuled in the already quoted phrase, "the gospel of God's love in Christ." The key paragraph is the first under the heading "United Methodists and the Christian Tradition." There it is said that Methodist theologizing does not begin *de novo*, but shares a "common heritage with all other Christians everywhere and in all ages." It is affirmed that there "is a core of doctrine which informs in greater or less degree our widely divergent interpretations." It is not clear whether "divergent interpretations" refers to the *oikoumene* or to Methodists themselves, but we may safely assume to both.

But here one thing becomes very clear: the well-known scene of ecumenical diversity is being applied by analogy to a single denomination (the Methodist), and that, partly on this analogy, the factual diversity *without* (as among denominations *inter alia*) is affirmed to obtain *within* Methodism as a fact but also as a norm. That is, I think, misuse of analogy, but it becomes another basic and unexamined postulate which contributes its unannounced support for the presiding thesis of "theological pluralism as a principle." An appropriate rejoinder may well be the question, With what right is factual doctrinal diversity among a plurality of separate churches taken to be a standard model in assessing the role and status of doctrinal standards in any *one* denomination? To assume that it is or may be modular or normative begs the question on an issue of maximum importance.

What, then, is "core of doctrine," and what is its status for "doctrinal standards" in The United Methodist Church? It is at this point that the assessment of the issue of loyalty will have to be played down to the wire. The core in our document is delineated under two aspects: (1) The first succinctly relates the principal doctrinal content of the universally shared Christian tradition on pages 71–72. This is the "common faith in the mystery of salvation in and through Jesus Christ," which includes overcoming our willful alienation through God's pardoning love in Christ and states that through faith, enabled by the Holy Spirit, we receive "the gift of reconciliation and justification." (2) The second aspect of the core of doctrine, presuming the common Christian tradition as above, singles out distinctive emphases or particular traditions of the Methodist heritage. These, with right, may be viewed as truly embedded in that tradition and as rooted in both the *Standard Sermons* of John Wesley and in the liturgy and hymnody, and exemplified in the Social

Creed of American Methodism. Since they are readily available, and for economy of space, I pass over their substance.

Such, then, is the "common," together with the "distinctive," core of the doctrinal heritage by which it is indicated our loyalty ought rightly to be claimed as a wholesome guide and check upon freedom in theologizing. This doctrinal core is, then, a norm claiming our respect, but evidently not our adherence. However, as we scrutinize the language of our document respecting the normativeness of the core of doctrine, a resilient ambiguity persists.

Four Successive Postulates and Theological Pluralism

On further examination, the ambiguity appears to rest upon a succession of mutually supportive unexplicated theological postulates that, collectively, reinforce the thesis of "theological pluralism . . . as a principle." This may indicate that the ambiguity is intentional or at least unavoidable in view of the premises.

The first postulate takes the form of a tacit definition of the nature and the status of the doctrinal heritage represented by the core in the following proposition: "From our response in faith to the wondrous mystery of God's love in Jesus Christ as recorded in Scripture, all valid Christian doctrine is born." Doctrine, then, is always faith's response to the mystery. Its nature and status are that it is *our response*. Such a status is also that of the traditions of doctrine which are later described as "the residue of corporate experience of earlier Christian communities." Actually, the postulate simply reiterates the earlier declaration of Section 1: "that God's eternal Word never has been, nor can be, exhaustively expressed in any single form of words." Here, then, the limit to finality — and now with respect, not simply to the Confessions but to the core of tradition — is not the historical relativity of any response of faith; it is, rather, the ineffability of the eternal Word or the wondrous mystery that is symbolized.

The seconding postulate occurs earlier in our document and is used to retire the older "confessional tradition" in favor of "our newer experiments in ecumenical theology." Apparently, there is here further unargued dependency on analogy earlier noted. Thereafter, the passing of the confessional tradition in favor of the ecumenical method in doctrine is justified by the seconding postulate: "The transcendent mystery of divine truth allows us in good conscience to acknowledge the positive virtues of doctrinal pluralism even within the same community of believ-

ers, not merely because such an attitude is realistic." Immediately thereafter, it is stated: "The invitation to theological reflection is open to all."

The third consummating postulate is, then, invoked in the paragraph
just mentioned, although carried over from its earlier formulation "as
the principle of the historical interpretation of all doctrinal statements"—self-styled as crucial, as already discussed. It is this hermeneutical principle that banishes any status of finality for standards and opens
the door to horizons unlimited in theological development. And it is this
that justifies not only the thesis of theological pluralism as a principle
but does so by way of the final postulate.

The fourth postulate functions as the conclusion of the series. It first
appeared and offered itself as a judgment of alleged historical fact, *viz.*,
that the Methodist fathers "declined to adopt the classical forms of the
confessional principle." It now appears in the succession of scantily
supported theological postulates as the conclusion: "No creed or doctrinal summary can adequately serve the needs and intentions of United
Methodists in confessing their faith or in celebrating their Christian
experience" (p. 79). This is, indeed, far-reaching in import and amply
supplies the rationale for the view that our doctrinal standards are
merely landmark documents. It also appropriately justifies the exordium,
viz., "The United Methodist Church expects all its members to accept the
challenge of responsible theological reflection." If there is no finally
reliable past in standards, perhaps hope may yet make a future! So be it,
but the concluding postulate, standing as an unsupported *ipse dixit*,
smacks rather more of academic sophistication than of the living piety
of generations of Christians who have found in the venerable language
of the Liturgy and the Creed more than enough light to illumine their
darkness, indeed more than they used.

A Brief Provisional Assessment

This critical analysis must be abruptly terminated without further
needed scrutiny of certain of the working postulates, consideration of
the role of "experience" in the Wesleyan tradition, or perhaps adequate
attention to a defined method for doctrinal development which does set
some bounds to conciliar "theologizing" that is otherwise enthusiastically enthroned. This methodology is developed under the heading "Doctrinal Guidelines in The United Methodist Church."

The treatment of guidelines is knowledgeable and skillfully ex-
ecuted. It invokes a fourfold reference to Scripture, tradition, experience,
and reason as guidelines in theological reflection. It finds them in Wesley

and attributes their centrality to the founding fathers. The method is briefly stated very early in Section 1. There it is allowed that the fathers did acknowledge a marrow of true doctrine, and states: "This living core, as they believed, stands revealed in Scripture, illumined by tradition, vivified in personal experience, and confirmed by reason."

In this viewpoint, attributed to the Methodist fathers, we seem to be within reach of some yardstick to measure loyalty to doctrinal standards. It may be inadvertent as it is, I believe, unfortunate that the later, more expansive treatment of "guidelines" does not recapture the centrality of Scripture or vindicate its primacy. On the contrary, it vitiates the greater decisiveness of the earlier passage in which tradition, experience, and reason are recognized, in that order, and are subsumed to the primacy of Scripture. Such a viewpoint might well have clarified the dialectic balance of loyalty and freedom, and likewise qualified the outcome, by way of appropriating faith, to be what Wesley did describe, among his sermons, as "Scriptural Christianity." Yet under "Doctrinal Guidelines," faith, though possibly presupposed, has no mention as requisite for operation of the guidelines. In fact, justifying faith has scant treatment in the entire document and is scarcely conceived as the presupposition of Christian theology.

This, too, contributes to the vitiation of the standpoint justly attributed to the fathers respecting the primacy of Scripture, but of course for faith. But the decisive vitiation of the admirable earlier statement quoted above and the resurgence of ambiguity ensues again with the following two sentences in summation of the Guidelines: "There is a primacy that goes with Scripture, as the constitutive witness to biblical wellsprings of our faith. In practice, however, theological reflection may find its point of departure in tradition, 'experience,' or rational analysis."

This statement takes back, it seems, with the left hand what it gives with the right. Moreover, the extraordinary second sentence in this binary formulation quite evidently gives covey to every species of theological partridge except one bred in the Reformation tradition or cognizant of the Pauline gospel. Allowing for whatever the qualifier, "in practice," may mean to the authors, the latter sentence allows to Scripture only par value with the other three norms. But, altogether astonishing, it gives back all that Part II has striven to deny, namely, the confessional principle or tradition, as a starting point in doctrinal formulation. Finally, it is an understatement to observe that *Christian* doctrine, of whatever provenance, has not often found its starting point in "rational analysis." This is a fatal sentence, but perhaps it illustrates a pervasive claim of the document that all theological reflection is historically conditioned.

So far as this analysis has taken us, ambiguity respecting the status of doctrinal standards remains largely unrelieved and the vindication of a true dialectical balance of loyalty and freedom seems unattained. Among things accomplished is a rather fervent postulation of fully liberated conciliarism conceived in virtual equivalence with twentieth-century ongoing interchurch ecumenical dialogue. Without adequate representation of the case, this is unhesitatingly proposed as the timely model for intramural doctrinal standards, both in status and in function. In addition to installing intramural theological pluralism on principle, Part II is correspondingly bent upon the eradication of what it recognizes as "classical forms of the confessional principle." Perhaps it has won favor because in The United Methodist Church, as doubtless elsewhere, theological "indifferentism" has for long been nurturing a favorable climate.

Chapter 6

THE WESLEYAN QUADRILATERAL—IN JOHN WESLEY

by Albert C. Outler[1]

For five full decades, John Wesley served as theological mentor to "the people called Methodists," with no peer and no successful challengers. Throughout that half-century, he was embroiled in one doctrinal controversy after another—with Anglican priests and bishops, with Calvinist partisans (clerical and lay) and with occasional dissidents within his own "connexion." Doctrinal consensus was a prime concern with him and a prerequisite for stability in the Methodist Societies. Thus, at the outset of his first "conference" with his "assistants" (1744), the first questions posed for discussion were:

(1) *What* to teach?
(2) *How* to teach?
(3) What to *do* (i.e., how to regulate our doctrine, discipline and practice)?

There was, of course, no question in anyone's mind as to who would have the final word in these conversations but everyone agreed that these were the right questions for a religious society within an established church.

As the Methodist movement spread and matured, Wesley supplied it with reams of theological and ethical instruction, in different *genres*: sermons, letters, tracts, exegetical notes, a huge *Journal*, even a full-length monograph (on *Original Sin*). But—and this, of course, is my point—there is only one instance in all of this of anything resembling a doctrinal credo (in his open "Letter to a Roman Catholic," 1749) and even this was an obvious borrowing from Bishop John Pearson's classic *Exposition of the Doctrine of the Creed*—the bishop's counterpart to the Westminster Confession and Shorter Catechism. Wesley seems never to have toyed with the notion of a *summa theologiae*—not even a catechism. What then did he expect his people to identify as their "standards of doctrine"?

His first move had been to abridge the first four Edwardian Homilies (of 1547) into a brief theological charter: *The Doctrine of Justification according to the Church of England.*[2] Then as the Revival gained momentum, he turned to the method of conciliar dialogue, gathering his assistants together by invitation. He himself recorded the upshot of their discussions and published this in a cumulative set of *Minutes of Conversations Between the Rev. Mr. Wesley and Others* (1744 *et seq.*). The theological substance of these "minutes" reflects the mind and spirit of early Methodism very well indeed. A version of them ("The Large Minutes") was accepted by the fledgling Methodist Episcopal Church in American and so may be considered as included within the scope of that notoriously ambiguous phrase in "The First Restrictive Rule" (1808) in the Methodist Book of Discipline concerning "our present existing, and established, standards of doctrine."

In 1763, in what came to be known as "The Model Deed" Wesley proceeded to stipulate the *negative limits* of Methodist doctrine—*viz.,* that preachers in Methodist chapels were to preach "no other doctrine than is contained in Mr. Wesley's *Notes Upon the New Testament* and four volumes of *Sermons*." This provided his people with a doctrinal canon that was stable enough and yet also flexible. In it, the Holy Scriptures stand first and foremost, and yet subject to interpretations that are informed by "Christian Antiquity," critical reason *and* an existential appeal to the "Christian experience" of grace, so firmly stressed in the *Explanatory Notes*. The "four volumes" mentioned in the "Model Deed" contained either forty-three or forty-four sermons, depending on whether or not one counts "Wandering Thoughts."[3] All this suggests that Wesley was clearly interested in coherent doctrinal norms but was equally clear in his aversion to having such norms defined too narrowly or in too juridical a form. Thus, he was content with exegetical "notes" (eager to borrow heavily from others), plus a sampling of sermons (he would have dismissed all haggling over the *number* of "standard sermons!")— and, of course, the Wesley hymns (Charles' and his own). These non-confessional norms served his people well for the better part of two full centuries.

Wesley's refusal to define "doctrinal standards" too narrowly was a matter of principle: it was in no way the sign of an indecisive mind. Such a notion makes no sense when one considers how confident his own theological self-understanding was (as reflected in his controversial writings), and in his arbitrary decisions as an editor. Take a single example from several hundred: in *A Christian Library* (vol. 31), he felt free to make some fairly drastic revisions of the *Westminster Shorter Catechism* and thus on his own authority to "correct" what was a semi-sacrosanct text! Then, too, there were his equally drastic revisions of the Book of Common Prayer, with his brusque self-justification for simply having omitted a large fraction of the Psalter, characterizing the excluded Psalms as "not fit for the mouths of a Christian congregation." No, Wesley's refusal to provide the Methodist people with a confession for subscription was the conviction of a man who knew his own mind on every vexed question of Christian doctrine, but who had decided that the reduction of doctrine to any particular form of words was to misunderstand the very nature of doctrinal statements.

But does this mean, then, that Wesley was indifferentist? *Mē genoito!* His working concepts of doctrinal authority were carefully worked out; they were complex and dynamically balanced. When challenged for his authority, on any question, his first appeal was to the Holy Bible, always in the sense of Article VI in the Thirty-nine Articles—to which he had subscribed but which he was prepared to quote inexactly. Even so, he was well aware that Scripture alone had rarely settled any controverted point of doctrine. He and his critics had repeatedly come to impasses in their games of proof-testing—often with the same texts! Thus, though never as a substitute or corrective, he would also appeal to "the primitive church" and to the Christian tradition at large as competent, complementary witnesses to "the meaning" of this Scripture or that. Even in such appeals, he was carefully selective. For example, he claimed the right to reject the damnatory clauses in the so-called "Athanasian Creed"; he was prepared to defend Montanus and *Pelagius* against their detractors. He insisted that "private judgment was the keystone of the Protestant Reformation."

But Scripture and tradition would not suffice without the good offices (positive and negative) of critical reason. Thus, he insisted on logical coherence as an authorized referee in any contest between contrary propositions or arguments. And yet, this was never enough. It was, as he knew for himself, the vital Christian experience of the assurance of one's sins forgiven that clinched the matter.

Thus, we can see in Wesley a distinctive theological *method*, with Scripture as its preeminent norm but interfaced with tradition, reason, and Christian experience as dynamic and interactive aids in the interpretation of the Word of God in Scripture. Such a method takes it for granted that faith is human *re*-action to an antecedent action of the Holy Spirit's prevenience, aimed at convicting our consciences and opening our eyes and ears to God's address to us in Scripture. This means that our "knowledge of God and of the things of God" is more nearly a response of trusting faith in God in Christ as Grace Incarnate than it is a mental assent to dogmatic formulations however true. This helps explain Wesley's studied deprecations of "orthodoxy," "theological opinions," "speculative divinity" and the like. It illumines his preoccupation with soteriology and his distinctive notion of grace, in all its modes, as the divine constant in every stage of the "order of salvation" (from repentance and justification, to regeneration, sanctification—on to glory). And it justified Wesley's willingness, given honest consensus on essential Christian doctrine, to allow for wide variations in theological formulation and thus for Christians "to think and let think." This was less a mood of doctrinal compromise than it was a constructive alternative to the barren extremes of "dogmatism," on the one side, and "indifferentism," on the other.

Wesley's theological pluralism was evangelical in substance (firm and clear in its Christocentric focus) and irenic in its temper ("catholic spirit"). It measured all doctrinal statements by their biblical base and warrants. He loved to summon his readers "to the law and the testimony," understood as "the oracles of God." But this reliance on Scripture as *the* fount of revelation was never meant to preclude a concomitant appeal to the insights of wise and saintly Christians in other ages. And it never gave license to "enthusiasm" or to irrational arguments. Finally, since the devils are at least as clear in their theological assents as believers are, real Christians are called beyond "orthodoxy" to authentic experience—*viz.*, the inner witness of the Holy Spirit that *we* are God's beloved children, and joint-heirs with Christ. It is this settled sense of personal assurance that is "heart-religion": the turning of our hearts from the form to the power of religion. Christian experience adds nothing to the substance of Christian truth; its distinctive role is to energize the heart so as to enable the believer to speak and do the truth in love.

This complex method, with its fourfold reference, is a good deal more sophisticated than it appears, and could be more fruitful for contemporary theologizing than has yet been realized. It preserves the primacy of Scripture, it profits from the wisdom of tradition, it accepts the disciplines of critical reason, and its stress on the Christian experience of grace gives it existential force.

The Edwardian reformers (Cranmer and Harpsfield in particular) had placed the Church of England under the authority of Scripture, but they had then refocused its use more largely in the liturgy (so that "the Christian folk could be immersed in Scripture as they prayed"!). The Scripture is equally the baseline of Anglican doctrinal essays, especially those born of controversy. One has only to notice the differences in method and intention in, say, Richard Hooker's *Laws of Ecclesiastical Polity* (1594 *et seq.*) to see how far Anglicanism stood apart from continental Protestantism. In Hooker, Scripture, tradition, and reason are carefully balanced off in a vision of natural law, "whose seat is the bosom of God, whose voice is the harmony of the world."[4] There is no contradiction between reason's discoveries of natural law and faith's discoveries of revelation.[5] Bishops John Bramhall and Simon Patrick had mastered "Christian Antiquity" and had put it to good use. Thomas Tenison (Archbishop of Canterbury when the brothers Wesley were born) had defined "the Protestant theological method" as the conjoint "use of Scripture, tradition, and reason" and had defended this against the Socinians (who had, as Tenison believed, downscaled tradition and ended up with nothing better than a tepid biblical rationalism). Even after Wesley, Francis Paget (Hooker's best editor) could claim, quite plausibly, that "the distinctive strength of Anglicanism rests on its equal loyalty to the unconflicting rights of reason, Scripture and tradition." This, then, was the tradition within which Wesley took his stand; before the judgment bar of "Scripture, reason, and Christian antiquity."[6]

It was Wesley's special genius that he conceived of adding "experience" to the traditional Anglican triad, and thereby adding vitality without altering the substance. What he did was to apply the familiar distinction between *fides quae creditur* and *fides qua creditur* (from a theoretical faith to an existential one) so as to insist on "heart religion" in place of all normal Christian orthodoxy (cf. "The Almost Christian"). He had found support for this in Cranmer's wry comment (in Homilies, IV) about the devils who *assent* to every tenet of orthodoxy, "and yet they be but devils still." It was this added emphasis on "experience" that led Gerald Cragg (in his *Reason and Authority in the 18th Century*) to entitle his chapter on Wesley, "The Authority of Revitalized Faith." Wesley would have amended that to read "The Authority of Vital Faith."

With this "fourth dimension," one might say, Wesley was trying to incorporate the notion of *conversion* into the Anglican tradition—to make room in it for his own conversions and those of others. It is not irrelevant that in his report of the so-called "Aldersgate experience" of May 24th, 1738, he takes us back to his very first conversion (to "seriousness" and self-dedication in 1725); thence on to his grand mystical illumination in 1727. After "Aldersgate" and after his ambivalent encounters with the Moravians in Herrnhut, the *Journal* recounts his rediscovery of a vital doctrine of justification by faith *in his own tradition*, in November of 1738. But this had been followed by a lapse into the depths of religious anxiety (in January 1739). The process then reached its climax in the spring of 1739, with the "discovery" of his true and life-long vocation as an evangelist and spiritual director.

The success of Methodism as a religious society within the Church of England bolstered his sense of freedom to amend Anglican customs without rejecting the Anglican heritage. He quietly ignored the possibility that, in the process of reforming the national church, he was opening a way for his "societies" eventually to "separate" and go it alone as "sects" trying to become "churches" on their own. Over against the Anglican tradition of the church as *corpus mixtum*, Wesley demanded more of his societies, as disciplined communities of true believers. Against the Anglican reliance on church as ministrant of the means of grace, Wesley opposed the doctrine of justification by faith *alone* (and argued, mistakenly, that this doctrine was novelty in Anglicanism!). To the Anglican tradition of baptismal regeneration he added conversion and "new birth" as a Gospel requisite. To the Anglican contentment with the Prayerbook as a complete blueprint, Wesley added a medley of "irregularities": field-preaching, extempore prayer, itinerancy, class meetings and the like. To the Anglican tradition of the "natural" alliance between church and state, he opposed the concept of church as a *voluntary association*. The effect of such changes was to put the question of authority into a new context: to relate it more nearly to the individual's conscience, to small-group consensus, and also to link it practically with the ideal of "accountable discipleship" (to use an apt phrase of David Watson's). The practical effect of this was to make every Methodist man and woman his/her own theologian. He nowhere gave his people an actual paradigm for their theologizing: somehow, he hoped that they would adopt his ways of reflection as their own. The truth is, however, that his bare texts, unannotated, did not suffice to make true "Wesleyans" out of those who have continued to bear his name and who honor him as patriarch. This is why the editors of the new edition of his *Works* hope that more ample annotations will help both "Wesleyans" and non-Wesleyans in the "discovery" of the richness and sophistication of his special sort of "folk-theology."

Even that cheerful thought may be thwarted, however, so long as the phrase "the Wesleyan quadrilateral" is taken too literally. It was intended as a metaphor for a four-element syndrome, including the fourfold guidelines of authority in Wesley's theological method. In such a quaternity, Holy Scripture is clearly unique. But this in turn is illuminated by the collective Christian wisdom of other ages and cultures between the Apostolic Age and our own. It also allows for the rescue of the Gospel from obscurantism by means of the disciplines of critical reason. But always, biblical revelation must be received in the heart by faith: this is the requirement of "experience." Wesley's theology was eclectic and pluralistic (and I confess my bafflement at the hostility aroused in some minds by such innocent adjectives). Even so, it was a coherent, stable, whole, deriving its fruitfulness from its single, soteriological focus in the

Christian evangel of *Jesus Christ*—"who for us men *and for our salvation* came down from heaven and was made *man*"!

When I first began reading Wesley's entire corpus with some care (after many years as a credentialed professor of the "history of Christian thought"), I was puzzled by the score or more brief summations of "the Gospel" that Wesley sprinkles almost casually along the way—never twice in the same form of words (which suggest that, before Coleridge or Wittgenstein, Wesley had come upon the secret that language [and the language of religion in particular] is, by its nature, "incomplete"). Little by little, it dawned on me that Wesley's purpose in these summaries was to refocus the entire range of his theological reflection upon the crux of the matter: which is to say, *salvation*. For example:

> "Let us prophesy according to the analogy of faith"—as St. Peter expresses it, "as the oracles of God"—according to the general temper of them, according to that grand scheme of doctrine which is delivered therein touching original sin, justification by faith and present, inward salvation. There is a wonderful analogy between all these, and a close and intimate connexion between the chief heads of that faith "which was once for all delivered to the saints."[7]

He is eager for theological dialogue, but his real concern is with "the most essential parts of real experimental religion," its initial rise in the soul, that goes on to "faith in our Lord Jesus Christ," which issues in regeneration, is "attended with 'peace and joy in the Holy Ghost,' " thence to our wrestlings with flesh and blood, and finally to "perfect love."[8]

All Wesleyans are familiar with his metaphors of "porch of religion," "door of religion" and "religion itself."[9] Similar encapsulations of the *ordo salutis* abound, some in obvious places but some in unexpected places — as, for example, in the "Preface" to the *Explanatory Notes upon the Old Testament* (the vast bulk of which was simply lifted from others):

> [In your reading of the Scriptures] have a constant eye to the analogy of the faith, which is to say, the connexion there is between those grand fundamental doctrines of original sin, justification by faith, the new birth, inward and outward holiness.

As an Anglican priest, he will assume a shared faith with "A Gentleman of Bristol" (Jan. 6, 1758) in

> the principles of the Church of England as being confirmed by our Liturgy, Articles and Homilies—and so also by the whole tenor of Scripture [notice this catch phrase; it is a favorite, repeated in many different contexts].

In another place, he summarized the essential Gospel in yet another set of theses:

1. That without holiness no man shall see the Lord;
2. That this holiness is the work of God, who worketh in us both to will and to do;
3. That he doeth it of his own good pleasure, merely for the merits of Christ;
4. That holiness is having the mind that was in Christ, enabling us to walk as He walked;
5. That no man can be sanctified till he is justified; and
6. That we are justified by faith alone.[10]

This comes in a sermon; this particular form of words is never used again.

The obvious methodological question posed by summaries like this is whether such variant expressions oversimplify or distort "the *essence* of the Christian Gospel." For Wesley, it was enough to point to its soteriological core in evangelical terms. As far as the full range of theological opinions is concerned, he is more relaxed—even to the point of tolerating the "overbeliefs" of the Roman Catholics and also the Reformed doctrines of election and predestination. It is this skillful balancing of the essentials off from the *adiaphora* that allows Wesley to escape both the rigidities of dogmatism *and* the flabbiness of indifferentism.

In the new edition of Wesley's *Works*, we have tried to alert even the casual reader to the extent to which Wesley was, as he claimed he was, *homo unius libri*. To an extent that I had not realized before I wore out the first of two concordances we used in tracing down Wesley's Scripture citations (quotations, paraphrases, allusions, echoes), the Bible was truly his second language. His rhetoric throughout is a tissue woven from the biblical texts and paraphrases and his own crisp Augustan prose ("plain truth for plain people"). His appeal to Scripture goes far deeper than the use of texts in support of his own views. His larger concern was to let each part of Scripture be pondered in the light of the whole, obscure texts in the light of the more lucid ones—and all of them, always, in the spirit of prayer, *coram Deo*. Scripture is not merely God's address to the believer—it is inspired by the Holy Spirit who in turn inspires the believer's understanding. The Bible is to be read *literally*, save where such a reading leads to an absurdity or to an impugnation of God's goodness. Scriptural commands are not to be construed legalistically; they are to be seen also as "covered promises." Even allegory is occasionally resorted to (as with the image of "The Wilderness State"). The Apocrypha may be used for edification, though not for sermon texts. Wesley was capable of partisan prooftexting; and yet also felt free to alter the *Textus Receptus* by appeal to older MSS; and he had no qualms in nuancing some Greek words arbitrarily (as with *paroxysmos* in Acts 15:39), where he insists that only Barnabas lost his temper, but never St. Paul. The clearest impression that remains after all the tedium of tracing Wesley's Biblical sources is of a man very much "at home" in the Bible and quietly confident of his understanding of its "general tenor."

There is another sense, however, in which the notion of Wesley as the man of "one book only" is patently absurd. He read voraciously and in all genres. He had a special fondness for "the Fathers" of the early centuries. He thought that the Greek theologians had understood the Gospel more profoundly and therapeutically than their Latin counterparts. He came at the Fathers with an Anglican bias (he had been at Oxford in the twilight of a great age of patristic scholarship), in the tradition of Richard Field, Henry Hammond, and Simon Patrick. He was not in the least intimidated by learned detractors of patristic wisdom (like Jean Daillé and Conyers Middleton).

What Wesley learned most from the Eastern fathers was the rich notion of the Christian life as a participation in the divine (i.e., salvation as the restoration of the ruined image of God in the human soul). The stage for his "Aldersgate experience" had been set by the Scripture with which he began that day: II Peter 1:4 (cf. Wesley's paraphrase: *ta megista hēmin timia epangelmata dedōrētai, hina genēsthe theias koinōnoi physeōs*, and the crucial phrase, "partakers of the divine *physis*." It was in this sense of "participation" in the divine life that Wesley had already understood the mysteries of grace and free will, of prevenient grace as the Holy Spirit's constant initiative, of "perfection" as a process rather than a completed act. There is much Anselmian language in Wesley ("acquittal," "imputation"), but there is even more that stresses the notion of healing (*therapeia psychēs*). He was neither "Augustinian" (indeed, he has some tart comments about the great bishop), nor "Pelagian" (he actually doubted that *Pelagius* had been a "Pelagian")—and he could interpret *dikaiosynē* not only as the "imputation" of Christ's righteousness to the repentant believer but also its "impartation" as well.

From the Latin traditions, he seems to have learned most from men like William St. Thierry—who had taught that love is the highest form of *knowledge*—and from the Victorines (Ruprecht of Deutz, Hugh, *et al.*) with their bold notion that God had used the Adamic Fall to bring about a greater total good than if Adam had not sinned (*O felix culpa!*).

All of this is a way of saying that, for Wesley, the Christian tradition was more than a curiosity or a source for illustrative material. It was a living spring of Christian insight. Reading Wesley against his sources amounts to an eccentric excursion through the length and breadth of the history of Christian thought. And because a lively sense of "tradition" has now come to be a prerequisite in ecumenical dialogue,[11] it is all the more important for "Wesleyans" (and others), to discover how much he had learned from the Christian past and thus also to learn for ourselves the importance of being truly "at home" in that past.

But Wesley was no antiquarian. We know of his inborn tendency to require a reason for everything from his father's well-known complaint to Susanna about his personal habits. He never discounted his university training in logic nor his life-long interest in contemporary science and culture. He lived in the perilous transition from an earlier theocentric rationalism that sought to reconcile religion and science (as in John Ray's *Wisdom of God in Creation*—the prototype for Wesley's *Survey of the Wisdom of God in Creation*) to the "Enlightenment's" outright rejection of supernaturalism (as in the deists and David Hume). To be a theologian in 18th century Britain was to struggle with deism and secularism (see Joseph Butler, William Paley, *et al.*). Wesley's acknowledgment of rationality as normative was both principled and pragmatic. He took logical order as a paradigm for the order of being itself (as any good Ramist would, or later, the Kantians). He remained a disciple of Locke and Aldrich all his days. But his vivid sense of mystery kept him aware of reason's limitations (as in "The Case of Reason Impartially Considered"). Richard Brantley has analyzed Locke's influence on Wesley.[12] But no one, to my knowledge, has provided a comparable study of Wesley and Malebranche, or the Cambridge Platonists, or John Norris, or Bishop Berkeley, *et al.*

Wesley's understanding of reason led him to a religious epistemology that hinges, crucially, on his view of intuition as a "spiritual sensorium" in the human mind that constitutes what is most distinctively human: *viz.*, our capacity for God. This is part of God's creative design and it points to the chief inlet of the Holy Spirit into the human soul and spirit. Just last year, a dissertation was accepted by Rome's Angelicum University on *The Perceptibility of Grace in John Wesley* (by Daniel Joseph Luby—a layman!). It is a superb probing of the importance, for Wesley, of "immediate perception" (of spirituality reality). Such unexpected developments remind us of how much we also need a full-fledged monograph on "*rationality* in the Wesleyan spirit." Even so, "our knowledge of God and of the things of God" does not come from intuition, inference, or deduction alone. Always it is a prevenient and unmerited *gift* and must, therefore, be experienced as an inward change of heart and head in which the mind's intuitions of the truth are *realized* in the heart (as when *Christus pro nobis* becomes *Christus pro me*).

Here a careful distinction is needed. The "experience of grace" is indeed deeply inward, but it is not a merely subjective "religious affection." It is an objective encounter (within "the heart," to be sure) of something not ourselves and not our own (something truly transcendent). It is an inward assurance of an objective reality, *viz.*, God's unmerited favor, his pardoning mercy, an awareness of the Spirit's prevenient action in mediating the grace of our Lord Jesus Christ to the believer. It is, therefore, the experience of a *given*—a divine action that can only be re-acted to, in trusting faith or in prideful resistance. It is this stress upon the sheer givenness of spiritual insight and of divine grace that distinguishes Wesley from Pelagius —and for that matter, from Arminius and Episcopius. Had he known of Kant (his younger contemporary!) Wesley would have agreed with at least the first two paragraphs of his first *Critique of Practical Reason* (1788):

> There can be no doubt that all our knowledge begins with experience. . . .
> In the order of time, therefore, we have no knowledge antecedent to experience and with experience all our knowledge begins.
> But though all our knowledge begins with experience, it does *not* follow that it arises *out of experience*. . . .

When, therefore, zealous and pious souls conclude that the intensity or inwardness of their own feelings is the measure of truth (and when they invoke Wesley's "strangely warmed heart" as a witness to such a correlation) nothing but pious sentimentality can ensue and, with it, a sort of narcissism that readily turns into an anti-intellectualism. The verb forms in the familiar phrase, "I felt my heart strangely warmed" give us an underdeveloped clue. "I felt" is in the *active* voice; "strangely warmed" is *passive*.

In this light, one may read with profit another of Wesley's "summaries," this one of the gist of Christian experience at its best:

> Indeed there are [no words] that will adequately express [and he was serious in his conviction that religious language is apophatic and, therefore, also polysemous] what the children of God experience. But perhaps one might say (desiring any who are taught of God to soften or strengthen the expression), the testimony of the Spirit is an inward impression on the soul, whereby the Spirit of God directly "witnesses to my spirit that I am a child of God"; that Jesus Christ hath loved me and given Himself for me; and that all my sins are blotted out, and I, even I, am reconciled to God.[13]

Dr. Sugden's comment on this passage, invoking the authority of W. B. Pope, takes Wesley to task for this emphasis on the *objectivity* of the Spirit's activity and of the human role as wholly reactive. This reminds us of how, in the history of Methodist theologizing, Wesley's heroic efforts to save us from subjectivity and sentimentality have so often gone so largely for naught.

Wesley's theological method was distinctive, and maybe unique (for one cannot identify any of his disciples who adopted it as a whole or in his theological spirit). Adam Clarke, Richard Watson, W. B. Pope, and others grasped much of the substance of the patriarch's teaching, but they were bent on remaking him into a *biblicist* (Clarke) or a *systematic* theologian (Watson and Pope). Indeed, Watson went so far as to entitle his own exposition of Wesleyan theology in the Calvinist fashion, *Theological Institutes*.

All Wesleyans have agreed on the primacy of Scripture and then differed (not always helpfully) in their hermeneutical perspectives. This seems to me to have come from a neglect of Wesley's own hermeneutical focus on "the analogy of faith"; I cannot cite a single essay by a Wesleyan exegete or theologian in which the *analogia fidei* is a governing notion. In the nineteenth century, Wesley's reliance on the Christian tradition as a whole (and especially "the Fathers") was quietly jettisoned (even by Methodist historians, like Sheldon and Cell). His confidence in reason, *within its proper limits*, has given way to an emotive anti-intellectualism or else its opposite: e.g., an overconfidence in reason (as in Bowne and Brightman). His focus on "experience"—*as a soteriological category*—has been turned into a variety of empiricisms, bolstered by a pragmatic appeal to "practical results."

The term "quadrilateral" does not occur in the Wesley corpus—and more than once, I have regretted having coined it for contemporary use, since it has been so widely misconstrued. But if we are to accept our responsibility for seeking *intellecta* for our faith, in any other fashion than a "theological system" or, alternatively, a juridical statement of "doctrinal standards," then this method of a conjoint recourse to the fourfold guidelines of Scripture, tradition, reason, and experience, may hold more promise for an evangelical and ecumenical future than we have realized as yet—by comparison, for example, with biblic*ism*, or traditional*ism*, or, rational*ism*, or empiric*ism*. It is far more valid than the reduction of Christian authority to the dyad of "Scripture" and "experience" (so common in Methodist ranks today). The "quadrilateral" requires of a theologian no more than what he or she might reasonably be held accountable for: which is to say, a familiarity with Scripture that is both critical and faithful; plus, an acquaintance with the wisdom of the Christian past; plus, a taste for logical analysis as something more than a debater's weapon; plus, a vital, inward faith that is upheld by the assurance of grace and its prospective triumphs, *in this life*.

The epoch that looms before us, whether we like it or no, is a postliberal age, in which the dogmatisms of the pre-Enlightenment orthodoxies and the confident dogmas of "liberalism" (e.g., "progress" and "human perfectibility") will come to seem increasingly outmoded. It is, predictably, a time of troubles for the whole world, with no assured future for our plundered planet or for a humanity addicted to self-defeating strategies masked with the illusions of good intentions. The still-divided fragments of the Christian community are more interested in honest doctrinal consensus than ever before. But this is also to say that it is a time when the study of Wesley has a distinctive contribution to make.

Neither the Wesley theology, nor his methods are simple panaceas. They are not like the TV dinners that can be reheated and served up quickly for immediate use. They call for imaginative updating in the new world cultural contexts (the sort of thing that John XXIII spoke of as *aggiornamento*—care in preserving the kernel, imagination in renovating the medium). Wesley's vision of Christian existence has to be reconceived and transvalued so that it can be as relevant in the experience of the late twentieth century as it was to alienated English men and women in 1740! This requires that it must be refocused in ways neither doctrinaire on the one hand, nor trendy on the other. Wesley avoided such barren polarizations and so, one thinks, we may also—if our theologians, like his, are as deeply immersed in Scripture ("at home" in its imagery and mystery), as truly respectful of the Christian wisdom of past ages, as honestly open to the disciplines of critical reason, as eagerly alert to the fire and flame of grace.

Wesley's complex way of theologizing has the ecumenical advantage of making fruitful linkages with other doctrinal traditions without threatening to supplant any of them and without fear of forfeiting its own identity. There are, however, at least two prior conditions for such linkages: that Wesley be rescued from the stereotypes in which his professed disciples have cocooned him and that we recover for ourselves the rich manifold of tradition from which he drew so freely and creatively. These conditions can be best met by learning more and more from Wesley himself (the whole Wesley, including "the later Mr. Wesley" as reflected in A Christian Library and *The Arminian Magazine*) and yet also learning more and more, and on our own, from the rich manifold of Christian traditions from which Wesley learned so much.

This is a daunting challenge and I freely confess that it is more of a task than I have myself been able to bring off to my own satisfaction. But I can testify, with great gratitude, that my communing with Wesley and his sources has been immensely enriching, in my theological concerns and in my own growth in grace. It is, therefore, with full assurance that I commend such explorations, not only to those who bear the Wesleyan insignia, but to all others who may care to extend their acquaintance with a rare man of God.

The 1988 Disciplinary Statement

Introduction

The 1984 General Conference, in response to many petitions, established a commission to review the theological statement in the Discipline. Bishop Earl G. Hunt, Jr. chaired the study group which published a draft of their statement in *The Circuit Rider* in February 1987 for public reaction across the church.

This early draft ignited some serious discussion that increased as General Conference approached. Many of the papers in this section present issues that were discussed in that intervening year. John B. Cobb, Jr., a member of the committee which prepared the 1972 theological report, expressed serious reservations about the published draft's treatment of authority in theological reflection, especially the roles of Scripture and reason. Thomas C. Oden mounted a sustained argument to affirm Wesley's *Sermons* and *Notes* as juridical standards of doctrine, responding in part to Richard P. Heitzenrater's historical study of doctrinal standards in early episcopal Methodism, published in "At Full Liberty." The General Commission on Christian Unity and Interreligious Affairs developed a response to the published draft, delineating several concerns that had become evident in the discussions. Ted Campbell outlined the historical development of the so-called "Wesleyan quadrilateral" and looked at problems associated with its interpretation. Thomas W. Ogletree, a member of the study commission, wrote a substantial statement, published at the time of General Conference, that presented the committee's position on several key issues as revised in the final document.

Two papers in this section recount the development and presentation of the 1988 doctrinal statement "In Search of Continuity and Consensus," by Richard Heitzenrater, who was chair of the sub-committee that wrote the doctrinal statement, describes the dynamics of the preparation of the document and its presentation to the General Conference. Thomas A. Langford in the article, "Conciliar Theology: A Report," describes the discussion of this document at General Conference in 1988, noting the changes that were made in the legislative process.

The selections included are intended to present some of the issues central to the development of the disciplinary statement on "Doctrinal

Standards and Our Theological Task," representing some of the diversity that typifies United Methodist theological endeavors. The draft statements that are the focus of these commentaries may be found in the February 1987 issue of *Circuit Rider* and the Journal of the General Conference as found in the *Daily Christian Advocate* (May 1988).

Chapter 7

IN SEARCH OF CONTINUITY AND CONSENSUS: THE ROAD TO THE 1988 DOCTRINAL STATEMENT

by Richard P. Heitzenrater[1]

The 1984 General Conference of The United Methodist Church, in response to a deluge of petitions, passed a resolution directing the Council of Bishops to appoint a "committee on our theological task, representative of the whole church, to prepare a new statement which will reflect the needs of the church, define the scope of our Wesleyan tradition in the context of our contemporary world, and report to the 1988 General conference."[2] Mark Trotter, the chair of the legislative sub-committee that made this proposal, speaking in the spirit of the 1972 doctrinal statement, indicated that it was time "to continue that conversation on our theological task," which was seen as "an ongoing task of the church."[3]

Although there had been some theological discussion in the church subsequent to the 1972 statement, many (including the prime author of that statement) had been disappointed by the lack of serious continuing theological study. This call for a new theological study committee, however, was primarily the result of some increasing dissatisfaction with the church's official doctrinal statement in the Book of Discipline, virtually unchanged since its adoption in 1972. The central feature of the proposal was the third section, ¶ 69, which proposed a theological methodology for encouraging and guiding responsible theological reflection.

From the outset, some of the statement's strengths were also perceived by some to be its weaknesses. The pervasive sense of theological freedom was perceived by some as a threat to the church's doctrinal integrity. The literary flair of the statement, using images and metaphors that were (sometimes intentionally) imprecise, was seen by some as resulting in more confusion than clarity. Clear priorities in some places in the statement were viewed as being diluted if not abandoned in other places within the statement, partially the result of a committee process. Doctrinal standards that were called "non-juridical" in one part of the

Discipline but functioned as a measure of doctrinal discipline for church trials presented a confusing discrepancy to many. The general avoidance of rigid dogmatism in the statement was viewed by many as contributing to a developing sense of apathy or indifferentism within the church.

From the beginning, many critics expressed concern with some particular views expressed in the statement.[4] An increasing number of people thought that it should be changed to reflect the current temper of the church. In recent years, an increasing number of voices were asking for more clarity in United Methodism's sense of doctrinal identity.[5] Minor changes were made to the doctrinal statements at the General Conferences of 1980 and 1984.[6] But no call for major change was adopted until the action of 1984. In addition to asking for a "new statement," the General Conference specified three issues that should be addressed in particular: "(1) the significance and proper use of the so-called Methodist Quadrilateral;[7] (2) the proper understanding of the catholic spirit, which is often spoken of today as pluralism; and (3) the contribution that United Methodism can make to the ecumenical-theological conversation."[8]

Organization of the New Study Committee

The Council of Bishops appointed the twenty-four member Committee on "Our Theological Task" (COTT) in December 1984. Its membership included five bishops, five academicians, five clergy, five laity, and four at-large members. It was representative in terms of race, gender, age, and geography (with European and Pacific members). The General Board of Higher Education and Ministry and the General Board of Discipleship provided staff assistance, their General Secretaries serving as consulting members of the committee.

Bishop Earl G. Hunt, Jr., convened the first meeting of the committee on February 18-19, 1985, in Atlanta, Georgia, and was elected its chair. Bishop Hunt began the deliberations of the committee by conveying the hope of the Council of Bishops that the committee would take into account the life and thought of the whole church and that our report would be both healing and invigorating.

The first task of the committee was to interpret the mandate given it by the General Conference, especially concerning the phrase, "to prepare a new statement." The consensus of the group was that the church would be best served, and the mandate of the General Conference met, by a careful revision of the 1972 statement. In the light of several issues that were immediately designated for attention, the group developed a statement of purpose. After quoting the mandate given by General Conference, the statement continued:

Its purpose is to prepare a statement that will:

1. Elucidate United Methodist doctrinal standards and guidelines, their nature, scope, and use.
2. Clarify an appropriate understanding of pluralism and the catholic spirit in The United Methodist Church.
3. Address the significance and proper use of the "Wesleyan quadrilateral."
4. Illuminate the relationship between The United Methodist Church's theological heritage and its mission, life, and polity.
5. Strengthen United Methodist participation in ecumenical conversations within the global context.
6. Reflect our global nature.
7. Strive for inclusiveness in concept and language.
8. Employ a literary style that allows the statement to be readily understood.

The Committee intends that its work will prove to be healing, invigorating, and edifying.

The last line summarized well the conscious intent of the committee and the tone of its deliberations as encouraged by its chairman.

In order to broaden the base of theological discussion, the committee decided to solicit suggestions from a variety of experts and representative church leaders, and expressed the need to keep in touch with the work of the other study commissions.

Preparation of a New Working Document

The second meeting of the COTT was held in November 1985 in Dallas. It was an occasion for absorbing a tremendous number of suggestions, brainstorming on both process and content, analyzing the 1972 statement section by section, and setting a structure for the new writing process.

The official sessions of the committee were preceded by an informal roundtable meeting which included several guests, including some clergy and laity from the Dallas area and the consultants who were invited to present position papers that weekend. The committee was presented several issues to consider, many of them related to the question, "How does the church teach authoritatively?"

The committee began its sessions by hearing a presentation by Albert C. Outler, chairman of the 1968-72 doctrinal study commission. He stressed the importance of knowing what was *intended* by the statements of 1968 and 1972, "born of the exigencies of merger." Some confessions of inadequacies in their 1972 statement[9] were followed by his urgent appeal to "reflect a spirit of real continuity in the development of a basic doctrinal identity in Methodism." He emphasized the need for the new committee to develop a credible statement concerning the church's doctrinal norms, keeping in mind that any tentative proposals must also develop into the growing consensus in the ecumenical Christian community.

Three consultants had been invited to present papers at the Dallas meeting: Dr. Paul Mickey, of Duke University,[10] Dr. Riley B. Case, district superintendent from Muncie, Indiana,[11] and Dr. Thomas A. Langford, Duke University. The common concern that crucial terms (e.g., sources, guidelines, norms, principles, standards) be used with care was developed more fully in a paper by Langford which examined the role of theology within the life of The United Methodist Church. His observations were based upon a careful distinction among three ways the church expresses its faith: as *dogma* ("the received apostolic faith"), *doctrine* ("the consensus of the mind of the church at a given time about its faith"), and *exploratory theology* ("exploration of fresh interpretations of faith"). He also agreed with several points of Robert E. Cushman's critique of the 1972 statement and welcomed any clarification the COTT could bring to some specific issues: the primacy of Scripture, the status of doctrinal standards, the nature of juridical norms, and the character of the faith response.[12]

Several specific proposals were made at this session: restructure the outline of Part II, show more grounding in the history of Christian thought, aim primarily at a United Methodist audience, write with theological integrity and ecumenical sensitivity, keep the statement as short as possible, and develop a study guide to help interpret the document to the church. A writing committee of eight members, representative of the whole and headed by Richard Heitzenrater, was assigned by the chair. The committee was encouraged to consider other doctrinal statements being developed around the world, such as the proposed Nairobi statement of the World Methodist Council.[13]

Wrestling with a Text and Raising the Issues

The first public draft from the writing committee was circulated to the whole COTT at its next scheduled meeting in Washington, D.C., in April 1986. The thirty-five page draft statement incorporated many of the basic concerns of the 1972 statement and drew upon nearly half of its rhetoric. The basic pattern of the document was set. Part II was divided into four sections —"Our Doctrinal Heritage," "Our Doctrinal History," "Our Doctrinal Standards," and "Our Theological Task."[14]

Two pages listing the "Characteristics of the draft" outlined some of the underlying assumptions that were operative in its creation. These were reflected in the way the draft (1) presented the United Methodist approach to theology as inclusive, corporate, and practical; (2) restructured the presentation of the "quadrilateral" in order to highlight the primacy of Scripture; (3) distinguished Wesley's use of the fourfold guidelines from our own practice, while making clear the senses in which his work is our model; (4) differentiated the various functions of the church's doctrinal standards; (5) explicitly endorsed modern biblical criticism; (6) developed liberation themes in the context of the discussion of tradition and experience, rather than relegating them to the end of the section; (7) acknowledged our diversity while stressing our desire to strive for convergent understandings of the Gospel; (8) retained an emphasis on ecumenical and interfaith dialogue; (9) reinforced the statement of distinctive Methodist theological contributions.

The introductory section of the document defined the distinctions between "doctrinal statements," "doctrinal standards," and "our theological task."[15] The main distinction was between doctrine and theology. *Doctrinal affirmation*, through both officially adopted (normative) standards and traditionally accepted (formative) standards, was seen as anchoring the church's attempt to enunciate its witness of the apostolic faith. *Theological reflection*, through both critical and constructive processes, was seen as the manner by which the community of faith continues to examine and explore as well as to express its faith. The committee suggested moving the paragraphs containing these definitions in order to improve the literary flow of the text. These portions were, in fact, subsequently removed from the text, but the basic distinctions (between the nature of doctrine and theology, and between the function of standards and statements) were adopted and provided an important part of the framework for the committee's subsequent deliberations. The group also expressed a strong (though not unanimous) feeling that it must clearly articulate the important function of doctrinal standards in order to strengthen the church's sense of doctrinal identity and provide a possible grounding for consensual developments. These steps represented major departures from the approach of the 1972 statement.

In addition to the concerns listed in the "characteristics" noted above, the last section of the document, dealing with the theological task, attempted some additional distinctions and definitions. The intention of the committee from the very beginning to highlight the primary authority of Scripture was visually accented by heading that portion of the discussion of theological guidelines, "The Primacy of Scripture," and subsuming the discussion of the other three guidelines into a single section entitled, "Tradition, Reason, and Experience." The concept of "guidelines" was in fact revised in order to use the more precise terminology, "sources" and "methods." This was subsequently refined to "sources and criteria," which allowed for a distinction between the ways in which each of the four elements might be seen functioning in different ways as *resources* for theological reflection on the one hand and as *authorities* for theological interpretation on the other.

The committee also desired to portray the theological task as more than a rational enterprise, to incorporate the concept of theology as the way the community lives out its faith, to recognize the prevenience of grace in the idea of faith grasping us, and to admit that we are confronted by both the reality *and* the mystery of God's love.

The attempt to use traditional theological language in the draft document clashed at times with the intent to use inclusive language.[16] A rather lengthy discussion at this Washington meeting resulted in a workable compromise ("Kingdom," "Lord," and terms within quotations being accepted for the time being), with the understanding that the discussion was not closed. The arguments against using the term "pluralism" were reiterated, while general satisfaction was expressed concerning the attempt to recognize the presence and value of diversity. The committee agreed with the basic presuppositions of the document, and stressed the need to present "red-flag" ideas with appropriate tactfulness without compromising principles involved.

The writing committee was instructed to incorporate all the new suggestions while reducing the overall length of the document.

Refining the Text and Debating the Issues

Another draft of the statement, the fifth major revision, provided the basis for the discussion of the COTT meeting in Madison, New Jersey, in October 1986. The meeting began with a report of specific critiques of the most recent draft by a wide range of reader-consultants. Most of the readers had responded with general enthusiasm for the document, mentioning as particular strengths its tone, revised outline, improved clarity in many areas, and use of traditional theological terminology. Several specific suggestions for improvements were taken very seriously by the committee, especially regarding the need for more clarity on the nature of the theological task, the nature of scriptural authority, and the implications of increased "Methodist" self-identity for continued ecumenical discussions.[17] Some of these suggestions had already been incorporated into the text for the meeting, such as the restatement of "The Nature of the Theological Task" in terms of five basic characteristics: critical, constructive, individual, communal, and practical.

The ensuing discussions of the committee moved beyond the polite exchanges that generally characterized earlier meetings and revealed some strong feelings that touched the heart of some of the issues. A proposal to affirm non-Christian (specifically Asian and Native American) traditions within the framework of the document provided the opportunity for debating the meaning of "tradition" as authority, and raised the need for distinguishing between "resources" that assist theological reflection and "criteria" that provide authoritative patterns for "Christian" assertions. That distinction also allowed for a broadening of the discussion of "experience," and affirming (beyond the Wesleyan sense of the quadrilateral) the experience of women, ethnic minorities, the poor, and other marginalized segments of society as having something important to contribute to our understanding of the gospel message. Working in these directions, the committee was able to make more explicit the interworking of the fourfold guidelines, not just by stating that they must all work together, but by showing (within the discussion of each of the four) how they do in fact have an integral relationship with each other in very specific ways.

The need for enhancement of the proposed statement on several points resulted in a new paragraph on eschatology, more stress on the Kingdom of God, and an attempt to illuminate a doctrine of the church. Proposed additions also included the concepts of atonement, resurrection, eternal life, and several specific adjectival additions to elaborate upon ideas such as perils, hopes, special theologies, and geographical areas.

The desire to be specific, precise, and all-inclusive resulted in the proliferation of multiple "laundry-lists" that were problematic from both a conceptual and literary point of view. Not only were the sentences awkward, but the committee found it increasingly difficult to make the lists accurate and complete—in many cases it was evident that no consensus was possible as to appropriate terminology and adequate specificity. Was "women's liberation theology" (1972 statement) to be called "women's theology"? "feminist theology"? "liberation theology"? Was "third-world theology" (1972 statement) still an appropriate term? As the lists grew out of proportion and the propriety of specific terms became more problematic, the committee decided whenever possible to use generic and conceptual language that would in the end be more inclusive and descriptive (and less subject to obsolescence) than any simple list of adjectives or nouns.[18]

The draft that emerged from this meeting in October 1986 provided the basis for selections that were published in the February 1987 issue of *The Circuit Rider* for reaction from across the church (as well as from the growing list of readers who were sent the text of the whole document in November).[19]

Preparing a Final Text

Responses to the published (eighth) draft of the document (and its fuller circulated version) began to arrive almost immediately and continued through the spring of 1987. In the most part, the response was very favorable, often pointing out that the new statement was an improvement over the 1972 document. Repeated commendations were expressed for the sections on "Basic Christian Affirmations" and "Distinctive Wesleyan Emphases," "Doctrinal Standards in American Methodism," "The Nature of Our Theological Task," and "The Primacy of Scripture." Many writers did also have suggestions for further improvement of specific wordings. Three or four letters were very critical of the tone and content of the document, distressed in particular with its position on Scripture, its reflection of more traditional rather than cutting-edge theological perspectives, its highlighting of doctrinal standards, and what was perceived as its faulty explanation of the fourfold guidelines (especially the primacy of Scripture).

The dozens of responses that contained specific suggestions were considered at a final meeting of the writing committee in July 1987. One of the more controversial issues focused on the manner of referring to the triune God. Differences of opinion, both from respondents and from some on the writing committee, on the matter of Trinitarian terminology led to the deletion of all controversial names, descriptive formulas, and elaborations of the Trinity (leaving references to "the triune God," which were felt to be of basic significance). The resolution of that issue was left to the larger committee or the General Conference.

The interworking of the fourfold guidelines, already stated in several contexts, was made more explicit by including additional comments concerning the specific ways in which they interact, especially the ways in which neglected traditions and a various human experiences can inform our understanding of Scripture and help shape who we are.[20]

Some statements which might be seen as expressions of "Methodist provincialism" were altered to reflect a more thoroughly ecumenical outlook, and the portion that dealt specifically with ecumenical commitment was given a separate heading for emphasis. The addition of comments recognizing the pervasive and systemic nature of evil and the occasional unfortunate uses of theology to legitimate injustices were part of a larger attempt by the writing committee to adjust the general tone of the document in ways that reflected a more balanced view of reality as well as hope.

The wording on Wesley's *Notes* and *Sermons* was adjusted further to emphasize their substantive authority as traditional doctrinal standards. At the same time, the fact that they do not lend themselves to juridical enforcement was restated to clarify their functional distinction from the *Articles* and *Confession*.

The committee also accepted the suggestion of an episcopal respondent who felt that the document could come to a fitting conclusion by quoting Ephesians 3:20-21. The writing committee also made many literary alterations. A few non-inclusive words that had eluded earlier detection were replaced (there was some debate over whether or not "dynamic thrust" was a male power term). Concern about the number of repeated terms and phrases was handled by a computer search.[21]

Final Meeting of the Committee

The final meeting of the COTT was held in Oklahoma City in October 1987. Besides dealing with the latest draft from the writing committee (re-written twice after its July meeting), the committee considered substantial responses from two sources, the General Commission of Christian Unity and Interreligious Affairs and one of the working groups of the Oxford Institute of Methodist Theological Studies (held in July). In spite of the increased interest in the statement across the church as a result of its publication earlier in the year, no monitors or observers from any special interest group attended this last meeting of the COTT.

Most of the substantive alterations at this meeting were made in the sections dealing with the fourfold guidelines. Some of the rationalistic language in the introductory section was removed (e.g., "to assure the authenticity and validity of the witness we make" became "to express faithfully the witness we make"). The interaction of the four guidelines was again restated and strengthened, noting that they are all "indispensable to our theological task" and that theological reflection "always involves" all four.[22] The "interrelationship and inseparability of the four basic resources for theological understanding" was seen as "a model that is present in the biblical text itself." Some of the adjectives used in relation to scriptural primacy were softened or deleted.[23] As a whole, the material was strengthened in ways that resulted in general satisfaction among the committee, perhaps for the first time on this section.

A few final touches were also made here and there, mostly at the beginning of "Our Doctrinal Heritage" (¶ 66) and within "Our Theological Task" (¶ 69). The temptation to flesh out some of the illustrative lists resulted in a few more examples being added to the strings of nouns and adjectives that had survived earlier extractions (this would continue in the discussions at General Conference). A new "Bibliographical Preface" was approved for the section on "Our Doctrinal Standards."[24] The last suggested alteration was virtually the only proposed change for "Our Doctrinal History" (¶ 67): to alter "identify a 'marrow' of Christian truth" to "identify the essentials of Christian truth." Fighting off fatigue, the committee, with a slight note of humor, voted to maintain that one modestly antiquarian touch.

Before calling for a final vote on the proposed document, chairman Hunt noted that although the committee had addressed all the concerns that had been communicated to it, there still might be critical questions remaining in the document and certainly there would be some remaining differences of viewpoint in the church as a whole. He asked that anyone on the committee who still had any problems with the tenor and basic content of the statement should voice them forthrightly. There were no comments, and the vote to approve the new statement for submission to the General Conference was unanimous. The work of the committee now completed, the final draft was submitted to the Secretary of the General Conference as a report and four petitions.[25]

The chair designated Richard Heitzenrater and Thomas Ogletree to represent the committee at General Conference, in addition to those members of the committee who were elected delegates. It was hoped that the committee would be allowed to make a presentation and that during the deliberations, those representatives would be able to interpret the sense of the committee on many of the controversial issues.

Transmitting the Statement to the General Conference

Bishop Hunt appointed the chair of the writing committee, Richard Heitzenrater, to go to the General Conference Briefing Session for heads of conference delegations in order to make the presentation of the committee's proposed statement in October 1987. Those comments attempted to describe the intentions of the committee and to outline the distinctive characteristics of its proposed statement.

The Committee on Our Theological Task was concerned that the new statement represent both *continuity* and *consensus*. In constructing the proposed statement, the committee tried to maintain the spirit and tone of the doctrinal statement that has served the church for nearly a generation. . . . The desire for clarity as well as self-critical understanding, as recommended in our document (as well as the 1972 document), were also evident in the manner of the committee's deliberations.

. . . We were not that uncomfortable with the 1972 statement as a whole. However, we recognized that much of the attractiveness of the previous disciplinary statement (the mystique of the document, if you will) lies in its ambiguity. It was our intent to try to clarify some of the issues in the statement and thereby help to do away with some misunderstandings that had developed on the basis of that ambiguity. Clarification in some cases entailed an apparent shift in emphasis.

One noticeable shift in emphasis is indicated by the absence of the term "pluralism" in our proposed statement. That does not mean that we have failed to recognize or to appreciate the richness of our diversity; it does not mean that we are less willing to encourage continued theological endeavors in a variety of directions and ways. We simply felt that it was difficult to use such a loaded term at this point in our history in a way that would be understood, [especially in the light of a growing] self-conscious desire for consensus or convergence—looking for those aspects of United Methodist doctrine and theology that represent areas in which we have a common identity not only among ourselves but with other Christians around the world. . . .

Another matter that occupied a great deal of our attention was the role of Scripture in the fourfold guidelines and the manner of the interrelationships among all four, Scripture, tradition, reason, and experience. It becomes apparent when you glance at the outline of our document that we have highlighted a traditional Wesleyan concept, even using it in one of our headings—the primacy of Scripture. We understand this not so much as a shift in emphasis as it is a clarification—you will find the terminology in the 1972 document. In fact, to use the concept and the phrase is not at all new to the United Methodist Book of Discipline. If you go back to 1968, our first Discipline, you will find a very strong statement on the place of Scripture: doctrinal guidelines and standards are "not to displace the direct and primary authority of the Bible. In all matters of faith and morals, the authority of Holy Scripture stands supreme." We have not used that strong language in our statement, but we have tried to maintain our tradition in this regard. . . .[26]

It is that understanding of the primacy of Scripture within the fourfold guidelines that we have simply tried to clarify as well as highlight. It would be a serious misconstrual of our design to see the present committee's work as "dismantling the quadrilateral," so to speak. We have maintained and made even more explicit the necessary interrelationships of the fourfold guidelines while giving proper place to Scripture in the process.

... If the church is to have vitality and integrity in its witness and mission, it must willingly embrace both doctrinal affirmation and serious theological reflection. We recognize the importance of the theological task as we attempt to minister to the world, and we also see the limitations that face us in that task. With a full sense of honesty, the committee began to draw its document to a close with the comment that "our faith witness cannot fully describe or encompass the mystery of God. Though we experience the wonder of God's grace at work with us and among us and though we know the joy of the present signs of God's kingdom, each new step makes us more aware of the ultimate mystery of God, from which arises a heart of wonder and an attitude of humility." In that spirit, we concluded our deliberations.

The 1984–88 Committee on Our Theological Task represents a cross-section of United Methodism, and the discussions of the committee have exemplified the richness of our diversity in theological dialogue seeking consensus. In the end, while each committee member individually may well have written a quite different document, the group as a whole accepted the proposed document with a unanimous vote.

Several of the basic assertions and distinctions in the proposed document, along with some carefully developed balances and tensions, were not noticed by some critics and commentators: the distinction between doctrinal affirmation and theological reflection (allowing for a wide range of diversity in theological exploration), the affirmation of Wesley's *Sermons* and *Notes* as doctrinal standards (distinguishing their function from that of the Articles and Confession), the functional differentiation for elements of the quadrilateral (distinguishing between their use as resources and/or authorities), and the necessary interplay of the fourfold guidelines (holding to the primary authority of Scripture) not only as a proposed methodological principle but also incorporated into the discussion of authority within the statement itself.

Some polarization of opinion began with the appearance of "The Houston Declaration," a statement produced by a group of evangelical clergy meeting in the Texas city. This document seemed to affirm the COTT position on the primacy of Scripture by quoting a small segment of the committee's document. It also prescribed using the traditional formulation of the Trinity, "Father, Son, and Holy Spirit," which related to concerns of the doctrinal statement. The Houston Declaration was countered by another document, "Perfect Love Casts out Fear," produced by a dozen pastors who took exception to the declarations of their colleagues and indicated that they saw "no compelling reasons" for changing the 1972 doctrinal statement.[27] Indeed, they stated their belief that the proposed COTT statement "would move our church into a narrow sectarian and repressive stance." Individuals and groups began to position themselves by aligning with one or the other of these two positions. Most conspicuous were the Good News caucus and the Chicago statement (organized by Dr. James Holsinger) supporting the former, and the Methodist Federation for Social Action and Women's Division of the Board of Global Ministries supporting the latter.

Additional controversy was stirred up by Professor Thomas Oden's claim that the new statement had "abandoned" Wesley's *Sermons* and *Notes* as doctrinal standards and had "eliminated every standard reference to them." Professor John Cobb also produced an article entitled, "Is Theological Pluralism Dead in the UMC?" In the view of many COTT members, the debate seemed to be developing on the basis of issues and fears projected by critics, rather than problems contained in the statement itself. This circumstance was addressed directly by Professor Thomas Ogletree, member of the writing committee, who wrote an *apologia* for the doctrinal statement, "In Quest of a Common Faith: The Theological Task of United Methodists."[28]

As General Conference approached, discussions of the executive committee of the COTT focused on the ways by which each of the criticisms could be met, either by pointing to material that was already in the proposed doctrinal statement or by suggesting modification to the text. Some of the specific concerns (such as those of Oden and Cobb) were worked out through personal communication and, in some cases, amended wordings to be proposed at General Conference. The committee was fairly confident that most of the concerns being expressed across the church either were already addressed by their proposed statement or could be incorporated with some minor adjustment to the text. Their main concern was that the document get a fair hearing at General Conference, based on the delegates' careful reading and clear understanding of the proposal, the last draft of which they felt had within its outline and text the possibilities of clearly meeting or easily accommodating nearly every criticism that had been expressed publicly.

General Conference

The COTT report and petitions were sent to the Legislative Committee on Faith and Mission at the meeting of the General Conference at St. Louis in April 1988. The chair of that committee, Dr. Thomas A. Langford, was instrumental in setting a tone of seriousness and openness and in ferreting out the main issues for discussion. The committee discussions were open and frank, with a high degree of participation from around the room. The group also took the unusual step of allowing the representatives from COTT into the bar of the committee as full participants in the discussion.

From the beginning, there were obvious and open divisions and tension. For some, their opening statements had less to do with the proposed statement than with the general state of affairs in the Church. The chair settled the agenda rather early by leading the committee to focus upon a refining of the document proposed by the COTT.[29]

Discussion proceeded through the three main sections of the statement, beginning with "Our Doctrinal Heritage" and "Our Doctrinal History." The conversations revealed a basic consensus on most of the text. As Dr. Langford later commented, "The document itself is structured in a way that allowed for convergence among the diversity present in the committee."[30] At the same time, differences were outlined in a spirit of rational integrity and mutual respect. The first actual vote, on adding specific terminology for the triune God (Father, Son, and Holy Spirit), was 41 to 39 and was the only close vote of the whole process. The questions surrounding the place of Wesley's *Sermons* and *Notes* were resolved by a sentence worked out by Ogletree, Oden, and Heitzenrater a month before the meeting, simply recognizing that the actions of the 1968 Plan of Union included these two sets of material as doctrinal standards. At the same time, the paragraph further describing them as "formative doctrinal standards" and "authoritative teaching" was deleted from the COTT document. The other major addition to the second section was a reiteration of the formula that expresses the interaction of Scripture, tradition, reason, and experience (adding a third instance to the two already in the proposed document).

Most of the time and attention of the legislative committee was focused on the final section, "Our Theological Task." Some of the potential controversy was avoided by initial consideration of proposals from the COTT representatives. The most significant, a proposed wording change to the introductory paragraph, spelled out the difference between the church's theological task and its doctrinal expressions. This distinction, which had been implicit in the work of the COTT and was an important presupposition to the section, was made more explicit by saying that "While the Church considers its doctrinal affirmations a central feature of its identity and restricts official changes to a constitutional process, the Church encourages serious reflection across the theological spectrum."[31]

Two other early proposals from the COTT representatives helped move the discussion along. The first was a simple change in the headings in the discussion of the fourfold guidelines, changing "Primacy of Scripture" to "Scripture," and giving the other three their own heading. This change was the only dilution of the basic concept, which was in fact more strongly reinforced in some other areas. Another early proposal that diverted unnecessary controversy was the substitution of suggested wording from the General Commission on Christian Unity and Inter-religious Affairs (submitted too late for full COTT consideration) for the section on "Ecumenical Commitment."[32]

Most of the other changes to this last section were additional sentences or terms. There were six major additions. The first was an introductory paragraph that introduced theological inquiry in terms of "our effort to reflect on God's gracious action in our lives."[33] The second was the inclusion of a paragraph on the "contextual and incarnational" nature of our theological task.[34] The third is another reiteration of the interworking of the fourfold guidelines, along with a strong statement that Scripture "occupies a place of primary authority among these theological sources."[35] A fourth is a sentence that points out how the four basic resources may become "creative vehicles of the Holy Spirit as they function within the Church."[36] The fifth, in the section on reason, makes more explicit that all truth is from God and that efforts to discern the connections between revelation and reason, faith and science, grace and nature are useful endeavors in developing credible and communicable doctrine.[37] The last adds a paragraph concerning the global character of the church, a concern that had been reinforced in other places by addition of a term or phrase.[38] Similar minor changes had highlighted God's work in creation and reinforced the church's responsibilities for evangelism and its recognition of systemic evil in society.

Much of the discussion focused on refinement of terminology in these proposals, so that concerns of the whole group were addressed. In most cases, adjustments were easily worked out in a spirit of good will and a recognition that the group was representing the whole church. It appeared to some observers that the conversations were at times characterized by catchwords and mottoes, but by and large, the members of the committee were listening carefully to each other and their chair, learning how to venture into the field of "conciliar theology."

The result was a document that was accepted by an overwhelmingly positive vote of over 90%, anticipating the action of the plenary session of the General Conference the next day. Two proposed changes made on the floor of the Conference drew little discussion and did not pass.

The successful passage of the statement can be attributed in part to the continual concern throughout the process for both *continuity* and *consensus*. From the outset, the COTT strove to keep the discussion rooted within the framework and themes of the United Methodism's original doctrinal statement (1972). It also attempted to highlight Methodism's solid rootage in and continuing role in the broader Christian tradition, as well as its continuing appropriation of the heritage of its Wesleyan, Methodist, and EUB forebears. The concern for consensus, born of an identity crisis of sorts, was persistently evident throughout the process of broad consultation, with a growing awareness of lines of convergence among the various theological perspectives within the church (exhibited by the unanimous vote of the COTT, which was then reflected in the heavy majority at General Conference).

In hindsight, it would appear that the basic theological work for the disciplinary statement was done within the Committee on Our Theological Task. The strength and resilience of the committee's text was based on its having taken into account the wide range of comments and criticisms from across the church. The COTT document therefore provided a ready medium for minor revisions at the General Conference and emerged with the integrity of its form and content basically intact.

I would disagree with those who were ecstatic at the sight of the General Conference "doing theology." What happened at General Conference was generally not very good theological discussion for the most part (with the exception of a few good mini-lectures by Tom Langford), but rather was political and programmatic maneuvering, with some theology by catchword and slogan. We must, however, also realize that such a thing is all part of the process of the Church (people in the Church) coming to claim the statement as its (their) own.[39]

These observations of the church adopting a doctrinal statement with such a spirit of consensus (even if marked by a note of compromise) should not lull us into a spirit of complacency, however. The section on "Our Theological Task" is not an answer to all our questions but an outline of how we should proceed in reflecting upon those questions. The document exhibits a certain carefully developed balance, but it also maintains some tensions that characterize our heritage. This is not a statement to comfort the church so much as to challenge the church. The intent is not to offer a final consensus but rather to challenge the church in its continuing task of serious theological exploration within a context of considered doctrinal identity. This statement declares that we are not hesitant to affirm the basic elements of our doctrinal heritage as a distinctive feature of who we are, and also that we will continue to seek even better ways of expressing the wonders of God's love.

Chapter 8

AT FULL LIBERTY: DOCTRINAL STANDARDS IN EARLY AMERICAN METHODISM

Richard P. Heitzenrater[1]

The distinction between doctrines and the standards used to enforce them can be understood as a tension between the weight of tradition and the force of law.

American Methodism has never been characterized by a strong inclination toward careful doctrinal definition. That is not to say that Methodism has had no concern at all for matters of doctrine. From the beginning, the Methodist preachers referred to "our doctrines" with a sense of pride; they likewise expressed concern about the dissemination of erroneous doctrines in their midst. As American Methodism shifted from a movement to an institution (from a society to a church), it quite naturally developed structures and procedures to protect and perpetuate its traditional identity. Such a process included not only the establishment of legal and constitutional means by which to guard the "standards of doctrine," but also the preservation of traditional doctrinal emphases to perpetuate the distinctive, if not well-defined, Methodist proclamation of the gospel which lay at the heart of the movement. The growing desire for order and discipline, in tension with a seeming ambivalence toward doctrinal formulation, provided the setting for a unique development in the constitutional history of Methodism in America that to this day has not received an interpretation that commands a consensus.

The General Conference in 1808 passed a set of rules for "regulating and perpetuating" the conference. Among the provisions that became recognized as constitutionally binding upon Methodism was the stipulation that the General Conference have "full powers to make rules and regulations for our Church," subject only to a list of six "restrictions" subsequently called the "Restrictive Rules." The First Restrictive Rule, still in effect in the United Methodist Church today, states that the General Conference shall not revoke, alter, or change our articles of religion, nor establish any new standards or rules of doctrine contrary to our present existing and established standards of doctrine.[2]

Questions of doctrinal standards[3] in Methodism are determined in large part by the interpretation of this rule. The issue of interpretation is often focused on the meaning of the last phrase ("our present existing and established standards of doctrine"), giving rise to no small amount of debate among Methodist theologians during the past hundred years or so.

The interpretation that has prevailed over the last century has been incorporated into the official documents of The United Methodist Church. The *Plan of Union*, approved in 1966–67, noted that, although the last phrase of the First Restrictive Rule had never been formally defined, the "original reference" would include, "as a minimum," Wesley's "forty-four *Sermons on Several Occasions* and his *Explanatory Notes Upon the New Testament.*"[4] That assumption provided the basis for subsequent interpretive statements passed by the General Conference in 1972. The "Historical Background" statement, still contained in Part II of the 1984 Book of Discipline, reiterates the claim that Wesley's *Sermons* and *Notes* were "by plain historical inference" among the "present existing and established standards of doctrine" specified by the framers of the First Restrictive Rule in 1808.[5] This view, however, like nearly every comment on the question during the last century, overlooks two key sources of evidence: the Discipline's own historical stipulations for enforcing doctrinal standards (beginning in 1788) and the manuscript journal of the General Conference of 1808 that passed the first constitutional rules. Careful consideration of this evidence challenges the current view and calls for a reconsideration of the assumptions that have prevailed regarding doctrinal standards.

The question of doctrinal standards in early American Methodism has taken on added significance with the decision of the 1984 General Conference to establish a study committee on "Our Theological Task." The committee's charge is "to prepare a new statement [Book of Discipline, ¶ 69] that will reflect the needs of the church [and] define the scope of our Wesleyan tradition in the context of our contemporary world." The First Restrictive Rule, of course, remains in force, and therefore a clear understanding of the intent of its framers (and thereby the meaning of its language regarding doctrinal standards) is crucial to the constitutionality of any updating of disciplinary statements concerning United Methodist doctrine. Of particular concern in this chapter is the relationship between matters that bear the force of law and those that rely on the weight of tradition.

The matter of ascertaining the meaning of the phrase "our present existing and established standards of doctrine" in the 1808 document hinges upon two questions: What do the official documents of the Methodist Episcopal Church from 1785 to 1808 stipulate (legally *establish* by definition or implication) as the doctrinal standards of the denomination at that time? and What did the persons who drew up those documents intend by their language? Two related, but different, questions are, What are the distinctive doctrinal *emphases* of early Methodist preaching? and What documents best exhibited those distinctive doctrines? The developments during the period from 1785 to 1808 are of primary interest in answering these questions regarding law and tradition, but the ideas and actions of the generations of American Methodists before and after that period also help illuminate the issues.

The constitutional developments at the turn of the nineteenth century have never been fully outlined or adequately examined in the light of material now available. These events are crucial to a full understanding of the issues today, however, and deserve our careful attention. We will therefore look at the constitutional activities of early American Methodism step by step with an eye toward discerning the tension and interplay between the force of law and the weight of tradition, in an attempt to contribute to a better understanding of the scope of the Wesleyan tradition in relation to doctrinal standards in The United Methodist Church.

Wesley and the Christmas Conference

The organizing conference of the Methodist Episcopal Church met in Baltimore in December, 1784, to consider the scheme of organization proposed by Wesley, as filtered through Francis Asbury and Thomas Coke. Its main concern was to establish a workable polity for American Methodists, *separate* from their former British connections yet still to some extent reliant upon Wesley, during his lifetime.

The question of doctrine remained largely in the shadows during those days of rewriting the *Minutes* of the British Methodist Conference (also known as the "Large Minutes") into a form of discipline for the American Methodist connection. In fact, the official minutes of the Christmas Conference do not refer at all to any action concerning doctrine as such. One oblique reference appears in a letter from Wesley "To Dr. Coke, Mr. Asbury, and our brethren in North America" that is prefixed to those minutes. The letter spells out Wesley's rationale for allowing the organization of a separate church in the American states in the light of the "uncommon train of providences" by which they had become independent. Wesley concludes by proclaiming that the American Methodists, being totally disentangled from the English state and church, "are now at full liberty, simply to follow the scriptures and the primitive church."[6]

Lest anyone think, however, that he was casting his American followers adrift in a sea of doctrinal tumult, Wesley sent to the new world, with Dr. Coke, a document that provided the liturgical and doctrinal framework for American Methodism. *The Sunday Service for the Methodists in North America*, received and adopted by the Christmas Conference, contained Wesley's abridgement of the Book of Common Prayer and his distillation of the Thirty-Nine Articles. Wesley may very well have conceived of these materials, along with the "Large Minutes," as providing the basic design for the organization of a Methodist church in America, much as John Fletcher and Joseph Benson had proposed to him in a nearly identical scheme for England in 1775.[7] The Methodist preachers in America not only adopted Wesley's revision of the Articles, but also apparently assumed that these materials from Wesley's hand furnished the necessary official doctrinal framework for an ecclesiastical organization, similar to the way the Thirty-Nine Articles provided doctrinal standards for the Church of England.[8] The acceptance of these documents *per se* did not diminish the American Methodists' regard at that time for Wesley's continuing leadership in matters of government or for his other writings as a traditional source of doctrine.[9] In fact, their high regard for Wesley's scheme seems to have convinced them that the specific documents he had drawn up and sent over were deliberately conceived for the purposes of establishing the new church, which now stood in a new and separate constitutional relationship to both the Church of England and British Methodism.[10]

The preachers meeting in Baltimore clearly understood themselves to be establishing an independent organization that *superseded* any previous arrangements that had existed. The minutes of the Christmas Conference point out that "at this conference we formed ourselves into an Independent Church." Also, the answer to Question 3 in their first Discipline, which they drew up in Baltimore, makes this point very clearly:

> We will form ourselves into an Episcopal Church under the direction of Superintendents, Elders, Deacons and Helpers, according to the Forms of Ordination annexed to our Liturgy, and the Form of Discipline *set forth in these Minutes*. [italics mine][11]

The British "Large Minutes," which formed the basis for these American "Minutes" as revised at the Christmas Conference were thus superseded and no longer had any binding effect on the American Methodists after January, 1785.[12]

There is no reason to suspect that the traditional distinctive doctrines preached by Methodists in America would have changed as a result of any action of the organizing conference. The preachers in the newly organized Methodist Episcopal Church would certainly be expected to preach the same message that had given life to their movement over the previous decade. No one would expect that Wesley's *Sermons* and *Notes* would suddenly be discarded by the Americans; they had long been an important resource for solid Methodist doctrinal preaching.

After 1784, however, a new legal situation had been established in which the *Sermons* and *Notes* would appear to function quite differently than previously. During the decade prior to the Christmas Conference, the American Methodist conference had on several occasions pledged itself to the Wesleyan scheme in both doctrine and polity. It had followed the stipulations of the British *Minutes* to the letter, as was appropriate, given their status as part of British Methodism, under leaders appointed by Wesley. Their chapels were secured by the "model deed" contained in those *Minutes*, which, among other things, (1) required that the preachers be appointed by Mr. Wesley, (2) "Provided always, that such persons preach no other Doctrine than is contained in Mr. Wesley's *Notes Upon the New Testament*, and four volumes of Sermons."[13] These guidelines for measuring the doctrinal soundness of Methodist preaching were certainly, by any definition, "doctrinal standards." As such, they applied equally in America up through 1784 and were reinforced by specific actions of the conferences of Methodist preachers in America.[14] But the Christmas Conference had established American Methodism as a separate organization with its own set of constitutive documents, similar in form but significantly different in content from the British counterparts. The differences in the legal situation and the tensions with the traditional understandings became evident in the development of American Methodism subsequent to 1784.

From the Christmas Conference to the General Conference of 1808

After 1784, the Methodist preachers in America no doubt remained committed to their traditional doctrines. But the question remains, what did the Methodist Episcopal Church understand their "established *standards* of doctrine" to be? The fate of the "model deed," which stipulated those standards in Britain, helps answer that question. As noted previously, the Christmas Conference spent a large part of its time revising the "Large Minutes" into the new American form of discipline, published as the *Minutes* of 1785. A comparison of the two documents indicates that, although some sections were altered, many sections were either omitted totally or adopted without change, depending on their applicability to the American scene. The section which contained the "model deed" was omitted.[15] The new Discipline in America therefore specified no doctrinal *standards*, as the British "Large Minutes" had, although it did have many references to specific doctrines and doctrinal writings.

The conference had, however, received and adopted another document, *The Sunday Service*, that did contain a specifically designed formulation of doctrinal standards, the Articles of Religion (printed at the end, in the same manner that the Anglican Thirty-Nine Articles appeared at the end of the *Book of Common Prayer*). These "rectified" Articles, as we have said, had been drawn up specifically by Wesley for the American Methodists. There seems to have been no need in the minds of the American preachers, given Wesley's intentional provision of these Articles, to specify any other *standards* of doctrine by which to measure American Methodist preaching and teaching. This assumption is further supported by the fact that the "model deed," which the Methodist Episcopal Church did insert into its Discipline beginning in 1796, not only (1) designated a new source of authorization for the preachers (the American conferences instead of Wesley), but also (2) specifically deleted the proviso concerning the *Sermons* and *Notes*, thus consciously deleting their force as legally binding standards of doctrine.[16]

A more direct clue to the Methodist Episcopal Church's understanding of its doctrinal standards can be found in the disciplinary provisions for maintaining and enforcing those standards. The *Form of Discipline* for 1788 introduces a section on the trial of "immoral ministers and preachers," in which Question 2 is "What shall be done in cases of improper tempers, words or actions, or a breach of the articles, and discipline of the church?"[17] (This same edition of the Discipline, coincidentally, also has "some other useful pieces annexed,"[18] one of which contains the Articles of Religion.) The first General Conference of the Methodist Episcopal Church, meeting in 1792, divided that question (the second in the section on trials of ministers) into two questions that distinguish between matters of discipline and matters of doctrine. The new Question 3 dealing with doctrine, reads, "What shall be done with those Ministers or Preachers who hold and preach doctrines which are *contrary to our Articles of Religion*?" (emphasis mine).[19] It is clear from this question that the only official measure or test of doctrinal orthodoxy (the function of doctrinal *standards*) within the Methodist Episcopal Church at that time were the Articles of Religion. In the same Discipline (1792) which contains this new question, the Articles were moved to a more prominent position at the front of the book, section II. The sacramental services were added to the volume and the title was changed to *The Doctrines and Discipline of the Methodist Episcopal Church in America*.

At no point in the early history of American Methodism were the Articles of Religion designated as standards that demanded positive subscription. Although not a creedal formula in that sense, they did function like the creeds of the primitive church in another way—they were used as standards by which to protect orthodoxy by determining heresy or erroneous doctrines, i.e, those doctrines that were "contrary to" the standards as found in the Articles.[20] No American Methodist candidate for ministry was required to make any positive doctrinal subscription, either to the Articles, to Wesley's *Sermons* and *Notes*, or to any other documents. The Articles served the purpose, then, of providing minimal norms or standards by which to measure the orthodoxy (not necessarily the adequacy) of doctrine held and preached by the Methodists.[21] The Wesleyan Articles of Religion provided a churchly doctrinal foundation for the new American Methodist ecclesiastical organization. They also presented an explicit doctrinal tie to the church universal and as such were a more appropriate standard of doctrine for such a church than the earlier British Methodist standards, Wesley's *Notes* and *Sermons*. In their original context, those British Wesleyan standards outlined what might be seen as a sectarian emphasis (for a movement rather than a church) under the larger umbrella of the Articles of Religion of the Church of England.

So far we have been looking at *standards* of doctrine as found in the Articles. That is not to say that good Methodist or Wesleyan *doctrines* were not to be found in other places. The Discipline itself, beginning with the first edition, contained two sections on doctrine (on perfection and against antinomianism) and explicitly recommended several other writings for specific purposes.[22] Beginning with the edition of 1788 (the "useful pieces annexed"), the Discipline contained several doctrinal tracts in addition to the two doctrinal sections already mentioned.[23] These were apparently not considered to be *standards* of doctrine in the same sense as the Articles since the provisions for the trial of a preacher on matters of doctrine were not altered in any way so as to take these doctrinal writings into account. These treatises certainly contained sound Methodist (if not always, strictly speaking, Wesleyan) doctrine, as did many other writings, but they were clearly never considered to be standards of doctrine.[24] The same can be said of the *Sermons* and *Notes*.

Whether or not the American Methodists understood all the ecclesial implications of their separate establishment, they apparently did accept Wesley's intention that their organization be grounded upon a doctrinal statement (the Articles of Religion) that provided basic doctrinal standards and had obvious ties to the larger church universal in both form and content. In this context, nevertheless, other Wesleyan writings continued to provide the distinctive shape of Methodist doctrinal teaching and preaching in America, fleshing out the basic Protestant norms provided in the Articles.

The General Conference of 1808

Twenty-three years after the Christmas Conference, only a dozen or so of the preachers from 1785 remained active in the Methodist connection in America. At about the same time, the passing of the earlier generations had led the British Methodist Conference in 1806 to ask, "Can anything be done for the security of our doctrines?" The answer in their *Minutes* was that Adam Clarke, Joseph Benson, and Thomas Coke were to "draw up a Digest or Form, expressive of the Methodist Doctrines." Their efforts resulted in two documents, both entitled *Articles of Religion*.[25] In America, a similar desire to protect and perpetuate the established doctrines and discipline of the church was apparently on the minds of Asbury and some of the other preachers at the General Conference in Baltimore in 1808.

On the fourth day of the conference, a committee was established to set rules for "regulating and perpetuating General Conferences in the future."[26] This "committee of fourteen," formed by two members elected by each conference, included all seven of the preachers in attendance (excepting Asbury) who had been in active connection since 1785: Philip Bruce, Ezekiel Cooper, Jesse Lee, John M'Claskey, William Phoebus, Nelson Reed, and Thomas Ware. The subcommittee designated to write the proposal was made up of three persons: Bruce, Cooper, and Joshua Soule, a young preacher who would soon make his mark on Methodism. Their report to the conference came from the hand of Soule, and proposed the following as the first "restrictive rule": "The General Conference shall not revoke, alter, or change our Articles of Religion, nor establish any new standards of doctrine, contrary to our present existing and established standards of doctrine."[27]

The report of the "committee of fourteen" also contained, as its first item, a controversial proposal to establish a delegated General Conference. The defeat of that part of the report, over the question of how the delegates would be selected (largely because Jesse Lee opposed the committee's proposal of seniority as a basis), seemed to doom the whole report, which was then laid aside. As the conference drew to a close, however, the question of designating a time and place for the next conference allowed for the reintroduction of the question of delegation, and Soule's motion that delegates be selected by the annual conferences "either by seniority or choice" broke the logjam and allowed for the rest of the report to be brought up and carried, item by item.

Along with the other rules for governing the conference, the First Restrictive Rule was then passed, including the important phrase in question, "nor establish any new standards or rules of doctrine, contrary to our present existing and established standards of doctrine."[28] The primary impact of that second part of the statement seems to be to allow for new standards or rules of doctrine so long as they are *not contrary to* the existing ones ("present existing and established"). The main intention, then, of the conference's adoption of the phrase seems not to have been to incorporate an additional body of material, such as Wesley's *Sermons* and *Notes*, to their "present and existing standards," the Articles. The primary intent was rather to protect the present standards, the Articles, and to stipulate narrow restrictions under which new standards could be developed.

The intention of the conference in the face of the tension between the force of legal standards and the weight of traditional ideas is made more evident in the actions taken almost immediately after the passage of the Restrictive Rules on the morning of May 24. The first action of the afternoon session was an attempt to clarify any ambiguity caused by the phrasing of the first rule. Francis Ward moved

> that it shall be considered as the sentiment of this Conference, that Mr. Wesley's Notes on the New Testament, his four first Volumes of Sermons and Mr. Fletcher's Checks, in their general tenor, contain the principal doctrines of Methodism, and a good explanation of our articles of religion; and that this sentiment be recorded on our Journal without being incorporated in the Discipline.[29]

Three things are significant about this motion: first, it indicates a willingness among some preachers to specify particular writings that "contain" the core of traditional Methodist doctrine and exposit the "standards" found in the Articles; second, that such sentiment was not inclined to rely solely upon Wesley's *Sermons* and *Notes* but to include also John Fletcher's *Checks Against Antinomianism*; and third, that this sentiment was somewhat hesitant, resulting in a desire for a "memorandum of understanding" only, that would be recorded in the journal of the proceedings but not explicitly stated in the Discipline. The most startling thing about this guarded and carefully worded motion is that it lost. The General Conference was *not* willing to go on record defining its standards of doctrine in terms of documents other than the Articles, not even Wesley's *Sermons* and *Notes*.

The rationale for the conference's negative vote on this motion is nowhere explicitly indicated. Nevertheless, in the light of the wording of the motion as well as the action taken, it seems obvious that the majority of the members present did not consider Wesley's writings to be "rules or standards of doctrine" in the same sense as the Articles of Religion. If the members of the conference had generally assumed such a correlation, the motion would not have been made in the first place, much less defeated. But what is confusing to the present observer is the conference's reticence to specify that the writings of Wesley and Fletcher "contain the principal doctrines of Methodism." This vote seems to be continuing evidence of a spirit of independence among the American Methodists that was more than simply anti-British sentiment, although that spirit can be seen flaring up at several points during the early years of the new denomination, including this period leading up to the hostilities of 1812. The tension between dependence upon and independence from Wesley had long been a mark of the Methodists in America, as illustrated clearly in the life and thought of Francis Asbury himself, who played a major leadership role in the conference of 1808. Asbury was apparently satisfied that the conference had sufficiently protected its Methodist heritage. Three days after passage of the Restrictive Rules he reflected upon the actions of that conference in a letter to Thomas Rankin, noting in particular that "we have . . . perpetuated in words the good old Methodist doctrine and discipline." Although this phrasing echoes the minutes of 1781, when the colonial conference reiterated its allegiance to the British Wesleyan standards, this comment by the bishop can be seen as an indication on his part that the actions of the conference had, without a literal return to their pre-1785 legal condition, preserved the original Methodist spirit in the face of new challenges from both heresy and sloth. Although the Articles of Religion seem to bypass some distinctively Wesleyan ideas, it appears that the Methodists in America accepted Wesley's design for protecting doctrinal orthodoxy through a brief and basic symbol of catholic doctrine, purged of Calvinist and Roman errors.

The intent of the 1808 General Conference thus seems to be clear. The majority desired to restrict Methodism's "established standards of doctrine" to the Articles of Religion that Wesley had provided in 1784 and to avoid even implying, by association or otherwise, that there were other specific writings that were authoritative *in the same manner.* The motion itself is, of course, an expression of the weight of the Wesleyan tradition coming to the fore, howbeit in a form considered inappropriate by most of those present and voting at the conference. The defeat of the motion seems to be conclusive evidence that the General Conference did not understand its standards of doctrine to include Wesley's *Sermons* and *Notes.* The Methodist Episcopal Church was left with a constitutional statement in the wording of the First Restrictive Rule, which refers specifically only to the Articles of Religion, and reiterates and reinforces the crucial importance of the Articles by referring to them as "our present existing and established standards of doctrine."

In the light of those actions of the 1808 General Conference, it is by no means strange that for two successive generations no one ever seems to have raised the question as to what the "present existing and established standards of doctrine" were. The Articles of Religion were the only standards of doctrine that had been "established" by the Methodist Episcopal Church, that is, adopted between 1785 and 1808 with provisions for enforcement as a measure of Methodist doctrine in America. The fact that writers in the last half of the century began to raise the question, and in fact make inaccurate speculations about the intentions of the framers of the First Restrictive Rule, can be partially explained by the absence of any mention of this motion (or attempted "memorandum of understanding") from the published version of the manuscript journal of the conference. A note in the margin of the manuscript journal explains the omission: "N.B. It was voted that this motion be struck out of the Journal." The whole paragraph mentioning the defeated motion regarding the *Notes, Sermons,* and *Checks* is struck through with a huge "X" and consequently deleted from the printed version of the journal. That entry is the only instance of such an action in the whole manuscript volume, which covers the general conferences from 1800 to 1828. The conference did not want to specify its Wesleyan measures for orthodoxy beyond the Articles, but it also did not want the public to know that it had been unwilling to go on record in that matter. The General Conference of 1808 manifested in its actions the continuing tension between dependence and independence, and, in its careful maneuvering, highlighted the distinction that is occasionally evident between the force of law and the weight of tradition.

119

The General Conferences of 1816 and 1828

The evidence outlined above would seem to be adequate to make the point that the doctrinal standards of early American Methodism were understood from a legal and constitutional point of view to be located solely in the Articles of Religion (though perhaps traditionally understood to be illustrated in other Wesleyan writings as well). However, further evidence to corroborate that view can be found in the actions of the General Conference during the two decades following the establishment of the Restrictive Rules of 1808. Two incidents in particular relate to this question, and both are coincidentally connected with Joshua Soule.

In the first case, the General Conference of 1816 decided to appoint a "Committee of Safety," which was assigned the task of inquiring "whether our doctrines have been maintained, discipline faithfully and impartially enforced, and the stations and circuits duly attended."[30] This committee consisted of Enoch George, Samuel Parker, and Soule (a most appropriate person to be in this group, providing continuity from the conference of 1808). The report of the Committee of Safety, apparently drawn up by the chairman, Soule,[31] was approved two weeks later. It begins with the following statement:

> After due examination, your committee are of opinion that, in some parts of the connexion, doctrines contrary to our established articles of faith, and of dangerous tendency, have made their appearance among us, especially the ancient doctrines of *Arianism, Socinianism,* and *Pelagianism,* under certain new and obscure modifications.[32]

The term "established articles of faith" is not precisely the same as "articles of religion," but the committee seems to have had those articles in mind, since the three erroneous doctrines listed are specifically contradictory of Articles II, I and IX respectively of the Articles of Religion.

In the second incident, the General Conference of 1828 exhibited again the relationship that some persons within Methodism saw between the Articles as doctrinal standards and other doctrinal writings accepted and used by the preachers as containing good Methodist doctrine. The conference heard the appeal of Joshua Randall, a preacher from the New England Conference, who, according to the wording of the *Journal,* "had been expelled from the Church, upon a charge of holding and disseminating doctrines contrary to our articles of religion." The charges were upheld by an overwhelming majority of 164 votes to 1. Encouraged by the tone of the conference, Lawrence M'Combs introduced a proposal that accused Bishop Soule (who was presiding at that session!) of preaching erroneous doctrine the previous year in a sermon at the South Carolina Conference. The motion claimed that in the sermon there was "in the opinion of some an apparent departure from several points of doctrine held by the Methodist Episcopal Church."[33] The matter was referred to the Committee on the Episcopacy, on which M'Combs sat. The committee's report was brought to the floor the following day by its chairman, Stephen Roszel, the only member of the group who had been at the General Conference of 1808. The report, adopted by the conference, cleared the bishop of the charges. It concluded by saying, "There is nothing in the sermon, fairly construed, inconsistent with our articles of religion, as illustrated in the writings of Messrs. Wesley and Fletcher."[34]

The conference thus stated its understanding of the relationship between the legal standards of doctrine and the traditionally accepted doctrinal writings. This statement is particularly illuminating in four ways: (1), it demonstrates the position of the Articles of Religion as *the* standards of doctrine; (2), it shows that the doctrinal material found in certain other writings in the Methodist tradition did actually function at that time in a supplemental and illustrative role in relation to the doctrinal standards in the Articles of Religion, similar to the manner expressed by the defeated motion of 1808; (3), it reveals that, among these other writings, the broad range of Wesley's work was considered useful in illuminating matters of doctrine, rather than just the *Sermons* and *Notes*; and (4), it clearly indicates that materials other than the writings of Wesley, in this case (again) the writings of Fletcher, were also considered to be important in this illustrative role. While the Articles of Religion functioned as juridical standards of doctrine, these other doctrinal writings, traditionally accepted as containing sound Methodist doctrine, were seen as exemplary illustrations of the Methodist doctrinal heritage.

Concluding Observations

The developments within early American Methodism indicate very clearly that the "historical inferences" that are "apparent" from the available evidence all tend to confirm the Articles of Religion alone as the "present existing and established standards of doctrine" that the "committee of fourteen" had in mind when it drew up the First Restrictive Rule. The founders of the Methodist Episcopal Church were not legally bound by any action previous to the Christmas Conference (1785) and seem to have taken Wesley's words to heart in considering themselves "at full liberty." At every point where the Methodist Episcopal Church had an opportunity to reiterate and reaffirm its allegiance to Wesley's *Sermons* and *Notes* specifically as doctrinal standards after 1785, it either consciously deleted the references, failed to mention them, or voted to the contrary. At every point where doctrinal *standards* are referred to, it is the Articles of Religion that are specified as the basic measure of proper Methodist doctrine.

That American Methodism was firmly grounded in the broader Wesleyan doctrinal heritage, however, can hardly be denied. Wesley had not only provided the new church with its Articles of Religion; even after 1808 his writings continued to provide the traditional exposition of the principal doctrines of Methodism, despite the General Conference's reticence to make that relationship explicit. The *Sermons* and *Notes* were quite likely alongside the Bible in the saddlebags of many preachers in America, along with *Primitive Physick*, the *Doctrines and Discipline*, and other basic resources of the circuit rider. Just as likely, Fletcher's *Checks* could be found in those same saddlebags, and, shortly, even Watson's *Institutes* and *Apology* would be considered appropriate baggage for a Methodist preacher. The relationship between these traditional doctrinal *statements* (accepted patterns of doctrinal *exposition*) and the established doctrinal *standards* (minimal measures of doctrinal *orthodoxy*) soon became confused as the constitutional distinctions became blurred in the minds of later generations.

By the middle of the nineteenth century, commentators began to read mysterious inferences into that phrase, "present existing and established standards of doctrine," and shortly began to alter the Discipline to conform to their new readings. Bishop Osmond Baker, in his 1855 manual of church administration,[35] was one of the first to claim that the Articles of Religion "do not embrace all that is included in 'our present existing and established standards of doctrine.'" His rationale was quite simple: "Many of the characteristic doctrines of our Church are not even referred to directly in those articles." He therefore suggested that "usage and general consent would probably designate Mr. Wesley's Sermons, and his Notes on the New Testament, and Watson's Theological Institutes" as "established standards of doctrine."

This line of reasoning, confusing traditionally accepted doctrinal statements with officially established doctrinal standards, was continued in southern Methodism by Bishop Holland N. McTyeire, who comments in his manual on the Discipline that "the phrase, 'doctrines which are contrary to our Articles of Religion,' is evidently elliptical." He goes on to mention those works which "usage and general consent" would include in the "established standards of doctrine," and adds to

Bishop Baker's list the Wesleyan Methodist Catechisms and the Hymn-book.[36]

In the 1880s, this broadened reading of the meaning of "established standards" was incorporated into the Discipline of the northern church in the section on the "Trial of a Preacher." The charge of disseminating "doctrines contrary to our Articles of Religion" was amended to add the phrase "or established standards of doctrine," thereby referring to a separate body of material.[37] The Ecclesiastical Code Commission that proposed this change to the 1880 General Conference was chaired by James M. Buckley. Buckley's published explanations of doctrinal standards confuses the clear distinctions of legal establishment and traditional acceptance, resulting in continual references to "*other* established standards of doctrine" (my italics).[38] Buckley, along with others who used this frame of reference, was forced into making distinctions between the way the Articles could be enforced and the manner in which these "other" standards functioned. He noted, for instance, that such a range of material provides for "substantial unity" while allowing "circumstantial variety" within Wesleyan Methodism.

The incorrect assumptions (as well as the new wording) of these constitutional historians became explicitly implanted in the 1912 Discipline of the northern church, which referred to "doctrines which are contrary to our Articles of Religion, or our *other* existing and established standards of doctrine" (¶245; my italics). This wording was subsequently carried over into the *Discipline of The Methodist Church* after 1939. In the meantime, the First Restrictive Rule had remained unchanged, though by now its original context and intent were fully misunderstood.[39]

The terminology for the section on trials in the present Book of Discipline (1984) is less precise, though perhaps more accurate (if understood properly) in its simple reference to "the established standards of doctrine of the Church" (¶ 2621.g). The phrase should be understood historically and constitutionally as referring to the Confession of Faith (from the Evangelical United Brethren tradition) and the Articles of Religion (from the Methodist tradition). These are the standards of doctrine that have been established as juridical standards and carry the force of law within the church. Any attempt to enumerate *other* "standards of doctrine" confuses the distinction between the constitutional history of the church and the development of its doctrinal heritage. To say that our doctrinal standards are not "legal or juridical instruments" (1984 Discipline, p. 72) is to ignore our own provisions for enforcing those standards. To say that a particular list of other historic doctrinal statements should in some way be considered "established standards of doctrine" is to confuse the weight of tradition with the force of law.

The task of defining "the scope of our Wesleyan tradition in the context of our contemporary world" includes much more than defining or redefining legal standards of doctrine, although that is also involved. Minimal legal standards of orthodoxy have never been the measure of an adequate witness to the tradition, be it Christian or United Methodist. The heart of our task is to discover how seriously we take our distinctive doctrinal heritage and how creatively we appropriate the fullness of that heritage in the life and mission of the church today.

Chapter 9

WHAT ARE "ESTABLISHED STANDARDS OF DOCTRINE"? A RESPONSE TO RICHARD HEITZENRATER

Thomas C. Oden[1]

"The General Conference shall not revoke, alter, or change our Articles of Religion or establish any new standards or rules of doctrine contrary to our present existing and established standards of doctrine" (Book of Discipline of The United Methodist Church, 1984, ¶ 16). The same sentence, known as the First Restrictive Rule, is in every Book of Discipline of The United Methodist Church and its predecessors from 1808 to the present. To what standards does this sentence refer?

The most commonly accepted interpretation is found in the 1972–84 Disciplines: "The Discipline seems to assume that for the determination of otherwise irreconcilable doctrinal disputes, the Annual and General Conferences are the appropriate courts of appeal, under the guidance of the first two Restrictive Rules (which is to say, the Articles and Confession, the *Sermons* and the *Notes*)" (1984 Discipline, ¶ 67). But is this interpretation historically correct and accurate in its textual specification of what the rules protect? That is what the current debate is about.

The thesis of this essay: John Wesley's *Sermons* and *Notes* have had an uninterrupted consensual history of being received as established standards of doctrine in The United Methodist Church and its predecessors. It sets forth reasons for retention of current language of the Discipline that specifies the *Sermons* and *Notes* as constitutionally protected doctrinal standards (1984 Discipline, ¶ 67). It sets forth a resumé of evidence for doctrinal standards from 1763 to the present, especially the disputed period of 1784–1808, showing that the *Sermons* and *Notes* were not rejected by the deeds of settlement, and that the conference of 1808 referred to them in the second clause of the First Restrictive Rule as "our present existing and established standards of doctrine." The undebated, nonconsensual view that the Articles only are protected by the constitution should not enter prematurely into the language of church law.

In 1749 Wesley drew up a "model deed," published in 1763, for all Methodist preaching houses, which restricted the use of the chapels to those who "preach no other doctrine than is contained in Mr. Wesley's Notes upon the New Testament, and four volumes of sermons."[2] The "four volumes of sermons" were the *Sermons on Several Occasions*, which since the 1840s have been generally referred to as the "Standard Sermons."[3]

The 1972–84 Disciplines specifically hold that there is a dual norm operative in the standards of doctrine referred to in the First Restrictive Rule: "The original distinction between the intended functions of the Articles on the one hand, and of the *Sermons* and *Notes* on the other, may be inferred from the double reference to them in the First Restrictive Rule (adopted in 1808 and unchanged ever since)" (1984 Discipline, ¶67). Here the Discipline clearly endorses the "two-clause theory" of the First Rule: "On the one hand, it [the constitution] forbids any further *alterations* of the Articles and, on the other, any further contrary *additions* 'to our present existing, and established standards of doctrine' (i.e., the Minutes, *Sermons*, and *Notes*)" (1984 Discipline, ¶67). The two-clause reading of the First Rule emphasizes the difference and complementarity between the two sources — Articles and other "established standards."

All Disciplines since 1972 affirm as an accepted view the theory that the 1784 Conference affirmed Wesley's *Sermons* and *Notes* as established sources of doctrine:

> From their beginnings, the Methodists in America understood themselves as the dutiful heirs of Wesley and the Wesleyan tradition. In 1773, they affirmed their allegiance to the principles of the "Model Deed" and ratified this again in 1784, when they stipulated that "The London Minutes," including the doctrinal minutes of the early Conferences and the Model Deed, were accepted as their own doctrinal guidelines. In this way they established a threefold agency—the *Conference*, the *Sermons*, and the *Notes*—as their guides in matters of doctrine. (1984 Discipline, ¶ 67).

There is no doubt that the 1984 Discipline regards the Sermons and Notes as constitutionally protected doctrinal standards. It is generally agreed that during the period from 1855 (Bishop Osmond Baker's *Guidebook*) to the present, the leading experts on American Methodist constitutional history (from Bishops Baker and Holland McTyeire to Albert Outler and Bishop Nolan Harmon) have included the *Sermons* and *Notes* along with the Articles as constitutionally protected doctrinal standards. Happily there is very little disagreement over the period from the inception of American Methodism to the Christmas Conference of 1784, during which time the *Sermons* and *Notes* were repeatedly stated in the Minutes (and incorporated legally into the deeds of Methodist preaching places) as doctrinal standards. That leaves at issue only a single disputed period—from 1784 to 1855, that is, between the Christmas Conference and the publication of Baker's *Guide-book*.

It has been argued by Richard Heitzenrater in this journal that during this period the *Sermons* and *Notes* were not regarded as legally binding doctrinal standards, and that only after that time did Baker's interpretation emerge as normative, whereby the *Sermons* and *Notes* were belatedly (and wrongly!) reinstated as binding doctrinal standards after a seventy-one year interruption.[4] Our purpose is to present evidence to the contrary, so as to provide a reliable historical basis for concluding that the *Sermons* and *Notes* have remained established doctrinal standards steadily and without interruption from the inception of American Methodism to the present Book of Discipline.

The first "query proposed to every preacher" of the American Conference of 1773 was: "Ought not the authority of Mr. Wesley and that Conference to extend to the preachers and people in America, as well as in Great Britain and Ireland?" "Yes." Second question: "Ought not the doctrine and discipline of the Methodists, as contained in the [British] minutes to be the sole rule of our conduct, who labor in the connection with Mr. Wesley in America?" "Yes."[5] These two questions established from the outset three key principles that would enter deeply into the spirit of American Methodism: (1) Wesley would exercise authority within the connection as long as he would live, and the distance to America did not weaken or diminish that, so that Wesley or his authorized representatives would govern personally as Wesley did in Britain and Ireland. (2) The doctrine taught in Europe and America was the same— hence there was not thought to be a Methodist doctrine taught in one country distinguishable from that in another. (3) More importantly, the doctrine taught had a specifically defined textual basis and reference— that contained in the British *Minutes* which included a "model deed" requiring that preachers preach "no other doctrine than is contained in" Wesley's *Sermons* and *Notes*.

The American Conference of 1780 established the pivotal principle that all deeds of American Methodist Church properties "shall be drawn in substance after that in the printed [British] *Minutes*," and thus would incorporate the restriction concerning the *Sermons* and *Notes*.[6] At the ninth conference of 1781 these same textual grounds were spelled out explicitly: "Ques. 1. What preachers are now determined, after mature consideration, close observation, and earnest prayer, to preach the old Methodist doctrine, and strictly enforce the discipline as contained in the *Notes*, *Sermons*, and *Minutes* published by Mr. Wesley. . . ?"[7] This was thought sufficiently important to require formal subscription: "The thirty-nine preachers assembled in the Conference subscribed their names to an affirmative answer."[8]

On five occasions between 1773 and 1784, supported by unambiguous documentation, the established standards of doctrine were clearly and textually defined as *Sermons* and *Notes*: (1) in the conference of 1773, (2) the conference of 1780, (3) the conference of 1781, (4) in Wesley's letter to the conference of 1783, and (5) the conference of May 8, 1784. All of these documents, criteria, and actions were well-known to American preachers when they met at the Christmas Conference in 1784. If there had been some rescinding or amendment of these standards in the period 1784–1808, one would expect that there would be some record of it. There is no record of it whatever, either in conference records or private memoirs, and furthermore, no hint of debate that these established standards were under challenge or even being questioned. This was the conference whose record shows that preachers were specifically urged to "be active in dispensing Mr. *Wesley's* Books."[9] This minute was retained in numerous subsequent issues of the Discipline in the disputed period from 1784 to 1808.

We will summarize Heitzenrater's case point-by-point and reply to each point. Heitzenrater has asserted that the omission of the "model deed" in the *Minutes* of 1785 constituted an implied rejection of Wesley's *Sermons* and *Notes* as binding standards: "The section which contained the 'model deed' was omitted. The new Discipline therefore specified no doctrinal standards."[10] This argument hinges on a curious assertion: that whatever ideas are omitted or not repeated annually from the previous minutes of a deliberative body constitutes an implied rejection of those ideas. If one should take this premise seriously, it must be applied and tested with other ideas besides the elimination of the *Sermons* and *Notes* as doctrinal standards. Taking this premise rigorously, here are several of the ideas that one must also consider as having been *rejected* by the Discipline of 1785 since they were *omitted* (or better, simply not repeated): that faith is a "divine conviction of things not seen" ("Large Minutes"); that the "office of a Christian Minister" is to "watch over souls, as he that must give account"; that the labor of private instruction is absolutely necessary; that one should inquire into the state of the soul of the unconverted.[11] All of these points were in the British "Large Minutes," but not in the American Discipline of 1785. By this reasoning, anything not included must be considered "consciously dropped" and deleted "as legally binding."[12] Only if one answers that the above items were intended to be consciously rejected, can one also answer that the *omission* of the "model deed" indicated a specific rejection of its doctrinal standards.

The more transparent reason we know that the *Sermons* and *Notes* were not rejected in 1784 is that the American Discipline of 1785 itself makes numerous references commending Mr. Wesley's *Sermons* and *Notes*: "We advise you . . . from five to six in the Evening, to meditate, pray, and read, partly the Scripture with Mr. *Wesley's* Notes, partly the closely practical Parts of what he has published." Among the 1785 instructions for preaching: "Frequently read and enlarge upon a portion of the Notes." "Searching the Scripture, by (1) Reading: *constantly*, some Part of every day; *regularly*, all the Bible in order: *carefully*, with Mr. *Wesley's* Notes. . . ." A document that affirms these things could not at the same time be deliberately rejecting Wesley's *Notes* as established doctrinal standards. Further, there are numerous references to key themes dealt with in more detail in Wesley's *Sermons*: "go on to Perfection"; "gradual and instantaneous change"; "holiness comes by faith," etc.[13] None of these themes are dealt with in the Articles, which would be the only binding standards of doctrine remaining if it is imagined that the conference had just eliminated the *Sermons* and *Notes* as binding doctrinal standards.[14]

The 1788 conference vigorously disavowed that it had changed any doctrinal standards. It specifically declared that it had taken actions "such as affect not in any degree the essentials of our doctrines."[15] Surely "our doctrines" could not be the Articles of Religion alone, since the amendments made at this conference had no reference whatever to any point covered by the Articles. The next Discipline of the disputed period, that of 1789, did not hesitate to acknowledge John Wesley as one who, "under God, has been the father of the great revival of religion now extending over the earth by the means of the Methodists" (1789 Discipline, p. 3), language that would be repeated in the Disciplines of 1790 and 1791. In the "Notes" written by Coke and Asbury for the Discipline of 1798, as prepared on request of the General Conference of 1796 and reconfirmed by the General Conference of 1800, the encomium toward Wesley would accelerate. There he was regarded as "the most respectable divine since the primitive ages, if not since the time of the apostles"(p. 7)! This does not sound like the language of those who had just devalued Wesley's established standards of doctrine. Had there been any serious proposal that the *Sermons* and *Notes* be demoted from binding status, surely such a great issue would have been rigorously debated and prominently reflected in the *Minutes* of some conference between 1784 and 1808. No such evidence has been forthcoming.

The most crucial turn in Heitzenrater's theory hinges conspicuously upon an argument from silence—the simple nonmention of Wesleyan standards—so as to allege broadly that the conference was "consciously deleting their force as legally binding standards of doctrine."[16] It is unconvincing to argue from silence that the simple absence of the Wesleyan standards in the deed of settlement constitutes a direct negation of, or withholding of approval from, them as standards for preaching. To the contrary, it is evident that the early Methodist preachers thought that they were holding fast to the "old Methodist doctrine."[17] Had changes been proposed, would not such an important matter have been widely debated by the preachers? Would not there have been a significant documentary residue of that debate? None exists. The more plausible hypothesis is that the American *Minutes* and the Disciplines following 1784 affirmed the existing standards of doctrine derived from the "model deed" so obviously as to require no further specification, definition, or extensive debate. It is *non sequitur* to conclude that since the "model deed" was *not repeated* in the American *Minutes*, its standards were implicitly being discarded.[18] For the *Sermons* and *Notes* were so familiarly known by Methodist preachers who had been solemnly bound by the "model deed," the Circular Letter, the "binding minute," and numerous conference actions, that they required no repetitious further specification in American *Minutes* that stood in such obvious continuity with the previous tradition of *Minutes*. The contention that the British "Large Minutes" were "superseded and no longer had any binding effect"[19] in American Methodism fails to take sufficiently into account the fact that Wesley's Circular Letter, to which Asbury assented, required that the American conference "cheerfully conform to the Minutes both of the English and American Conferences."[20] This does not imply that the American conferences after 1784 remained bound in perpetuity to the British *Minutes*, but rather the doctrinal continuity between them was affirmed even while disciplinary refinements were being contextually adapted to the American situation.

There was a succession of similar deeds that eventuated in the "deed of settlement" enacted by the General Conference in 1796. They were: (1) Wesley's "model deed" of 1763; (2) the virtually identical deed that appeared in the "Large Minutes" of 1776 and following; (3) the deeds written in America after 1780 that were to be drawn up in accord with the "model deed" printed in the "Large Minutes"; (4) the English Deed of Declaration to provide for succession of property rights after Wesley's death, enrolled in chancery in 1784; (5) the anomalous absence of any printed deed in the revised Discipline of 1785, which Heitzenrater questionably takes to be an outright rejection of the previous deed; (6) with the decease of Wesley in 1791, the "deed of declaration," making the British conference a self-governing body, conveying to the conference powers that had been vested under law to Wesley during his lifetime; and (7) the "deed of settlement" that appears in the *Journal of the 1796 General Conference*. In this entire succession of deeds, there is no evidence of debate that doctrinal standards were being formally revised, amended, re-evaluated, or even debated.[21]

Heitzenrater has argued that after 1784 a new doctrinal standard prevailed in American Methodism, that the standards of the earlier *Minutes* were "thus superseded and no longer had any binding effect on the American Methodists after January, 1785."[22] But seven years later, in the record of the General Conference of 1796, we find that its first action was to reassure all American Methodists that *no doctrinal changes* had been made, and that, however the disciplinary language had been prudently restated for the American situation, its intent was not to alter doctrine. The second major action taken, after specifying the boundaries of the annual conferences, was to provide a plan for "a deed of settlement." This was the standardized, legal, post-Revolutionary American version of the "model deed." It was a legal instrument enabling properties to be set aside for a particular use: Methodist preaching. The purpose of the deed was to allow to be built a "place of worship, for the use of the members of the Methodist Episcopal Church in the United States of America, *according to the rules and discipline*" (italics added),[23] rules which since 1773 had legally required trustees to allow preaching of "no other doctrine than is contained in" Wesley's *Sermons* and *Notes*. There is nothing in the deed of settlement that suggests that the Articles of Religion had displaced the *Sermons* and *Notes* as the only binding criteria for preaching in Methodist meeting houses. Had that been the conference's extraordinary intent, one would reasonably expect that there would have been some note on it, or evidence of debates. None exists. The "rules and discipline" to which the deed of settlement referred had long before provided that no preacher could join the connection without agreeing to "abide by the Methodist doctrine and discipline published in the four volumes of sermons and the notes."[24] It is in this way that the same doctrinal standards continued after 1796 to impinge upon the use of church property.

Heitzenrater has argued that, in the procedure for trial of ministers, the reference to "a breach of the articles and discipline of the church" (1789 Discipline, Q. 2, ¶XXXIII) must be a reference limited exclusively to the Articles of Religion. Following the language of the Discipline of 1792 he concludes "that the only official measure or test of doctrinal orthodoxy within the Methodist Episcopal Church at that time was the

Articles of Religion." He thinks that the American Articles superseded "the earlier British Methodist standards, Wesley's *Notes* and *Sermons*."[25] Yet these procedures for trial do not anywhere specifically prohibit other standards of doctrine from applying. The question rather is, simply: "What shall be done with those ministers or preachers, who hold and preach doctrines which are contrary to our articles of religion?" (1792 Discipline, Q. 3, continuing through 1804 Discipline, Q. 3, p. 41). Upon this thread Heitzenrater hangs the theory that the Articles *only* have binding relevance as doctrinal standards. Pertinent to this issue are the notes written by Coke and Asbury for the Discipline of 1798, especially as they apply to trial. They specified that one of the legitimate reasons for trial of a preacher would be if the preacher should "oppose the doctrines of holiness" (1798 Discipline, p. 113). These doctrines are not specifically to be found in the Articles of Religion, but are prominently addressed in Wesley's *Sermons* and *Notes*. Hence the Articles could not have been considered by Coke and Asbury in 1798 to be the only standard doctrines, even in the case of trial.

There are in fact two very different contexts in which doctrinal standards may apply: (1) the recurrent and primary task of preaching; and (2) the rare and exceptional situation of the trial of a minister, where a much more concise, specific, definition is needed than is applicable to preaching. The conferences may have decided that they did not want to encumber the difficult situation of trial with the details of all four volumes of *Sermons* and the extensive *Notes*. It could have been thought prudent to narrow, for trial purposes alone, the criteria of culpable offenses. Keep in mind that the designation of the *Sermons* and *Notes* as doctrinal standards for preaching occurred long before (1763) the designation of the Articles as standards that may have had special applicability to trial (1792).

The Discipline that the conference of 1808 had in hand when it wrote the Constitution and Restrictive Rules was the Discipline of 1804. When the members of the conference constitutionally prevented subsequent General Conferences from altering "our present existing and established standards of doctrine," they surely must have assumed that the Discipline of 1804 was consistent with those standards. If the standards were "present and existing," it is difficult to see how they could not be existing in the 1804 Discipline. That Wesley's *Notes* were assumed as normative in the 1804 Discipline is evident in the section on the duty of preachers, who are required to read the notes carefully, "seriously" and "with prayer," "every day" (1804 Discipline, Sect. 12, Q. 2). "From four to five in the morning and from five to six in the evening, to meditate, pray, and read the scriptures with notes, and the closely practical parts of what Mr.

Wesley has published" (1804 Discipline, p. 38). The *Sermons* and *Notes* were widely distributed already, and obviously did not need (and could not have allowed) quadrennial updating, as did the rules of discipline. This is the simple and transparent reason why they were not bound with the Discipline—not because they were rejected. Since the Articles were much shorter, they could easily and conveniently be bound with the Discipline, but that does not imply that they were distinctly preferred or had higher constitutional status.[26]

The preamble of the 1808 conference began on a rigorously conserving tone: "It is of greatest importance that the doctrines, form of government, and general rules of the United societies in America be preserved sacred and inviolable," and it was precisely for this purpose that the constitution was written.[27] This preamble shows that matters of doctrine were not being debated at this time, but were generally understood and viewed in a settled way as being "established standards of doctrine." Such a consensus could not have occurred quickly. Consensual reception does not develop or become "established" in a single month or year, but only over decades, and this had in fact occurred during the years between 1773 and 1808. What other understanding of "doctrine" could have been assumed than that which had been consensually shared for thirty-five years in the case of the *Sermons* and *Notes* and twenty-four years in the case of the Articles?

The language of the First Rule contained two clauses: (1) the first clause specified the "articles of religion" received from Wesley, as distinguished from the older criteria, (?) the "standards of doctrine," which by long consensual tradition had been textually specified as the *Sermons* and *Notes*. These two clauses conceptually distinguished the two norms of classical Methodist doctrine: the tightly constructed twenty-five Articles of Religion, as distinguished from the much longer four volumes of *Sermons* and extensive *Notes on the New Testament*. Leading constitutional historians (McTyeire, Tigert, Neely, and Buckley) have subsequently read the rule as indicating this "duplex norm"[28]—first clause: "The General Conference shall not revoke, alter, or change our articles of religion"; second clause: "nor establish any new standards or rules of doctrine, contrary to our present and existing and established standards of doctrine."

Heitzenrater has argued that the entire Restrictive Rule refers only to the Articles of Religion. Yet if the intent of the 1808 conference had been to specify a single document, the Articles of Religion, as the only norm, it would not have required two clauses, but one. Under Heitzenrater's hypothesis, the second clause becomes redundant, and one is left with the curiosity of why the constitution writers not only added it, but rigorously required that it not be changed. The major clue is the fact that the second clause is not stated in the singular (so as to imply a single document) but in the plural (implying more than one document of doctrinal standards). If one hypothesizes that "standards of doctrine" refers to the Articles of Religion alone, one is left with the dubious alternative that the plural—"standards"—refers to each separate article of the Articles of Religion. To the contrary, the rule required two clauses to convey the two dimensions of Methodist doctrinal accountability: first, to the teachings of the Reformation (Articles), and secondly, to the more specific Methodist teachings (Wesley's *Sermons* and *Notes*). It is precisely these doctrinal norms that the 1808 conference was determined to protect and ensure that they could not be casually revoked.

The two clauses can be compared and contrasted as follows:

ARTICLES OF RELIGION	SERMONS AND NOTES
Confessional form	Homiletical-exegetical form
The ecumenical consensus	The Methodist emphasis
Anglican theology	Wesleyan themes
Concise	Five volumes
Criterion for trial	Criteria for preaching
Shorter history (as amended in 1784) of consensual reception	Longer history (since 1763) of consensual reception
Textually specified by the constitution	Implied by the constitution by "plain historical inference"

The vast majority of leading American Methodist constitutional historians have affirmed the two-clause interpretation of the First Rule. Buckley stated the principal reason why: "The Articles of Religion, so far as they go, contain only the faiths of universal Protestant and evangelical Christendom, and the 'other existing and established Standards' contain, in addition, those Methodist teachings which in substance or mode of statement are not universal among Protestant evangelical Churches."[29]

Why did the question of doctrinal standards not recur in each subsequent General Conference? Because once settled in 1808, having entered unalterably in the constitution of American Methodism, there was no need (and indeed no way) to return to it, unless one wished to try to amend the constitution. If one takes the odd view that the *lack of mention* of the *Sermons* and *Notes* in General Conference *Minutes* constitutes deliberate dissent from them, then the same criteria must be applied to other ideas acted upon once in the General Conference minutes and then not mentioned again.

Heitzenrater has argued that "at every point where the Methodist Episcopal Church had an opportunity to reiterate and reaffirm its allegiance to Wesley's *Sermons* and *Notes* specifically as doctrinal standards after 1785, it either consciously deleted the references, failed to mention them, or voted to the contrary."[30] Yet this claim assumes that the *Sermons* and *Notes* are not already embedded in the First Restrictive Rule, an assumption as yet insufficiently debated. Heitzenrater stands almost alone among major American Methodist constitutional interpreters of the last hundred years in this assumption. The alternative hypothesis is more plausible: that the very purpose of the First Restrictive Rule was to guarantee that these established standards (*Sermons, Notes,* and more recently *Articles*) not be amended. Hence, once acted upon, as it was so definitively in 1808, the matter of doctrinal standards needed no further mention or definition because this matter was decided as absolutely and irrevocably as any constitution-making body could possibly act—i.e., by strictly limiting the ability of the legislative process to amend these "established standards of doctrine."

Heitzenrater has argued that the 1816 General conference's reference to "established articles of faith" was a reference to the Articles of Religion alone, and not the *Sermons* or *Notes*.[31] But that could not be the case, because of the very nature of the issues to which they were attending, which focused specifically upon the defense of distinctively Wesleyan doctrines not even mentioned in the Articles of Religion. Among these doctrines "as defended by Wesley," the following were cited by the General Conference Committee of Safety: the doctrines of "the direct witness of the Holy Spirit, and of holiness of heart and life, or gospel sanctification."[32] Hence, when the General Conference approved the resolution of the Committee of Safety, it could not have been limiting its view of "established articles of faith" strictly to the Articles of Religion.

Since more than sixty editions of Wesley's *Sermons on Several Occasions* were published in the years 1784–1860 (the years in which some have argued that Wesley was decreasing in influence and virtually ignored in American Methodism, when these sermons presumably were not regarded as binding doctrinal standards), why were so many editions required? Why was Wesley so avidly read? Why were most of these editions published under the official direction and with the standard publishing houses of the Methodist Episcopal Church? Would General Conferences that had denigrated or demoted the sermons to secondary status continue to issue, finance, and distribute so many editions?

Similarly, Wesley's *Explanatory Notes Upon the New Testament* were republished frequently in the American connection, specifically in the following years: 1791, 1806, 1812, 1818, 1837, 1839, 1841, 1844, 1845, 1846,

1847, 1850, 1853, 1854, 1856, and 1856–60.[33] These editions were largely published under the direction of the General Conference and issued by the same presses that printed the *Sermons* and Discipline. Other editions of the *Notes* were available during this period through other presses in Canada, England, and Ireland. The *Notes* were republished in the United States during this period as frequently as they were in Britain, where no one doubts that the *Sermons* and *Notes* were doctrinal standards for the Wesleyan connections.

Heitzenrater has argued that after 1784 American Methodists thought their constitutive documents, inclusive of doctrinal statements, were "significantly different in content from the British counterparts."[34] Resolutions from the General Conferences of 1820 and 1824 indicate the opposite: that "Wesleyan Methodism is one everywhere—one in its doctrine, its disciplines, its usages."[35] The affinity of American, Canadian, and British Methodist doctrinal standards was repeatedly reaffirmed and publicly stated by actions of American General Conferences. In 1820 the conference affirmed its doctrinal affinity with British and Canadian Methodists: "The British and American connections have now mutually recognized each other as one body of Christians, sprung from a common stock, *holding the same doctrines*"[36] (italics added). If American and British Methodists had viewed themselves as possessing two different standards (as Heitzenrater argues), then these official actions would have been wholly inappropriate. If there was *only one recognized international standard*, as it appears from these quotations, then the *Sermons* and *Notes* must have continued as American doctrinal standards during this disputed period.

Heitzenrater rests much of his case upon one curious incident: the defeat of Francis Ward's motion during the General Conference of 1808. He regards this as "conclusive evidence that the General Conference did not understand its standards of doctrine to include Wesley's *Sermons* and *Notes*."[37] Francis Ward, it should be noted, was the assistant secretary of the conference, and could have been himself writing down the minutes that we now have in manuscript. On Tuesday, May 24th, 1808, at 3:00 p.m., it was "moved by Francis Ward and seconded by Lewis Myers, that it shall be considered as the sentiment of this Conference, that Mr. Wesley's Notes on the New Testament, his four first Volumes of Sermons, and Mr. Fletcher's Checks, in their general tenor, contain the principal doctrines of Methodism, and a good explanation of our articles of religion; and that this sentiment be recorded on our Journal without being incorporated in the Discipline." We do not know whether or how the motion was debated, or what particular reasons led to its defeat. In the original manuscript of the Minutes of the conference at the United

Methodist Archives at Drew University, however, it is noted as "lost," and there is a note in the margin in the same hand: "NB: It was voted that this motion be struck out of the Journal."[38] The motion has a single large "X" through it. That is all we know, with no further explanation.

The fact that it was not included in the printed proceedings of the conference does not, as Heitzenrater assumes, imply outright hostility to the tenor of the motion. It is clear that the conference did not accept the motion, but it is not clear why.

For what possible reasons could the conference have preferred not to accept this motion at this time in this form? Heitzenrater concludes: "The General Conference was *not* willing to go on record defining its standards of doctrine in terms of documents other than the Articles. . . ."[39] Is this the only possible or self-evident conclusion? If the conference members had meant their defeat of the Ward motion to be a publicly declared positive rejection of its entire substance and intent, they would have been much more likely to have left it in the record *as acted upon*, as Albert Outler has suggested. The X-ing suggests that there was a consensus that preferred the whole affair expunged, left in limbo, or to be returned to later after more study and reflection.

There are at least seven possible alternative reasons for the deletion of this motion other than the Heitzenrater hypothesis. We do not know which one or combination of these hypotheses might be correct, because we do not have enough written evidence, but there are numerous plausible possibilities, of which the first and last are the most credible:

(1) Ward's motion was quite likely rejected because the conference did not wish to get into a highly controversial debate about *Fletcher*. The motion asked for an enormous *innovation* never before suggested, to my knowledge, in the previous literature on Methodist doctrinal standards: that Fletcher be inserted into the well-known list of traditionally received standards provided by the deeds and conference minutes since 1773. This would have been a controversial proposal at any time, but at this delicate time, it was quite impossible. The motion asked that the constitution protect against any future amendment not only those doctrines contained in Wesley's *Sermons* and *Notes* but also those in "Fletcher's Checks"! The Fletcher issue alone could have been enough to defeat it. For it constituted an intrusive innovation totally inconsistent with the rigorously conserving spirit evident elsewhere in the conference.

There are other potential reasons that a motion of this sort might be defeated:

(2) It could be that the motion was rejected not because it was too strong, but too weak; or (3) not because it was too decisively Wesleyan,

but not decisive enough; or (4) because it was proposed as a mere "sentiment of the conference," only to be recorded as such, and hence could be taken frivolously. (5) It could be that it was simply thought to be unnecessary, and so obvious as not to require formal action; or (6) it could have been regarded as poorly worded, or inappropriately formulated.

The more likely explanation, however, in addition to the Fletcher issue, is (7) that it was exquisitely ill-timed. The conference was not ready at that time to act on such a broadly stated and potentially controversial, innovative motion made without due consideration, referral, and deliberate study. At this critical stage of constitution-building, where many votes had been extremely close, alliances fragile, and many issues yet to come up, the deliberative body understandably may have felt (without any demeaning of theological debate) that it was more prudent not even to enter this hazardous territory and try to settle upon delicate language at this stage. Plenty was on its plate yet to be debated.

The conference had convened on May 6, and this motion did not come up until very late, May 24th, 1808, the nineteenth day. During those days many motions had been moved, debated, and defeated. Numerous amendments were made and lost. A motion to determine whether Coke would continue in Europe till called by the annual conferences lost by 54 to 67.[40] Numerous motions were made and then withdrawn. Many motions were made with no action reported in the minutes. Soule's motion for electing presiding elders was defeated 53 to 61.[41] On May 24, the Restrictive Rules were at length debated, and the hapless Ward motion came up in the afternoon session after the language of the Restrictive Rules had been settled upon. All of this is reported in order to show that the Ward motion for a *change* in doctrinal standards (to include Fletcher) was too much to handle under these sensitive circumstances. It was defeated and stricken, I believe, because it innovatively and abruptly required that Fletcher be added to the received texts of doctrinal standards, and because it was very poorly timed, *but not for the reason that Heitzenrater gives*—that the conference was deliberately rejecting Wesley's *Sermons* and *Notes* as binding doctrinal standards. Had that been the case, there surely would have been some residue of debate.

Many times a motion is tabled or defeated without any implication that every clause or aspect of that motion is rejected. If such reasoning were consistently applied (that loss of a motion implies rejection of each particular clause of that motion), then a deliberative body could be immobilized because it would know that its rejection of a single clause of a motion might be interpreted as implying the rejection of all other clauses. Sometimes ambiguous or nonconsensual wording in a single clause may cause a deliberative body to defeat a proposal at hand, in order to make a new start, especially if it seems inappropriate to wrangle about it under those circumstances. Heitzenrater argues that the defeat of Ward's motion implied a rejection of each clause of that motion, instead of its single most troublesome clause—that on Fletcher.

Heitzenrater's historical speculation focuses primarily on why the conference struck the Ward motion from the record. Could it have been struck precisely for the reason of avoiding the kind of speculation that has been advanced? Heitzenrater bases much of his historical argument upon a motion that was stricken intentionally from the record quite probably to circumvent precisely this sort of uninhibited conjecture as to its meaning. Therefore is it not rudely transgressing upon the "intent" of the American Methodist founders to bring this stricken motion again to the center stage of awareness, let alone to make it a linchpin of a new hypothesis with far-reaching ramifications?

Since there is no record of the discussion surrounding this issue, and since it was stricken from the record (the only instance of such action in the whole volume of the manuscript *Journal*), would it not be more prudent and respectful of the delegates' intent if we would also avoid such speculation? And particularly not to base a major reversal of a long-held constitutional interpretation on such a speculation?

Asbury later wrote that the conference of 1808 had perpetuated in constitutional form and language "the good old Methodist doctrine and discipline."[42] How could the "old Methodist doctrine" have been perpetuated if the conference, according to this conjecture, was avidly resisting or circumventing Wesley's *Sermons* and *Notes*? What could Asbury have meant *if* the conference had been "reticent" to specify Wesley's writings as doctrinal standards?

Heitzenrater's attempt to reconstruct the intent of the constitution writers leaves out exactly half of the duplex norm of the First Rule. It provides a dubious conjectural basis upon which the *Sermons* and *Notes* might quietly be revoked as doctrinal standards 179 years later. No matter how diligently the General Conference of 1808 and 1832 tried to protect the First Restrictive Rule, it is now ironically in danger of being subtly reinterpreted in a way that the writers would have found inconceivable, and in a way that the central tradition of constitutional interpretation has repeatedly rejected. Heitzenrater speculates on "the main intention" (p. 16) of the 1808 General Conference as if it were to *block any legally binding use* of Wesley's *Sermons* and *Notes*—at best a conjectural, at worst a projective hypothesis that stands contrary to virtually everything else known about the constitution writers.

Heitzenrater has argued that the case against the *Sermons* and *Notes* appears to be an objective, historical argument characterized by "careful consideration" of evidence.[43] On closer inspection, it appears to espouse a hermeneutical predisposition which guides the selection of data to be investigated. The historical case is weakened by three deficits: (1) Its most important conclusions are based upon *an argument from silence*. (2) Its reasoning is focused speculatively upon discerning the *intent* of founders in constitutional documents when documentary evidence for that is lacking. (3) The argument concentrates attention upon highly *selective* portions of the written record. It is hardly by accident that the argument concludes by conjecturally interpreting the intent of the language of early General Conference actions in a way that tends toward the limitation of binding doctrinal standards to their slenderest documentary ground.

Suppose one were to ask Asbury or Bangs or Timothy Merritt or Jesse Peck (all of whom wrote during the "disputed period") whether Wesley's *Sermons* and *Notes* were standards of doctrine among Methodists of the early nineteenth century; could one imagine them answering with Heitzenrater: They were "clearly never considered to be standards of doctrine" after 1784?[44] If this assertion applies only to trials, that should be clarified. But if more than that, it strains the imagination, forcing one to hypothesize that some other expression of interest predisposes this hermeneutical bent. The underlying hermeneutic possibly may be explained by reference to the contemporary situation of ecclesial pluralism, and the tendency toward theological indifferentism (which Heitzenrater strongly denies concerning his own view and intent, but which exists among those to whom he is apparently willing to accommodate, who wish to reduce the formal force of traditional Wesleyan influence within United Methodism).

Heitzenrater argues for a sharp distinction between "legal standards of doctrine" and "the traditionally accepted doctrinal writings." The former he thinks should include only the Articles of Religion, "*the* standards of doctrine." The latter he expands broadly to include not only Wesley's *Sermons* and *Notes* but "the broad range of Wesley's works" and "the writings of Fletcher," but all of these function merely "in a supplemental and illustrative role," serving not as "doctrinal *standards*" but "as exemplary illustrations of the Methodist doctrinal heritage."[45] There are five principal objections to this distinction: (1) The proposed distinction is an invention of Heitzenrater that has little precedent in the previous 179 years of constitutional interpretation. (2) It needlessly adds to the corpus of "traditionally accepted doctrinal standards" the "writings of Fletcher" which have never gained sufficient consent to be given equal categorical status with Wesley's *Sermons* and *Notes*. (3) It takes away from the *Sermons* and *Notes* the long-accepted status of "Standard Sermons" or "established doctrinal *standards*" and reduces them to "*statements*."[46] (4) It neglects to distinguish the special place of the *Sermons* and *Notes* as doctrinal guides within the larger Wesleyan corpus. (5) Having invented this questionable distinction, he then projects it back upon the history of constitutional interpretation, and regards virtually all major previous interpreters of constitutional Methodism as "confused" and in error.[47] The twofold distinction is insufficiently discriminating and descriptive.

To avert these problems, a threefold definition is more in accord with the facts of the received tradition, which would show that there are two types of doctrinal standards protected by the constitution: (1) the concise standard that stands alone and separable only in the case of the trial of preachers (the Articles of Religion), and (2) the broader standard that applies to preaching and interpretation ("our present, existing and established standards of doctrine," the *Sermons* and *Notes*). In addition to these constitutionally protected standards of doctrine, there is (3) a third category of other writings of doctrinal instruction received by wide usage, that includes the Six Tracts printed at various times in the Disciplines of 1784–1808, the remainder of Wesley's Works, the Wesleyan hymns, the doctrine contained in the "Large Minutes," and the catechism.

All Disciplines from 1972 to 1984, since the Plan of Union, have contained a paragraph that cannot easily be circumvented by subsequent General Conference action—a statement of fact concerning what the Plan of Union decided:

> In the Plan of Union for The United Methodist Church, the Preface to the Methodist Articles of Religion and the Evangelical United Brethren Confession of Faith explains that both had been accepted as doctrinal standards for the new church. It was declared that "they are thus deemed congruent if not identical in their doctrinal perspectives, and not in conflict." Additionally, it was stipulated that although the language of the First Restrictive Rule has never been formally defined, Wesley's *Sermons* and *Notes* were specifically included in our present existing and established standards of doctrine by plain historical inference. (1984 Discipline, ¶ 67)

This paragraph is a simple, factual report describing accurately the premise of the Plan of Union and its reasoning about doctrinal standards. The Plan of Union cannot now be legislatively refashioned by a subsequent commission of a General Conference, for the Plan of Union brought together the constitutions of two bodies so as to form a new church. Even if the phrase is omitted by a later General Conference, that does not revise the terms of union. If a General Conference should attempt substantively to redo the Plan of Union (which is highly unlikely), that would eventuate, doubtless, in a complex series of judicial challenges.

With few exceptions, the only portions of the Discipline of 1808 that have been retained without change are those protected by the Restrictive Rules. Almost everything else has been repeatedly tinkered with, often every four years. The constitution writers of 1808 grasped an early version of Murphy's Law, that "anything that can be amended will be amended." We can be grateful that they had sufficient sagacity to prevent our doctrinal experimentation and superficial "improvements" for 179 years. But now a new situation has emerged. The Rule may be able to be circumvented, not by amendment, but by an imaginative reinterpretation of history.

Chapter 10

RESPONSE TO THE REVISED STATEMENT ON "DOCTRINAL STANDARDS AND OUR THEOLOGICAL TASK"

Robert Huston, Jeanne Audrey Powers, Bruce Robbins[1]

Introduction

A comparison of the present 1984 Book of Discipline with the proposed draft document, "Doctrinal Standards and Our Theological Task" (herein called the *Study*) reveals striking shifts in The United Methodist Church's perception of doctrine and theology. In this response we will highlight what seems to us to be the critical issues, especially as seen through ecumenical and interreligious perspectives. We will begin by making several general comments and then look specifically at the text in certain sections. We hope these will lead to some further reworking of the draft, for there is much which we find problematic in the material.

First, The United Methodist Church has not been traditionally a confessional or a doctrinal church. By that we mean that our tradition has, through its history, been accepting of a diversity of theological opinion—yet firmly rooted in the same apostolic faith. The *Study* drafters do recognize our heritage of diversity for they have chosen to retain what the Discipline calls the "ecumenical watchword": "In essentials, unity; in non-essentials, liberty; and in all things, charity." Yet, that fundamental affirmation of variety and diversity in The United Methodist Church is retained **without** keeping the support and praise of "theological pluralism" which has also been at the heart of The United Methodist Church. The *Study* moves us in the direction of narrower, more specific doctrines while, at the same time, changing the place of doctrine within The United Methodist Church. For instance, *disciplinary* statements indicating that the Articles and the Confession are not "positive, juridical norms for doctrine" are eliminated by the *Study* in favor of a statement emphasizing the historic role of the Articles "as the basis for testing correct doctrine" (14) in the church.

Similarly, the *Study* does not retain from the Discipline key sentences that put the church's doctrine in its broadest context. For instance, the Discipline describes how our church rejected a "confessional principle" that contained legally enforceable doctrinal standards and chose instead a "conciliar principle" that represented a "collective wisdom" of the living Christian pastors, teachers, etc. The *Study*, on the other hand, through many of its changes, moves us in the direction of developing narrow, doctrinal standards. In fact, what the Discipline calls "guidelines," the *Study* now calls "standards." We have difficulties with these subtle but profoundly significant shifts in our church's official position.

Second, we recognize the *Study* to be much more historical in perspective than the Discipline. By itself, the addition of a historical dimension is welcome. United Methodists will profit by this educational material. But, the added historical dimension is hindered by an unbalanced assertion of Methodism's connection to the Reformed heritage at the cost of the "catholicity" of its tradition. In more than half a dozen places, the "reformed" perspective is intentionally added to the existing statement. In an examination of "Tradition" we will see the cost of such an emphasis.

Third, the most critical shift evident in the *Study* concerns Scripture and its place relative to Tradition, experience, and reason. A considerable portion of this document will pertain to that issue. Our criticism of the changes do not stem from a lack of appreciation of the absolutely necessary role Scripture serves within the Christian church. Rather, we reject the attempt to isolate Scripture both from the Tradition, experience, and reason out of which it has flowed and from its transformative power when practiced by the believers. We appreciate the new developments in biblical interpretation which emphasize the "hermeneutical circle," the understanding that how we read the Bible is continually influenced by our social structures and everchanging life context. The *Study*, despite its emphasis upon the primacy of Scripture, has actually *less* focus upon the place of Scripture within experience, Tradition, and reason than did the Discipline. Our concern is *not* that the Bible is overemphasized; rather, our concern is the tendency of the *Study* to objectify the Bible (and doctrine) by moving it further away from the life and community in which it is lived and read.

The following are our specific comments related to the text.

Scripture

The 1984 Book of Discipline (p. 78) states that "our present existing and established standards of doctrine" ("not to be construed literally and juridically") are methodologically determined by:

> . . . our free inquiry within the boundaries defined by four main sources and guidelines for Christian theology: Scripture, tradition, experience, and reason. These four are interdependent; none can be defined unambiguously. They allow for, indeed they positively encourage, variety in United Methodist theologizing.

And in the next paragraph, "United Methodists share with all other Christians the conviction that Scripture is the primary source and guideline for doctrine."

On page 25 of the *Study*, it is clear that the Discipline's principle of "interdependency" (with "Scripture as primary source and guideline for doctrine") is no longer to be the primary means by which United Methodists will pursue their theological task. In the *Study* "The Primacy of Scripture" is singled out—with "Tradition, Reason, and Experience" grouped together in a different sub-section. Note the repeated and single-minded way Scripture is then described: "the sacred canon for Christian people," "the decisive source of our Christian witness," "the authoritative measure of our theological statements," "the basic criterion by which the truth and fidelity of any interpretation of faith is measured." In addition, direct quotes from the Articles of Religion (Methodist) and the Confession of Faith (EUB) are no longer understood as "foundation documents," but rather as "doctrinal standards." The *Study* states, "Our standards affirm the Bible as 'the source of all that is necessary and sufficient unto salvation' (Articles of Religion) and 'the true rule and guide for faith and practice' (Confession of Faith)." All the phrases that have just been quoted (apart from the quotations from the Articles and the Confession) are totally new additions to our Discipline.

Indeed, it is in the comparison between the Discipline and the *Study* that one discovers the significant intentions which are behind the new statement. For example, the Discipline says

> United Methodists share with all other Christians the convictions that Scripture . . . is the primitive source of the memories, images, and hopes by which the Christian community came into existence and that still confirm and nourish its faith and understanding. Christian doctrine has been formed, consciously and unconsciously, from metaphors and themes the origins of which are biblical (p. 78).

These sentences have been dropped entirely from the *Study*, because of the new and restricted understanding of how we are to use the Bible. No longer do words such as "memories," "images," and "metaphors" offer promise for suggestive ways of wrestling with Scripture. In discussing Scripture, terms such as "sacred canon," "decisive," and "authoritative" now emerge in the next paragraph. And in the last paragraph of the sub-section on Scripture in the *Study*, note the use of words such as "careful handling," "legitimately," "basic criterion," and "by which the truth and fidelity of any interpretation of faith is measured." Scripture is no longer *first among equals*. It is even more than "primacy"; it is singular!

Another example indicates how the *Study* changes our understanding of Scripture as much by what it omits from the Discipline as what it retains. The Discipline states that as we study and understand Scripture, "both the core of faith and the range of our theological opinions are expanded and enriched" (p. 78ff). The *Study* states that as we open our minds to the Word of God our understanding deepens and "the possibilities for transforming the world become apparent." While no one would disagree with the importance of faith in "transforming the world," what is significant is what has been *dropped* in the *Study*. In the dropping of the phrase "the range of our theological opinions are expanded and enriched," the implication is that whatever the "core of faith" is, it is static and determined, and the "range of theological opinions" is not acceptable.

A final example is one of the descriptive phrases with regard to "God's self-disclosure." The Discipline states that such self-disclosure appeared "in the world's creation, redemption, and final fulfillment" (p. 78). The *Study* replaces this by paralleling it with "in the pilgrimage of Israel." One might say that the Church, rather than the world, is now the place of emphasis for God's self-disclosure.

Again, it will be very important for readers to review what has been omitted in the *Study* as carefully as they review the *Study* itself.

Tradition

In the understanding and place of Tradition in the life of the Church, a shift has occurred in the *Study* from a large "T" to small "t" understanding of "tradition." The 1984 Discipline points to three understandings of the word "tradition" (p. 79) that have been delineated in the contemporary Faith and Order discussions. We believe the Consultation of Church Union's *Consensus* contains the clearest and most succinct statement of Tradition available today. There the meanings of traditions and Tradition are spelled out in keeping with the well known break-through in ecumenical understanding of the 1964 Montreal World Faith and Order conference:

> There is an historic Christian Tradition to which every Christian body inevitably appeals in matters of faith and practice. In this Tradition three aspects can be distinguished, although they are inseparable. [a] By "*Tradition*" (with a capital "T") is meant the whole life of the Church insofar as, grounded in the life of Christ and nourished by the Holy Spirit, it manifests, confesses, and testifies to the truth of the gospel (I John. 1:1–4). This uniting Tradition comes to expression in teaching, worship, witness, sacraments, way of life, and order. [b] Tradition is also the *process of transmitting* by which this living reality of Christ is handed on from one generation to another. [c] And, since Tradition is this continually flexible and growing reality as it is reflected, known, and handed on in the teaching and practice of the Church, Tradition is also embodied and expressed more or less adequately in a variety of concrete historical *traditions* (lower case "t").[2]

One cannot however, look at Tradition without recognizing the place of Scripture in it. Because the interrelationship of Scripture and Tradition is so crucial to any such discussion, the following paragraph is also noted from *Consensus*:

> In the Church, Scripture and Tradition belong together, since each is a manifestation, by and for faith, of the reality of Christ. They are related in at least these ways. [a] Scripture is itself included in the Tradition. Christian Tradition, drawing on and in many ways continuous with the traditions of Israel, antedated the formation of the Church's biblical canon. [b] Scripture is the focal and definitive expression of the Tradition of the apostles. As such, it is the supreme norm and corrector of all traditions. The Church has acknowledged this by binding itself to the Scripture as its canon. The use of Scripture in worship and the authority of Scripture over the teaching of the Church are essentials in the life of the Christian community.[3]

The *Study*, however, has collapsed Tradition into the section grouped with reason and experience, diminishing its importance and its rela-tionship to Scripture. Of more serious consequence, the *Study* directs our attention to "traditions" (notice the small "t" and the plural "s"). It seems inadequate to begin an understanding of this term of multidimensional meaning not with the core of the Church's faith, but rather with the variations in its expression. In the way in which the first two paragraphs in the tradition sub-section is written, there is a conclusion that all these separate traditions (otherwise read "denominations" or "communions") are simply part of the history of Christianity and therefore *merely an historical process*. Once traditions are emphasized and articulated rather than "Tradition," then claiming the authority of Tradition is possible for any one of the segments of it, including the Wesleyan Teaching.

Further, in affirming "the multiplicity of traditions," the *Study* selects only *certain* ones and shifts its theological trajectories from our Catholic and Anglican heritage into the Reformed and pietistic one. Wesley was first and foremost a "catholic Christian" before he was an evangelical and pietistic Christian one. The historical church, rather than the free church, marked his understanding of the Body of Christ. Almost dismissing the first fifteen centuries of the Christian Tradition rather cavalierly (presumably affirmed in the phrase "the Patristic and Reformation teachings"), the *Study* looks primarily to eighteenth century wisdom as "keystone of our doctrinal heritage."

Equally serious, once all Tradition is reduced to "multiplicity of traditions," then it is easy for the *Study*, in its selectivity, to dismiss all *contemporary* theological work that carries other descriptive names. The contemporary theologies are not even recognized as "theologies": Black theology has become the "Black struggle for freedom"; feminist liberation theology reads "the movement for full equality of women in church and society"; and liberation theology is called "the quest for liberation." The *Study* views these theologies as merely "dimensions of Christian understanding." A variety of forms of contextual theology such as Minjung theology (Korea), or "people's theology" (Philippines), or "water-buffalo theology" (Thailand) are not recognized in the *Study* as a discipline in themselves, but rather are generally described as "rediscovering the biblical concern for the poor, the disabled, the imprisoned, the oppressed, the outcast." The *Study* seems to demonstrate little understanding of theology as an ongoing self-correcting process of "thinking about God."

In many ways, this section is not conservative enough, i.e. it does not understand the historic Christian Tradition of two thousand years (large T and singular) as one of the primary guidelines for our church's theological pursuit. The *Study* does not invite us to "remember our baptism and be thankful." It does not require us to be *of* the trunk of the tree instead of being satisfied as one of its many branches. At the same time, it is *too* conservative because it marginalizes and diminishes many of the contemporary theological traditions (small "t" and plural). Using selected parts of Wesleyan theology (with its prescientific reason, its Western or British experience, and its predating of form criticism of Scripture), it suggests that we look back—but only part way—for our wisdom from the Tradition (which the *Study* calls "traditions").

Methodist Triumphalism

Another great concern emerges from the last paragraph in the section on Tradition. There, when there are conflicting truth claims, "We examine such conflicts in light of Scripture and the doctrinal stance of *our own* church. It is by the discerning use of *our* standards that we understand ourselves as maintaining fidelity to the apostolic faith" (emphasis ours). Is it not possible that at certain points in the development of United Methodism we have been wrong or have overemphasized certain elements or have much to learn from others? The triumphalism in this paragraph is echoed elsewhere, too.

On page 5, para. 2, of the *Study* "ecumenical commitment" is to "gather our own distinctive doctrinal emphases into the larger Christian unity, there to be made more meaningful in a richer whole." That is a near quote from the 1984 Discipline (p. 76) repeated in the *Study*. But when you look at what has been omitted from the Discipline, you will see the intention of the *Study*. The very next sentence in the Discipline says, "But this requires a deliberate effort on our part to engage in critical self-understanding, as church, if we are to offer our best gifts to the common Christian treasury. Such self-knowledge is prerequisite to any and all productive ecumenical partnership." The articulation of the need for a self-critical understanding has been omitted from that section of the *Study*.

In other words, a *critical* self-understanding, a *critical* self-knowledge, was thought necessary in 1972 before we could even *dare* to claim that we have unique traditions that ought to be offered to the larger Tradition. In the *Study* "reconciled diversity" is the name for understanding what it means to be "church." It is the route on the ecumenical journey without that search for the larger Tradition in which we may all dwell together in the Household of Faith, the route which has more interest in proclaiming our own very small piece of the world-wide Christian Church's members. It is the route which sees our relationship to other Christians as objects merely of "partnership and conversation." We would hope the *Study* might convey a larger commitment to the wholeness of the Church.

Nature of Christian Unity

It is not surprising, in light of the above analysis, that at the end of the *Study*'s thirty-three page paper, only two paragraphs are given to Christian unity. Ecumenism is restricted to "entering into ecumenical dialogue with the major confessions of the church universal." Since the

149

Study emphasizes that we are to "maintain fidelity to the apostolic faith . . . according to the doctrinal stance of our own church," rather than the other way around, a minimal understanding of Christian unity is an obvious conclusion. The intention is to make sure that those who differ with us might see our critique of them, not theirs of us. Such a perspective blocks genuine experience in any ecumenical journey.

The *Study* suggests that "engagement within our own traditions equips us . . . [for] ecumenical dialogue with the major confessions of the church universal." But the choice of the phrase "major confessions of the church universal" reveals that such dialogue will take place between the confessional *families* (the Lutheran World Federation, the World Alliance of Reformed Churches, the Roman Catholic Vatican Secretariat for Christian Unity, the World Methodist Council, etc.). It means, fundamentally, a "live and let live" perspective: "You have your traditions, we have ours. You have your authorities, we have ours. We will engage in dialogue together." According to this perspective, future ecumenical directions will be characterized by what we (who have the truth) offer to others who need it. In fact, the *Study* even suggests that we will indoctrinate our United Methodist representatives so that they will "interpret our heritage faithfully in ecumenical discussions." (The shift of the title of this material from the Discipline's "doctrinal guidelines" to the *Study*'s "doctrinal standards" makes clear the intention.)

What is most surprising about this document even though written in the late 1980's is its lack of expressed awareness of ecumenical advancements *unprecedented* in Christian history which have taken place since the Doctrinal Guidelines of the Discipline were first printed in 1972. The implications of Vatican II have radically affected Christian theology and ecclesiological agreements. Agreements between Catholics and Lutherans on "justification by faith alone," between United Methodists and Catholics and Lutherans on grace, baptism, spirituality, and the church, to mention only a few major topics, could not have happened in the late 50's. And within the multilateral arena, the WCC *Baptism, Eucharist, and Ministry* convergence and the COCU *Consensus* form the basis for a far more contemporary view of previously assumed divisions in doctrine. The *Study* gives no indication that these significant developments have any bearing whatsoever on a statement of "United Methodist Doctrinal Standards and Our Theological Task."

The Means Toward Christian Unity

Ecumenical responsibilities of The United Methodist Church, according to the *Study*, "begins with affiliated autonomous Methodist churches in Asia, Africa, and the Caribbean and Europe." These churches are the products of Western missionary expansion (American or British Methodist or EUB) and have now been recognized in the global ecumenical community as national churches in their own countries. To assume that these churches comprise The United Methodist Church's first circle of ecumenical responsibility is to pre-empt their own decision making. They may well see church life in their own countries as the locus of their own national ecumenical relationships. For The United Methodist Church to encourage further fragmentation within already fragmented Protestant communities is to assume that our denomination is in a position to set the priorities of either autonomous churches or Central Conference United Methodist Churches in Third World countries.

Our next "ecumenical" commitment is supposed to be toward the predominantly black Methodist denominations and the super-conservative Wesleyan denominations in this country. Each of those Methodists pose particular problems in ecumenical life: the first, who have indicated willingness to engage in an ecumenical future only in a larger multilateral situation, and the latter, who are the least likely ecumenical partners in any local situation. The fact that we all sing Wesley hymns on a Sunday morning does not make us more likely ecumenical partners.

Only, finally, does the *Study* suggest that "ecumenical councils and consultations" (and that in only one sentence) might be included in our ecumenical responsibilities. Such is the response of the *Study* to thirty-nine years of active United Methodist membership in the World Council of Churches, thirty-seven years in the National Council of Churches of Christ in the USA, and twenty-five years in the Consultation on Church Union.

Interreligious Concerns

It is unfortunate that the developments carefully made in the United Methodist approach to interreligious dialogue and concerns are not reflected in the *Study*. As in many other cases, one only needs to compare sentences from the Discipline and the *Study* to see the step backward taken by the drafters of the *Study*. Even though the material in the *Study* comprises a short paragraph, we point to three significant changes:

(a) The General Conference has affirmed in the Discipline and in a 1980 statement, *Called to be Neighbors and Witnesses,* that God works through all peoples, Christians as well as people of other faiths. The *Study* has deleted any such reference. To anyone sensitive to the issue, the omission is highly significant. The Discipline specifically states that "we must also be conscious that God has been and is now working among all people."

(b) The *Study* calls only for "respectful conversations" and "practical cooperation." Our mandate as Christians is not to simply coexist and be respectful with people of other faiths as suggested in the *Study*. Besides affirming that God works for the "salvation, health, healing, and peace" for all people, the 1984 Discipline calls us to "raise all such relationships to the highest possible level of human fellowship and understanding." Why are these strong statements attesting to our constantly growing relationships with other faiths excluded from the *Study*?

(c) The Discipline, after raising the vision of the "highest possible understanding" of other faiths continues, "To this end, a self-conscious and self-critical understanding of our own tradition, along with appreciative, accurate understandings of other traditions, is necessary." As we have indicated before, the 1984 Discipline contains a dimension of humility as it calls for a self-critical understanding in several places in Part II. The sense of modesty we believe so critical to the Discipline and to our own understanding of faith is omitted, much to the detriment of the *Study*. The importance of retaining the phrase is twofold: it calls for a degree of humility to offset the history of triumphalism that has infected Christianity historically, and it calls us to the greatest possible understanding of other faiths in contrast to the stereotypes that we have often assumed and even promoted.

Instead of suggesting a rewrite of the *Study*'s attempt to speak about interreligious concerns, we recommend the retention of the pertinent paragraphs in the 1984 Book of Discipline with only slight changes to eliminate the gender exclusive language referring to God.

Conclusion

A comparison of the final section of each document reveals the 1984 Discipline's focus on methodological principles, stated frequently in an almost poetic way. The *Study*, on the other hand, seeks to capture mystery and symbol in statement and doctrine. Though it acknowledges the mystery of God, it does claim that this *Study* enables one to "know more fully what is essential for participation in God's saving work." In such it comes dangerously close, as H. Richard Niebuhr warned in *The Purpose of the Church and Its Ministry* to "confusing the symbol with what is symbolized and the subject with the object." He states that "Protestantism" is "the principle of protest of every tendency to do just that." It is precisely for those reasons that we have raised our objection to the *Study*'s attempt to replace "distinctive emphases" and "doctrinal guidelines" with doctrinal "standards, sources, and criteria."

Chapter 11

THE "WESLEYAN QUADRILATERAL": THE STORY OF A MODERN METHODIST MYTH

Ted A. Campbell[1]

In 1982 the Oxford Institute of Methodist Theological Studies met in Keble College, Oxford. Towards the end of that Institute, an international committee was formed to consider the subject and venue for the next Institute (which was held in 1987). A number of North American delegates suggested that the subject of the next institute should be the "Wesleyan Quadrilateral." British delegates were puzzled at this proposal, but put on a brave face, none admitting publicly that they didn't know what a "Wesleyan Quadrilateral" might be. A Cambridge professor turned to a befuddled colleague and explained in whispers, "I think that's meant to refer to Wesley's use of scripture, tradition, reason, and experience." Of course, by that time, the term had become a commonplace in North American Methodist circles.

Indeed, since the adoption of a new theological statement in 1972 which held up scripture, tradition, reason, and experience as "Doctrinal Guidelines in The United Methodist Church,"[2] this fourfold locus of religious authority has gained remarkable acceptance as a tool for theological analysis and as a starting-point for the recovery of the Wesleyan theological tradition in a modern ecumenical context. The fourfold pattern has served as an important teaching tool in United Methodist and other theological seminaries and in church-school literature, and has provided a critical means for evaluating theological claims within our tradition.[3] Although its specific formulation has shifted, the four-fold pattern of "Theological Guidelines" survived the serious revision of the United Methodist doctrinal statement by the 1988 General Conference.[4] In discussing the "myth" of the "Wesleyan Quadrilateral," then, I do not mean at all to devalue the importance of this fourfold pattern. The very fact that it has provoked serious debate among Methodists on a central theological issue is convincing evidence of its service.

The formulation has presented problems, however. From a systematic viewpoint, the 1972 statement of this pattern seemed to many to lack sufficient clarity in general, and, in particular, to lack a sufficiently clear assertion of the primacy of Scripture in doctrinal and practical reflection, and this concern prompted the 1988 General Conference's revision of the statement of "Theological Guidelines." From an historical perspective, the notion that this fourfold pattern can be attributed to, or easily found in the works of, John Wesley has to be seriously questioned. This article addresses the latter issue, in particular, by attempting to give a narrative of how United Methodists came to hold the notion of the "Wesleyan Quadrilateral," and by considering what basis this notion may have in the teachings of John Wesley.

The Development of the "Wesleyan Quadrilateral"

The notion of the "Wesleyan Quadrilateral" basically developed from the work of mid-twentieth-century Methodists engaged in various phases of the ecumenical movement. There had been an earlier debate about Wesley's understanding of religious authority, sparked when in the late nineteenth century some Anglicans and Methodists, influenced by the Oxford Movement, pointed to Wesley's fondness for Christian tradition.[5] They were answered by trumpet-blasts from George Croft Cell and others early in this century who were intent on showing Wesley's affinity to the Protestant Reformers, including his affirmation of *scriptura sola*.[6] Following a somewhat different line, some early twentieth-century Methodists in Britain and North America claimed Wesley as a kind of foreshadowing of Schleiermacher in his stress on the centrality of religious experience. None of these, however, attempted to show the interplay of these various sources of authority in Wesley's thought, as some versions of the "Quadrilateral" would try to do.[8]

The notion of the "Wesleyan Quadrilateral" was foreshadowed in Colin W. Williams's consideration of "Authority and Experience" in his influential textbook, *John Wesley's Theology Today* (1960).[9] Williams, an Australian Methodist, wrote from the perspective of the Ecumenical Movement, attempting in particular to interpret Wesley's relevance for Methodists relating to that movement. It was this concern that structured Williams's attempt to understand Wesley's doctrine of authority in relation to that of various confessional traditions, and that perhaps led Williams to focus on Wesley's *sources* of authority. Williams's five subject headings reflect these sources: the first two have to do with Scripture, the rest discuss tradition, experience, and reason. Thus, the four elements of the "quadrilateral" were already present in Williams's account. This was a critical development, because *John Wesley's Theology Today* became the standard textbook for students of Wesley's thought in the 1960s and beyond.

Williams's discussion began by outlining three distinctive understandings of theological authority: the "Catholic" (focusing on tradition), the "Classical Protestant" (focusing on Scripture), and the "Free Church Protestant" (focusing on immediate inspiration).[10] His conclusion was that Wesley essentially reflected a "Classical Protestant" doctrine of authority grounded in the final authority of the Bible, but he argued that Wesley's view was nuanced (and ecumenically relevant) in its positive attitudes towards tradition and religious experience.[11] In this way, Williams combined the late-nineteenth-century Anglican claims about Wesley's "high Church" attitude towards tradition and the early-twentieth-century claims about Wesley's revival of a distinctively Protestant doctrine of biblical authority. His work lay in the immediate background of the "Wesleyan Quadrilateral."

It was within a decade of Williams's text that the fourfold pattern of religious authority emerged in Methodist theological discussion, at first as a result of the merger of the Evangelical United Brethren and The Methodist Church. The 1968 General Conference that united these denominations mandated a Theological Study Commission to develop a new doctrinal statement based on the Methodist Articles of Religion and the E.U.B. Confession of Faith. The committee, chaired by the late Professor Albert C. Outler, began its work and by the specially called General Conference of 1970 was able to issue an interim report.

The interim report of 1970 indicates that the Committee had scrapped the idea of combining the Confession and the Articles, and had begun to focus on the development of a new doctrinal statement. It enunciated the fourfold pattern of religious authority under the heading of "The Wesleyan Concept of Authority." "Wesley," the document states, "was sensitive to the demand for credible authority and he tested his own teaching, and that of others, within a four-element compound of interdependent norms," which is referred to later in the document as a "quadrilateral."[12] In a series of paragraphs (all under the general heading of "Authority"), the document discussed Scripture, tradition, experience, and reason.

The use of the term "quadrilateral" to describe the fourfold pattern would have come naturally to Professor Outler, who first used it (though not without regrets later).[13] The "Lambeth Quadrilateral" of 1888 was well known in ecumenical circles. In it, the Lambeth Conference of Bishops of the Anglican communion laid out what they understood to be four essential conditions for a reunited Christian Church. Professor Outler borrowed the term from this context as a description for what he understood to be John Wesley's fourfold understanding of religious authority.

Between 1970 and 1972 the notion of the quadrilateral clearly caught on, for the doctrinal statement adopted by the United Methodist General Conference of 1972 (with less than twenty dissenting votes, and after only brief discussion) expanded on the 1970 document's section delineating the fourfold pattern. Some significant changes occurred in the 1972 statement, however.

In the first place, the 1972 statement did not utilize the term "quadrilateral," and did not attribute the fourfold pattern to John Wesley in the way that the 1970 statement had done. Rather than being titled "The Wesleyan Concept of Authority" (1970), the 1972 discussion of the four-fold pattern falls under the heading of "Doctrinal Guidelines in The United Methodist Church."[14] Thus, the 1972 statement purported to be a *contemporary* statement of guidelines for theological reflection in The United Methodist Church.

In the second place, the 1972 statement expanded all of the sections on religious authority, including the section on Scripture, but left the earlier assertion of the primacy of Scripture in a considerably more ambiguous state. The statement placed Scripture, tradition, reason, and experience under equal subject headings, thus conveying an impression of equality among them. A concluding section on "These Guidelines in Interaction" did assert that "There is a primacy that goes with Scripture, as the constitutive witness to the biblical wellsprings of our faith. In practice, however," the statement goes on to say, "theological reflection may find its point of departure in tradition, 'experience,' or rational analysis."[15] Although the second sentence does not strictly falsify the first, the connective "however" left the notion of scriptural primacy in some doubt.

Finally, it is worth noting that in the 1972 statement both "experience" and "reason" are assigned distinctly contemporary meanings: "experience" refers both to specifically religious experience and our general experience of the world, and "reason" is taken to mean "rational analysis" ("logical coherency" in the 1970 statement). In both cases, Wesley's stresses are missing, both his stress on "experimental religion," and his typically eighteenth-century British sense of reason as reflection on experience.

Despite the near-unanimous vote which approved it, the 1972 statement did not go long without criticism. Professor Leroy Howe of Perkins School of Theology criticized what he perceived as the general ambiguity of its statement on religious authority.[16] Dean Robert Cushman of Duke Divinity School criticized the ambiguity of its assertion on scriptural primacy: it ". . . takes back with the left hand what it gives with the right," as he put it.[17] Later criticisms were enunciated by the Nazarene historian Timothy Smith, who felt that United Methodism had jettisoned scriptural primacy in giving equal authority to Scripture, tradition, reason, and experience; the quadrilateral, as he saw it, was construed as an "equilateral."[18]

The United Methodist General Conference of 1984, aware of these criticisms, established a new Theological Study Committee, chaired by Bishop Earl Hunt, to revise or replace the 1972 statement. From the first, the Committee was determined to make the primacy of scripture more explicit, and this intent was clearly carried through in the statement that was adopted by the 1988 General Conference. In early drafts of their proposed statement, the four elements of the quadrilateral were not given equal subject headings: one section was entitled, "The Primacy of Scripture," and a subsequent section was entitled "Tradition, Experience, and Reason."[19]

In the statement as passed by the General Conference of 1988, however, the four subject headings were retained.[20] Like the 1972 statement, the 1988 statement does not utilize the term "quadrilateral," and does refer to the four elements as "Theological Guidelines." The statement is expanded in two important respects: the four "Guidelines" are understood as both "sources" and "norms" of theological reflection, and the description of each has been thoroughly revised. Like the 1972 statement, the 1988 statement purports to be a contemporary assessment of theological guidelines, and not a historical description of Wesley's thought. But the new statement is preceded by a historical preface explaining how "Wesley believed that the living core of the Christian faith stands revealed in Scripture, illumined by tradition, vivified in personal experience, and confirmed by reason."[21] The statement goes on to detail some particular aspects of Wesley's uses of each of these authorities. In this respect, the statement is more careful about the historical claims it makes, but only raises in a critical way the historical issues surrounding Wesley's own understandings of theological authority.

It is interesting to note that throughout this process, the fourfold pattern, whether stated as a historical pattern or a contemporary theological formulation, has come to be referred to almost uniformly by United Methodists as "the Wesleyan Quadrilateral," despite the fact that the 1972 statement did not claim it as Wesleyan. Presumably what has happened is that the language of the 1970 statement (which was a statement about Wesley's understanding of authority) was remembered in a kind of oral tradition or communal memory, and so was applied rather inappropriately to the 1972 statement. One might speculate that the quadrilateral notion was found helpful by Methodists principally as a means of combating uncritical views of scriptural authority. Here would be a powerful, subliminal motive for attributing the fourfold pattern of the 1972 statement to John Wesley: it would give the rejection of uncritical views of scriptural primacy the weight of Methodism's deepest roots. But put in this way—attributing the fourfold pattern as such to John Wesley—the notion of the "Wesleyan Quadrilateral" is quite problematic.

The Fourfold Pattern and John Wesley

In order to examine the extent to which the "Wesleyan Quadrilateral" may be grounded in Wesley's teachings, it will be important to note, in the first place, what can be said in defence of the "Quadrilateral" as a "Wesleyan" conception. Professor Outler defended the fourfold pattern as grounded in John Wesley in an article entitled "The Wesleyan Quadrilateral —in John Wesley."[22] He made several cogent points in this article. In the first place, Outler pointed out that Wesley did use throughout his career what we recognize as Scripture, tradition, reason, and experience as doctrinal norms. That is to say, Wesley was not in any simple sense a *homo unius libri*.[23] Moreover, and perhaps even more critically, Outler showed that there are in Wesley certain indications of conceptual patterns which link various ones of these four elements together, and from which a fourfold pattern might be inferred. Wesley fell heir to an Anglican theological tradition in which Scripture, Christian antiquity, and reason all functioned together in the formulation and evaluation of Christian teaching and practice.[24] There are two passages in Wesley's works where such a framework is given. Wesley's doctrinal treatise on "Original Sin" (1756) is formally titled "The Doctrine of Original Sin, according to Scripture, Reason, and Experience."[25] So at least those three stand as conceptually linked categories of doctrinal authority. Second, the preface to the first collected edition of Wesley's *Works* (1771) has the following statement: "So that in this edition I present to serious and candid men my last and maturest thoughts, agreeable, I hope, to Scripture, reason, and Christian antiquity."[26] "Christian antiquity," Professor Outler reasoned, is an element of Christian tradition, other elements of which Wesley utilized on other occasions as doctrinal authority. Thus, putting these two statements together, and understanding "Christian antiquity" as representing at least an element of Christian tradition, one could infer the fourfold "Quadrilateral" of Scripture, tradition, reason, and experience as a conceptual framework implied in Wesley's works.

There are at least two problems involved with this inference. In the first place, I think, it is not appropriate to conclude on the basis of these two passages that there must have been a consistent, fourfold conception of religious authority *in Wesley's mind or thought*. As in so many other areas, Wesley's theology and practice developed over the years, sometimes with major shifts in theological emphasis (such as his being convinced of the doctrine of assurance by the Moravians), sometimes with relatively minor shifts in emphasis. One cannot infer a static (or simply consistent) fourfold conception on the basis of an emphasis in 1756 on three of the four elements, and an emphasis fifteen years later on two of those three with another added to them.

A more crucial problem with the fourfold pattern involves the identification of "tradition" as an element in the pattern. I do not mean at all to deny that "Christian antiquity" or the teachings and practices of the Church of England would fall under what we would term as "tradition" in a post-Tractarian or modern ecumenical sense of the term. But here is precisely the problem: whereas "Scripture," "reason," and "experience" stand as clear conceptual categories in Wesley, I am not aware of an eighteenth-century conceptual category (or a term) answering to "tradition," in its modern sense. In fact, the term "tradition" very often carried negative connotations in the Reformation and post-Reformation periods. Wesley would have been familiar with the assertion in the first Homily of the Church of England that one must rely upon Scripture, and not "the stinking puddles of men's traditions."[27] There are indeed two places in Wesley's works where he linked together in a conceptual framework Scripture, Christian antiquity (or "the primitive church") and the Church of England, but this does not answer to the conceptuality of the fourfold pattern, since this broad description of the sources for Wesley's thought includes Scripture.[28] To restate the point: there simply doesn't seem to exist in Wesley a conceptual category answering to "tradition" as conceived in the "Quadrilateral," that is, as describing God's work in the church after the scriptural period, in the same manner as there *are* conceptual categories for Scripture, reason, and experience. The fourfold pattern, then, is asymmetrical in its mixing of properly eighteenth-century and non-eighteenth-century conceptual categories, and so should not be attributed to John Wesley as such. At this point, I would recall that the 1972 and 1988 statements in the United Methodist Discipline can be excused, at least insofar as they do not overtly attribute the fourfold pattern to John Wesley (although the preamble to the 1988 statement comes very close). The "myth" is the continuing legitimation of the fourfold pattern by historically attributing it to John Wesley.

Conclusion

I have been tempted, after a couple of years of reflection on these issues, to make a case that here we have an instance of the development of a modern version of the traditioning process. Perhaps we could identify Colin Williams as "E," Albert Outler as "J," and the 1970 draft of the Theological Study Commission (the only official text in which "quadrilateral" appears) as "P," with Wesley himself as a kind of *Urtext*. The notion of the "Wesleyan Quadrilateral," then, would be an intricate composite of these sources, formed under the crucible of Methodist involvement in the ecumenical movement, and then found almost indispensable by Methodists themselves in their defense of a progressive attitude towards biblical authority.

But this might lessen the contemporary significance of the "Wesleyan Quadrilateral," which, as I have remarked at the outset, has been remarkably helpful. A rather odd thing has happened: the Methodists, who at mid-century were accused of being "short on theology,"[29] have forged in the last thirty years a powerful tool for discussing the classic issues of the theological *prolegomena*. This tool has precedents in the Christian tradition in general, in the Anglican tradition in more particular respects, and specifically in John Wesley. But for all these precedents, it should be clear that the "Quadrilateral" is a distinctively *modern* tool, and perhaps for that reason all the more remarkable.

Chapter 12

Is Theological Pluralism Dead in The U.M.C.?

John B. Cobb, Jr.[1]

"Liberalism" has many meanings in contemporary theological usage. Chiefly it has come to name something the speaker dislikes. But the liberal spirit has continued in an affirmation of theological pluralism— an appreciation and attentive acceptance of a variety of theological programs. Sometimes this has meant that various historic Christian traditions have affirmed the legitimacy of each other's differences in articulating the faith. Sometimes it has meant that such diversity could be affirmed even within a single denomination. The United Methodist Church has accepted theological pluralism in both of these ways. However, the second is now under attack.

In late April the denomination's General Conference will convene for its quadrennial session. Decisions made at General Conference determine the denomination's practice so far as that can be settled by legislation at least until the conference meets again. Among the crucial issues to be decided this year is the denomination's openness to continuing its tradition of theological pluralism.

The U.M.C.'s authoritative document is called the Book of Discipline. In the present Discipline the church affirms its openness to divergent theological traditions and projects, declaring that the U.M.C.'s "theological spectrum . . . ranges over all the current mainstream options and a variety of special interest theologies as well." It asserts that the denomination's doctrinal guidelines allow for, indeed they positively encourage, "variety in United Methodist theologizing." The breadth of this openness is made explicit by reference to "neofundamentalism, new pentecostalism, new forms of Christian naturalism and secularity, as well as black theology, female liberation theology, political and ethnic theologies, third world theologies, and theologies of human rights."

This commitment to openness has not been without cost. For example, it too easily passes over into theological indifferentism. When theological faculties try to help students work out their own convictions in encounter with a variety of voices, many students find their freedom burdensome. Some prefer to be told what to believe. Even when students do successfully begin the task of articulating their own theological convictions, Boards of Ordained Ministry are often dissatisfied with the results. Thus candidates increasingly feel the need to know what answers will satisfy the boards.

A still more serious problem is that the denomination's erstwhile unifying vision of its mission has faded. Methodism came into being to meet individual and societal needs that were not being dealt with by other church institutions, first in England and then elsewhere, especially on this continent. In the late nineteenth century the parent bodies now joined together in The United Methodist Church threw their energies into extending Christ's reign around the world. Since World War II, however, only limited parts of the church are aroused to sacrificial giving and service by these visions and no vision has emerged to give focus and direction to the denomination. Inevitably, the U.M.C. turns in on itself to find its reason for existence and a basis for action. When it does so, many understandably seek unity of belief to replace the disappearing unity of purpose. Some of these individuals are disturbed to find the denomination's official statement so accepting of diversity.

The concern to resolve problems surrounding theological pluralism was a main factor leading the 1984 General Conference to seek the Council of Bishops' appointment of a Committee on Our Theological Task. That committee is to report to the upcoming 1988 General Conference.

The committee accepted the implicit mandate to reject theological pluralism; even the factual existence of pluralism is barely acknowledged in its report. "United Methodists as a diverse people continue to strive for consensus in understanding the gospel. . . . In the name of Jesus Christ we are called to work within our diversity while exercising patience and forbearance with one another." In this passage diversity appears as an impediment to unity, and it is not clear, even here, that the reference is to diversity of theologies. Nowhere is it suggested that the life of the denomination may be enriched by a variety of theological approaches.

Once the denomination commits itself to homogeneity of theological approach, the question of the one acceptable approach becomes critical. The present Discipline limits diversity only by insisting that theology must justify itself in relation to four sources and guidelines. Scripture is the primary source and guideline "as the constitutive witness to biblical wellsprings of our faith," but tradition, experience, and reason also function as sources and guidelines, and in practice "theological reflection may find its point of departure" in any of them.

The statement proposed to replace this one formulates the relationships quite differently. Scripture is no longer merely first among equals; it is treated in a separate section, with the other three grouped together as resources to be used in interpreting it. The passage on "Tradition, Experience, and Reason" begins by asserting that "while the community of faith acknowledges the primacy of Scripture as a norm in theological reflection, it is nevertheless the case that tradition, experience, and reason are invariably at work in our attempts to grasp its meaning." The passage's concluding paragraph asserts that "in theological reflection, the resources of tradition, experience, and reason are integral to our study of Scripture without displacing its primacy for faith and practice." The structure of the report, combined with these explicit statements, indicates clearly that what is called for is biblical hermeneutics.

However, the call is not for the mainstream of biblical hermeneutics in scholarly circles. There the multiplicity of diverse strands making up the Scriptures is emphasized. The report's insistence is on the harmonious unity of all these strands. All texts are to be interpreted "in light of their place in the Bible as a whole." Wesley's practice is held as normative. "At all times he sought to portray the unity of the biblical witness."

The document recognizes a certain problem in that "Scripture comprises a variety of diverse traditions, some of which reflect tensions in interpretation within the early Judeo-Christian heritage." But it points toward their harmonization. "However, these traditions are woven together in the Bible in a manner that expresses the fundamental unity of God's revelation as received and experienced by the people in their own lives." The report calls on reason to "organize the understandings that compose our witness and render them internally coherent." In short, the approved form of theology is what was known during the 1950s and 1960s as "biblical theology."

The Committee on Our Theological Task wanted a unifying document rather than a divisive one. Hence, it has been responsive to criticism, and the final version of the report includes many points missing from the earlier draft. These new points exist in some tension with the report's basic structure. The question is whether the goal is possible of achievement; to reject pluralism and yet satisfy the real plurality of theological concerns.

The tensions within the report can be examined by considering the document's implications for particular theologies and programs, for example, black theology, Minjung theology, Latin American liberation theology, feminist theology, philosophical theology. Can these forces justify their continued role in The United Methodist Church on the basis of the new report?

There is no question but that the report's authors are sensitive to the concerns of oppressed people and committed to hearing their views:

> We are now challenged by traditions from around the world which accent dimensions of Christian understanding that grow out of the sufferings and victories of the downtrodden. Some of these traditions help us to rediscover the biblical regard for the poor, the disabled, the imprisoned, the oppressed, the outcast. They underscore the equality of all persons in Jesus Christ. They display the capacity of the gospel to free us to embrace the diversity of human cultures and appreciate their values. They reinforce our traditional understanding of the inseparability of personal salvation and social justice. They deepen our commitment to global peace. A critical appreciation of these traditions can compel us to think about God in new ways, enlarge our vision of shalom, and enhance our confidence in God's provident love.[2]

We may assume that at least some forms of black theology and Minjung theology are thus affirmed, for they both interpret Scripture in just such ways as these. But what about black theology that draws on pre-Christian African traditions as a source, or Minjung theology that draws on the historic experience of the Korean people as well as on Christian Scriptures and tradition? Can these be affirmed? In the draft version of the document the answer seemed to be No. But two insertions in the final report may alter this situation. First, in the paragraph just quoted there is reference to appreciating the values of diverse cultures. Second, in the discussion of experience there is now an important new clause: "Our theological task is informed by the experience of the Church *and by the common experiences of all humanity*" (my emphasis). Third, in discussing interreligious relations, the final report states that "recognizing that the Spirit of God is at work everywhere, we listen thoughtfully to the wisdom and insights that others share with us." None of these phrases offers as clear a basis for black or Minjung theology as does the 1984 Book of Discipline, though they do offer it a foothold in the denomination.

Latin American liberation theology also functions emphatically as a biblical hermeneutic and in this respect is encouraged. But in most such theology social analysis plays a strong, constitutive role. Two sentences in the discussion of reason in an earlier version of the report could be taken to support the use of such analysis: "By reason we relate our witness to the full range of human knowledge and experience," and "By our quest for reasoned understandings of Christian faith we seek to grasp and express the gospel in a way that will commend itself to thoughtful persons who are seeking to know and follow God's ways." In the final version, a further statement is added: "By reason we ask questions of faith." This addition helps to counter the impression left by the earlier draft that reason is used only triumphalistically to display biblical truth and not penitently to criticize Christian beliefs and practices. Critical social analysis may thus be allowed entré into theology.

The report affirms feminist theology insofar as it is an aid to biblical interpretation that can be a part of a harmonized whole and insofar as it constitutes a call for equal treatment of women in church and in society. But many feminists want more than that. Engaging in a critique of the one-sided, masculine perspective that dominates our whole Western tradition, including the Scriptures, they take women's experience seriously as a source for transforming Christian theology. The only principle the report offers for inclusion of such a view has already been quoted: "Our theological task is informed . . . by the common experiences of all humanity." Whether this general statement allows for women's distinctive experience to be a source for transforming traditional Christian teaching may some day be an issue for the Judicial Council to decide.

Finally, one must ask whether the committee would allow confirmation of philosophical theology within United Methodism. In most such theology, philosophy's function is not limited to being a tool of biblical interpretation. Instead, it is usually supposed that a range of questions important for Christian theology can be dealt with better with the aid of the natural and social sciences and the humanities, including philosophy, than by biblical interpretation alone. In the form of personalistic idealism, philosophical theology has played a major role in Methodism.

One could interpret the several passages on reason quoted above as providing a basis for the practice of philosophical theology. And there is another already present in the first published draft. Near the beginning of the section "Our Theological Task," the report states that "our theological task . . . is critical in that we test various expressions of faith by asking, Are they true?" It could be argued that this question opens the way for testing those expressions against the findings of natural and historical sciences and of philosophy. The text continues: "Our theological task is constructive in that every generation must appropriate creatively the wisdom of the past." This notion could be interpreted to include the scientific and philosophical wisdom which would then be integrated with biblical wisdom in an inclusive theology, although this interpretation is in tension with the flat assertion that reason is "not itself a source of theology."

If the report is adopted by General Conference, these footholds for a variety of theological programs may become extremely important for individual United Methodist theologians. But even if they allow some continued diversity in theological programs within the denomination, the theological climate will change. Theological options that have heretofore been fully accepted as part of the conversation will be forced to defend their right to continue as such. Those who want to rid the denomination of its theological confusion by suppressing diversity will be strengthened. Presumably this was intended by many of those opposing theological pluralism along with the full recognition of tradition, experience, and reason as sources and guidelines for theology.

Whether the committee statement, if adopted, will ever be used as a basis for such serious procedures as heresy trials cannot now be predicted, but that it will be used by Boards of Ordained Ministry in screening candidates can be confidently stated. Seminaries will be under pressure to prepare students for doctrinal examinations judged by these boards. In that role the statement is likely to be read more in terms of its main drift toward biblical theology than in terms of the slight affirmation it accords other theological programs. In all of these developments, recent trends will be strengthened. The era of real theological pluralism in United Methodism will draw to an end.

Chapter 13

IN QUEST OF A COMMON FAITH:
THE THEOLOGICAL TASK OF UNITED METHODISTS

by Thomas W. Ogletree[1]

It is no simple matter for a contemporary Protestant denomination to engage its people in a corporate process of theological reflection. Such an enterprise is especially difficult for a denomination as large, complex, and diverse as The United Methodist Church. To be sure, virtually all Protestant denominations have formal doctrinal standards of some sort—creeds, articles of religion, confessions of faith. Yet only The United Methodist Church has ventured an official account of guidelines for the ongoing task of theological inquiry amid the changing circumstances of the church's life. This account, occasioned by the formation of The United Methodist Church in 1968, was adopted by the 1972 General Conference as ¶ 69 of the Book of Discipline, entitled "Our Theological Task." In combination with ¶ 67, "Historical Background," and ¶ 68, "Foundation Documents," it describes the "Doctrine and Doctrinal Standards" of The United Methodist Church (Part II).

Many United Methodist people have experienced the 1972 treatment of "our theological task" as a mixed blessing. Its strength is that it directs us to ongoing theological inquiry in which we relate the promises of the gospel to the challenges and perils of our modern world. It summons us to take responsibility for our critical judgments, specifying only in general terms the reference points pertinent to our thinking. Its weakness is that it appears uncertain and apologetic about whether there are any clear standards of doctrine to which we are all answerable when we speak to and for the church. This impression is conveyed by its celebration of theological pluralism and by its warnings against doctrinal rigidity. Despite its disclaimers, it has tended to legitimate theological "indifferentism," the attitude that just about any sincerely held belief is acceptable among United Methodists.

The 1984 General Conference mandated the formation of an episcopal committee to prepare a new statement on the theological task of

United Methodists. Advocates of the new statement were pleading for a stronger account of our doctrinal standards and their normative authority in our church's teaching. The resolution adopted by the General Conference specified a statement that sets forth the full scope of our Wesleyan heritage in its bearing on the mission of our church.

The Council of Bishops appointed the Committee on Our Theological Task, which has been at work throughout the quadrennium preparing the statement called for by the 1984 General Conference. In the course of its work, the committee found that it could not simply revise or rewrite ¶ 69 without also rethinking the whole of Part II of the Discipline. It has therefore, produced a new version of Part II, now composed of four paragraphs: 66, "Our Doctrinal Heritage"; 67 "Our Doctrinal History"; 68, "Our Doctrinal Standards"; and 69, "Our Theological Task." The first paragraph recounts classic and reformation doctrinal traditions and describes the distinctive emphases of the Wesleyan movement in relation to those traditions. The second paragraph discusses the doctrinal histories of the denominations which compose The United Methodist Church. The third paragraph contains the "foundation documents" as before, but it calls them quite directly, "our doctrinal standards." The final paragraph is a new formulation of our ongoing theological task.

In the fall of 1986, the committee published a preliminary draft of its report, soliciting responses from church leaders.[7] In light of numerous thoughtful criticisms, the committee then amended its statement, in some respects significantly, and adopted a final draft in the fall of 1987. This draft will go to the 1988 General Conference as a possible replacement for Part II of the current Discipline.

Though the new statement involves a fairly extensive rewriting of the disciplinary paragraphs on doctrinal standards, it is, nonetheless, in essential continuity with their central intent. In both form and content, it builds upon the present statement, frequently retaining the exact wording of individual sentences and phrases. The purpose of the new statement, then, is not to reform the doctrinal standards of our church; it is to adjust our official account of those standards in response to the church's present needs and concerns. If adopted, the committee's report, like its predecessor, will doubtless require further reworking from time to time, just as we periodically prepare new hymnals and books of worship.

From the Celebration of Pluralism to the Quest for Consensus

The new statement differs from the old in its overall tenor; it drops any explicit affirmation of theological pluralism and stresses instead the urgency of a renewed quest for common grounds of theological understanding. In this notable shift of emphasis, it accepts as valid the contention that United Methodists can and should be more forthright about their doctrinal standards, and that such forthrightness is crucial to the recovery of a shared mission.

Currently the Discipline speaks of "the positive virtues of doctrinal pluralism." It notes that "the theological spectrum in The United Methodist Church ranges over all the current mainstream options and a variety of special-interest theologies as well" (p. 73). It cautions against relying on "infallible rules" or "reflex habits" or "precedents for simple imitation" in doctrinal matters (p. 72). Such rules or habits would, presumably, dampen the lively inquiry which has been a special strength of the United Methodist traditions.

In my view, pluralism is a blessing when it expresses the richness of a diverse and vital church with a sure sense of its center. Such a church can readily "become all things to all people that it might by all means save some" (cf. I Corinthians 9:22). At the same time, pluralism is a problem when it signals a lack of accountability for critical standards of Christian teaching, or when it sanctions an avoidance of serious theological engagement with sharp and potentially divisive controversies within the church. Indeed, in these latter circumstances I do not believe that we have pluralism at all, but rather a fragmentation of the church's life and thought. When we face such fragmentation, we are obliged to redirect our energies toward clarifying afresh the convictions that express our common identity.

The new statement reflects a judgment that the principal threat to United Methodism at the present time is not doctrinal rigidity or narrowness, but theological confusion and fragmentation. Without necessarily precluding, still less repressing, the range of theological perspectives which are presently found within our church, it seeks to identify the standards to which we are properly subject when we represent the teachings of our church.

The new statement presumes that as United Methodists we do in fact have authoritative doctrinal standards. It provides an account of those standards and the criteria they generate for testing our theological judgments. Its aim is a heightened sense of our unity in faith. Drawing upon our doctrinal standards, it summons us "to articulate our vision in a way that will draw us together as a people in mission."

The emphasis on collective accountability will not suddenly resolve the conflicts that presently disturb our common life. In the short run, it could even intensify those conflicts because it impels us to take one another seriously and to engage one another theologically regarding the soundness and pertinence of our conceptions of the church's message. The new statement stresses, therefore, the need for patience and forbearance in pursuing our theological discourse. The accent unquestionably falls, however, on the task of renewing, sustaining and extending a common faith.

The Place of Scripture among the Sources and Criteria of Theology

A second notable change in the new statement is that it reorganizes the discussion of the basic sources and criteria of theology. It treats Scripture in a separate section, highlighting its primacy. It then links tradition, experience, and reason closely to the interpretation of Scripture.

In my view, this change has more to do with the form of presentation than with matters of substance. Both old and new statements attest the primacy of Scripture, and they also insist equally upon the necessity of bringing all four resources to bear upon every doctrinal consideration. The 1972 statement, however, has frequently been misconstrued as suggesting that the primary "guidelines" to theology are more or less equal partners, a misconception encouraged by their popular portrayal of "sides" of a "quadrilateral." The new statement corrects against this misconception, while continuing to insist that our appropriation of Scripture always involves tradition, experience, and reason. In actual practice, the four sources and criteria interact reciprocally, so that each illumines and is illumined by the others. Thus, the primacy of Scripture is a reality for us not apart from the other three resources, but only in and by means of their full operation.

The new statement expands the discussion of the sources and criteria of theology in a number of striking ways. It acknowledges, for example, the importance for our theological task of "neglected traditions" within the church, particularly traditions arising out of "the sufferings and victories of the downtrodden." Likewise, without in any way minimizing the centrality of the experience of new life in Christ, it also directs attention within the discussion of the sources and criteria of theology to wider senses of experience. It specifically mentions human experiences of terror, hunger, loneliness, and degradation, and the everyday experiences of birth and death, growth and life, and wider social relations.

171

The present disciplinary statement itself takes note of experiences such as those just cited, but only in its description of "theological frontiers and new directions." It lifts up such experiences, in other words, because they present us with special challenges as we go about our theological task. It does not yet include them within the internal processes of theological inquiry. In recognizing how essential these experiences are to our most elemental efforts to understand the biblical message, the new statement is a clear advance over the old.

It has been suggested that the emphasis on the primacy of Scripture establishes as normative one particular theological option: namely, "biblical theology." I would contend instead that any approach to theology is permitted, even encouraged, which clearly acknowledges the primacy of Scripture and recognizes at the same time the indispensable role of tradition, experience, and reason in appropriating the biblical witness into our total understanding of reality. Where United Methodists disagree, it is not over the primacy of Scripture, but over the way Scripture is received and interpreted.

In this connection, the new statement recognizes the usefulness of "highly theoretical constructions of theology," among which I would readily include personalism and process thought. The legitimacy of more speculative forms of Christian thought is also noted in the discussion of reason, where attention is called to the significance of relating the biblical message to "the full range of human knowledge and experience." To be sure, reason is described not as a "source of theology," but as a "necessary tool." This assertion may be troubling for some since in popular usage "reason" is frequently taken to refer to anything we are capable of knowing independently of divine revelation. Conceived in such a broad and encompassing manner, reason is unquestionably a source of theology. In a stricter sense, however, reason refers simply to the formal standards of valid human thought and discourse. In this usage, reason in itself is devoid of content! It gains content from human experiences of the natural and social worlds, especially as these experiences are formed in human cultures and traditions. Even the experiences of divine revelation are mediated thorough human cultures and traditions.

In a similar vein, by emphasizing the place of experiences of oppression and liberation in theological reflection the new statement makes direct contact with recent discussions of liberation theology. Key themes from the latter are lifted up: regard for the poor, the disabled, the imprisoned, the oppressed, the outcast; the equality of all persons in Jesus Christ; the openness of the gospel to the diversity of human cultures with their distinctive values.

I mention these two types of contemporary theology because some critics have argued that the new statement places them in a highly problematic position. My own contention is that the new statement does not favor any particular school of interpretation which we can readily identify. It rather shows how our standards, rightly understood, can provide a framework within which our people can critically assess the contributions to our theological task of a whole range of classical and contemporary options in Christian thought. In the final analysis, the test of any theological formulation is whether it can help us express the saving promises of the gospel in "plain words for plain people."

The Sermons and Notes as Doctrinal Standards

There is a third matter which deserves special mention. According to the present Book of Discipline, the Plan of Union for The United Methodist Church, while acknowledging that the language of the First Restrictive Rule in the Constitution has never been formally defined, stipulated that Wesley's Sermons and Notes "were specifically included in our present existing and established standards of doctrine *by plain historical inference*" (p. 49, italics mine). The new statement drops this claim, basically because the available historical evidence simply does not support the alleged inference. To be more specific, the 1808 General Conference of the Methodist Episcopal Church apparently did not intend to place Wesley's Sermons and Notes under the protection of the First Restrictive Rule.[3]

My colleague, Thomas C. Oden, has argued that the stipulation in the Plan of Union, noted above, has in itself the effect of including the Sermons and Notes in the First Restrictive Rule. He goes on to assert—erroneously, it would appear—that such inclusion was a constitutional act which cannot be "legislatively refashioned by a subsequent General Conference."[4]

The Plan of Union which was submitted to the annual conferences for adoption contained four parts: (1) the Constitution and the enabling legislation; (2) doctrinal statements and the General Rules with preface; (3) the Social Principles with preface; and (4) legislation on organization and administration.

The contention that the Sermons and Notes were intended by the phrase "our present existing and established standards of doctrine" occurred only in the preface to the second part, "Doctrinal Statements and the General Rules."[5] It did not appear in the main body of that section. Even in the preface, the claim was not offered as a proposition for debate and possible action, but as a statement asserting a historical judgment about the "original reference" of the second clause of the First Restrictive Rule. Finally (and this may be the crucial point), the "Message from the Joint Commissions," which serves as an introduction to the Plan of Union, specifies that the annual conferences are to vote only on Part I, the Constitution and enabling legislation. The remaining parts were submitted only for information.[6]

In short, the Plan of Union can be said to have stipulated that the *Sermons* and *Notes* are covered by the First Restrictive Rule only in the sense that the General Conferences of the two uniting churches accepted a particular historical judgment about what might have been the original reference of the First Restrictive Rule. Like any critical reconstruction of past events, this judgment remains open to historical review. Further, the action which included this stipulation in the Plan of Union had the status only of General Conference legislation. It simply cannot be described as a constitutional matter.

The next General Conference may still wish to interpret the First Restrictive Rule as covering the *Sermons* and *Notes*. However, it cannot do so any longer on the basis of an allegedly "plain historical inference." Nor can it claim constitutional protection for the *Sermons* and *Notes* merely by amending the document offered by the Committee on Our Theological Task. Such protection can be secured only by a constitutional amendment.

The new statement deals with the normative status of the *Sermons* and *Notes* by developing the distinction between *formal* doctrinal standards, which enjoy constitutional protection, i.e., the Articles of Religion and the Confession of Faith, and *traditional* doctrinal standards, which have their authority by their constant usage as major resources in doctrinal instruction, in particular Wesley's *Sermons* and *Notes*.

The two sorts of standards differ in both form and function. The formal standards consist of succinct propositions officially adopted as authoritative formulations of sound doctrine by specific ecclesiastical bodies. These propositions constitute the operative standards where judicial proceedings are involved. The traditional standards consist chiefly of full expositions of selected biblical texts and doctrinal themes by the principal teacher of the early Methodist movement. The latter are of vital importance in the teaching activities of our church. Because of their expository character, however, they are hardly suited to furnish constitutional standards of doctrine, especially not for use in judicial processes.

This proposed restatement in no way implies that we are about to "abandon" the *Sermons* and *Notes* as normative doctrinal standards.[7] On the contrary, the new statement is pervaded by Wesleyan thought, indeed, to a degree that surpasses the present disciplinary discussion. What is changed is the basic conceptualization of the normative standing of these Wesleyan writings. The new statement claims that the authority of Wesley's *Sermons* and *Notes* resides not in an article of the Constitution, but rather in the actual daily practice of our church.

The anomaly created by the new statement, of course, is that the articles which enjoy constitutional protection do not strongly articulate some of our most distinctive Wesleyan emphasis: prevenient grace, the universal love of God for all creation, assurance, disciplined communities, the connectional polity.[8] For my part, I do not believe that we have grounds to fear the loss of Wesleyan teaching. It is strongly present in the life of our church, especially in ministerial preparation. If we are concerned about this matter, however, then we should venture some additional articles which succinctly state the essential matters, and undertake the process of constitutional amendment which would incorporate them into our formal standards. We would not be well served by trying to place the whole of Wesley's *Sermon on Several Occasions* and *Explanatory Notes upon the New Testament* under the restrictive rules of the Constitution.

Conclusion

The new statement on doctrine and doctrinal standards is by no means perfect. Personally, I would welcome the freedom to modify this sentence or that, adding a bit here, eliminating a bit there. On the whole, however, I believe it is a good statement, an appropriate advance over what we now have. While the new statement may fully satisfy no one, it does promise to encompass the major doctrinal sensibilities presently at work in our church. Insofar as it does, it can strengthen the bonds which hold us together as a church.

Chapter 14

CONCILIAR THEOLOGY: A REPORT

Thomas A. Langford[1]

The Legislative Committee on Faith and Mission of the 1988 General Conference was constituted to engage in theology. It had received the report of the Committee on Our Theological Task which was proposed for inclusion in the Discipline. A study report is to the General Conference as a Presidential study commission (for instance on the stock market) is to Congress. Once the report is completed it is turned over to and becomes the property of the General Conference. The Conference may do with the report what it will.

General Conference holds the teaching office in United Methodism. It is the final authority and officially speaks for the Church. The procedure of General Conference is to refer all petitions to a legislative committee which then brings a report to the entire Conference for final action.

The Legislative Committee on Faith and Mission had ninety members. These people understood themselves to be engaged in theological activity as a church and for the church. They were challenged to model how The United Methodist Church actually does its theological work. They were reminded that this was a new legislative committee and, therefore, they were part of a new venture. They were commissioned to seek truth and serve the church; the spirit and quality of their work would leave its mark.

The gathered committee came with diverse opinions—some with publicly expressed support for or opposition to the proposed statement. The statement already in the Book of Discipline was approved in 1972. The fruit of the union of The Methodist Church and the Evangelical United Brethren Churches, it was produced by a distinguished team headed by Albert C. Outler. The statement possessed literary style, helpfully interpreted the denomination's theological history, was characterized by theological openness, and perhaps made its most lasting contribution by developing the so-called "Wesleyan quadrilateral," that is, the interaction of Scripture, tradition, experience, and reason in theological construction and exploration. This quadrilateral is a systematization of Wesley's theological sources. It is not found, as such, in Wesley, but it is true to Wesley's interest and intention.[2] This quadrilateral has become a pervasive and identifying character of United Methodist theology. No one on the committee questioned its importance; the chief issues of the discussion were the balances and modes of interaction in interpreting the quadrilateral.

The 1972 and 1988 Statements

Loyalty to the 1972 statement was strong, especially among those who found it to be a proclamation of freedom in theological work. The document used the word "pluralism" in describing United Methodist theology and many people found this an endorsement of creative theological activity.

Enthusiasm for the proposed 1988 statement was also evident. The resetting of the role of Scripture in the quadrilateral was its chief attractiveness. This new approach was especially clear in the fourth section on "Our Theological Task." It was here that the crux of the debate would center.

A large number of committee members came to the 1988 General Conference convinced that alterations would have to be made in either document if it was to be acceptable for the Book of Discipline. Their loyalty was more to crucial issues than to either statement.

The 1972 and the 1988 statements may be understood as two autobiographical accounts of the same community. To recount one's life at two points in time inevitably reveals continuities but also different evaluations of one's experience; so, for instance, one may reevaluate childhood influences, formative friendships, or decisive events. This was an underlying, if not fully conscious, frame of reference for the committee's discussion.

A strong aspect of committee work—and perhaps a chief contribution to its success—was openness and freedom in the exchange of ideas. Everyone could speak to any issue and a high percent of committee members did participate by discussion and everyone by voting on proposed changes. Consistency of position was balanced by respect for other opinions. When votes were taken there was a sense of clarity about options and decisions were accepted as representative of the body's best judgment. Differences remained and strong argument continued, but steps, as taken, were accepted as foundations for the next step.

Beginning

The first meeting revealed sharp divisions and tension. Members broke into small groups, then were asked individually to list on paper the issues they thought were paramount and which needed to be discussed. These suggestions were to be used to organize the discussion on the next day. The notes came in with exclamation points and polarized declarations. The chief issues were, pro and con, "pluralism" (over thirty references), "primacy of Scripture" (over twenty references), and Wesley's *Sermons* and *Explanatory Notes upon the New Testament* as doctrinal standards. Subordinate concerns were "ecumenicity," "denominational identity," and "trinitarian language" (one reference). Positions seemed sharply drawn and held with determination.

Initial discussions bore out the indications. The first shots across the bow were statements of positions. "Pluralism" and "primacy of Scripture" were two sides of the same coin. For some, slogans became theology. For most, the issues would have to be discussed in the context of a written statement with careful attention given to specific language.

An important juncture was reached when the 1988 document was accepted as the statement the committee would refine and perfect. It was decided to work on the document paragraph by paragraph. After the initial effort, one member favorably commented, "we are working with a Woody Hayes model: three yards and a cloud of dust." Slow, cautious, short, tentative steps were taken. For many, an underlying suspicion remained—would this procedure, in the last analysis, lead to an acceptable statement?

Section 1—Our Doctrinal Heritage

The arrangement of the materials in the document proved helpful. Differences were initially engaged over historical material where resolution was easier because of more objective points of reference. Discussion of Section 1 revealed basic consensus. The most critical issue was the reinsertion, after the reference to the Triune God, of the names, "Father, Son, and Holy Spirit" (as in earlier drafts of the document). After discussion, it was agreed by a majority of 41 to 39 votes that it is as important to say who God is as to speak of what God does (that is, as Creator, Redeemer, and Sustainer). Both ways of speaking (of God's person and of God's activity) were retained. Also of importance, a level and spirit of discussion was being established as arguments with theological and rational integrity were presented in a context of mutual respect.

"Pull off a few covers and United Methodists share a great deal in common." This awareness became increasingly clear as the group persistently worked through the sections on "Our Common Heritage as Christians," "Our Distinctive Heritage as United Methodists," and "Doctrine and Discipline in the Christian Life." The recognition of common roots, shared primary emphases in regard to theological affirmation and ethical mission created the foundation for further corporate agreement. The document itself, as prepared by the Committee on Our Theological Task, was structured in a way that allowed for convergence among the diversity present in the legislative committee.

Editorial revision gave new headings to aspects of our heritage so that under "Grace" the themes of "Prevenient Grace," "Justification and Assurance," "Sanctification and Perfection," "Faith and Good Works," "Mission and Service," "Nurture and Mission of the Church," and "General Rules and Social Principles" are clearly emphasized.

Section 2—Our Doctrinal History

Some members expressed uneasiness: would there be attempts to distort our history by reinterpretation or special interest? Discussion of Section 2 drew some issues to sharper focus. In the first paragraph the issue was faced: "What did Wesley intend to include in his sermon on 'Catholic Spirit?'" The statement said that it allowed "Christians to disagree on matters such as forms of worship, structures of church government, or modes of baptism." How about theological differences? Was theological diversity included in generous Christian acceptance of fellow believers? After debate—and with some fusion of Wesley's perspective with contemporary Methodists'—the committee included the words "theological explorations" in the list. With these two words, accepted by a close stand-up count vote, an important point was established. Subsequent decisions were now, in principle, being formed.

Immediately following, a moment of fundamental historical self-understanding came to the fore. In the section, "Doctrinal Standards in American Methodism," the question was whether Wesley's *Sermons* and *Explanatory Notes upon the New Testament* were to stand on equal footing with the Articles of Religion and the Confession of Faith. The proposed document did not say so. Pre-General Conference debate had been intense. Richard P. Heitzenrater, a principle author of the 1988 statement had, on investigation of the 1808 General Conference, come to the conclusion that only the Articles of Religion had legal sanction historically in early American Methodism as doctrinal standards. Thomas C.

Oden and Robert E. Cushman argued against this conclusion on the grounds that distinctive Wesleyan teaching, the actual practice of the Methodist tradition, and the plan of Union in 1968 made their equal status imperative in United Methodism. Sharp public debate, representing historical and theological argumentation, resulted. Before General Conference, Heitzenrater and Oden agreed to a paragraph which brought the interests together, including all four as "standards" and distinguishing two ways in which they function. This was accepted by the committee, which included the new sentence stating clearly the status of the *Sermons* and *Notes*, and then adding these to the documents listed in "Section 3—Our Doctrinal Standards and General Rules."

A major procedural matter must be noted. Two of the chief writers of the 1988 document were present as observers, Richard P. Heitzenrater and Thomas W. Ogletree. The committee, in an exceptional expression of good will and collegiality, invited both to participate in the discussion in order to interpret the document and help to keep coherence of subject and style in the refined statement. Both men participated in a helpful, non-defensive manner. They and the committee deserve commendation for the way they worked together. The committee understood it was responsible for decisions about the statement but it wanted to make informed decisions. The two consultants kept issues of larger context and specific reference before the committee and even made suggestions about the wording of changed passages.

It should also be noted that a change was made in the title of Section 3 from "Foundational Documents" to "Standards of Doctrine." This represented a difference which strengthened the core of United Methodist theological identity.

Clarifying and making firm the doctrinal standards was seen by many as a major strength of the new statement.

Section 4—Our Theological Task

The most controversial part of the document was now faced. All of the issues converged in Section 4. Had the preparation of working through the first three sections provided enough common ground to make agreement possible on this final part? We entered the discussion without certainty. With the controversial issues directly before us, could agreement be found? Could there be acceptable unity within our obvious diversity?

The first sub-head, "The Nature of Our Theological Task," engaged the issues. The first two paragraphs were inverted and rewritten and then an entirely new paragraph was placed before them. The present opening paragraph, written in committee, is of basic importance because it put primary emphasis on grace and hereby relates to a central theme of our tradition and sets the stage for the ensuing discussion.

To understand what was happening, it is necessary to understand a basic distinction between doctrine and theology made in the 1988 statement. The title of the entire statement, "Doctrinal Standards and our Theological Task," indicates this distinction and the first paragraphs of Section 4 make it explicit. One way of illustrating this difference is to say that doctrine is like a house that a religious communion already inhabits. It represents a communal agreement about what is essential to and characteristic of their faith. Theology, or theological exploration, is the proposal of blueprints for remodeling or extending the house. Often individually drawn, these blueprints represent creative efforts to suggest new construction which will make the home more welcoming or adequate. Such theological exploration must be free and newly suggestive, but it must also be brought back to the doctrinal community for its consideration, for acceptable new construction must "fit onto" the existing structure. To extend the illustration, which the statement by extrapolation suggests (but only suggests, for this illustration is not in the text), Jesus Christ is the foundation of the house and Scripture is its vestibule or entry hall.

The discussion of the theological task (for now the document moves in a strict sense from doctrine to theology) centered on the issue of freedom of theological investigation and the acceptance of diverse theological perspectives by our denomination. The reordering of the initial paragraphs and the insertion of a new paragraph on the contextual and incarnational nature of theology were indications of an open and learning spirit. This section merits careful study because of its content and the change in emphasis.

The interaction of parts of the quadrilateral became the next major issue and the matter was sharply debated. A motion was made to insert a paragraph from the 1972 document on the interrelationship of the four elements to complement the sentence which concluded the introductory section on "Theological Guidelines." In this reused paragraph, Scripture is reaffirmed as the "primary authority among these theological sources," but the point of departure for theological exploration may be any one of the four sources. "What matters most is that all four guidelines be brought to bear in faithful, serious, theological consideration." The motion passed, again with a count vote. The dynamic interplay within the complete quadrilateral was again reinforced. New, parallel headings of "Scripture," "Tradition," "Experience," and "Reason" emphasized the interaction. This was a critical move in shaping this part of the document.

The primary place of Scripture in the quadrilateral was affirmed in both the 1972 and the 1988 documents. What was in debate was the understanding of primacy and the role of Scripture (which has a secure place in each of the doctrinal standards) in theological exploration. In what sense is Scripture primary? The revised introductory paragraph to the section on "Scripture" (including three new sentences prepared by a team that struggled to say a great deal in a short space) asserts that the Living Word, Jesus Christ, has true primacy, and that Scripture possesses first place as witness to Jesus Christ. Further, Scripture is God's word as it is interpreted under the guidance of the Holy Spirit. Hence, Scripture stands at the point of intersection where the Word of God is conveyed through its words as they are illumined by the Holy Spirit. In this role, Scripture is "the primary source and criterion for Christian doctrine."

In the discussion of "Scripture," one issue was debated in Committee and again on the floor of the Conference. An amendment was offered to insert the words, "Scripture contains both authoritative witness to the word of God and expressions of human and cultural limitation." The argument made for this inclusion was that it represents an honest statement of where United Methodism is in regard to its understanding of Scripture. Opponents argued that as a matter of pastoral concern we should not have such a statement in this document since it opens issues in the current debate about biblical infallibility and could confuse as easily as clarify our church's position. In the committee it was also argued that the latter part of the paragraph put textual criticism positively, "We draw upon the careful historical, literary, and textual studies of recent years which have enriched our understanding of the Bible." The amendment did not carry in either arena.

The role of the Holy Spirit is made clearer in the revised document (for a lively doctrine of the Holy Spirit prevented the United Methodist traditions from moving to biblical literalism or infallibility). This emphasis is reinforced by extending a quoted phrase from the Confession of Faith to include the words "to be received through the Holy Spirit . . ." and by emphasizing that tradition, experience, and reason are significant as they "become creative vehicles of the Holy Spirit."

The sections on Tradition and Experience are basically unchanged, with only the insertion under Tradition of the words "witness to God's special commitment to the poor," and in Experience a sentence from the 1972 document is reused to end a paragraph, "All religious experience affects all human experience; all human experience affects our understanding of religious experience." Reason is brought to more equal status than the original report suggested, principally by deleting the sentence, "Although not itself a source of theology, reason is a necessary tool." The interaction of the quadrilateral was now stated to the satisfaction of the committee. The independent headings given to Tradition, Experience, and Reason, assigned them clear and explicit importance. This represented a concession by those who had argued for distinct emphasis on the primacy of Scripture.

Under "The Present Challenge to Theology in the Church," a new paragraph on the global character of United Methodism was added to affirm our theological interdependence with world Christianity and with United Methodists from other cultures and diverse experiential backgrounds. Delegates from Great Britain, continental Europe, and Latin America made significant contributions to both the formulation and the refining of the statement. There were leaders from the signees of the "Houston Declaration" and the "Pacific Declaration" on the Legislative Committee. There were delegates from both local churches and general agencies. Women and ethnic minority persons made strong contributions. This was a representative body of world United Methodism.

Finally a revised version of the "Ecumenical Commitment" paragraphs were accepted which express clearly the permeative and persistent ecumenical commitments of United Methodism.

The three-paragraph Conclusion was unchanged.

The Vote

The Committee had completed its work. What had started with a sense of clear differences and tension had changed into mutual respect, willingness to understand, suggestions for acceptable changes, and building upon committee judgment. A common project had evolved.

Most important, clarification of the importance of doctrinal standards in United Methodist self-identity had allowed for endorsement of free and responsible theological exploration.

The Legislative Committee voted. On the first three sections the vote was 75 for, 4 against, and 2 abstentions; on the fourth section the vote was 73 for, 5 against, and 2 abstentions.

A nice touch of good will and ownership of the document was expressed by fifteen persons, lay and clergy, who volunteered to stay after the legislative committee adjourned and type a clean copy of the statement. They did this under the leadership of the Committee Secretary. The last of these volunteers left at 1:45 A.M. Through this effort the document was submitted to the *Daily Christian Advocate* the next day for publication.

Presentation to General Conference

In presenting the Committee's work to the plenary session of General Conference, the chair made the following comments.

This theological document is the result of a significant process within our church and within this General Conference.

The history goes back to 1968 with the establishment of a theological study commission at the time of merger. The document produced for the 1972 Discipline carried the explicit hope that theological inquiry would continue to be characteristic of our emerging quest for United Methodist identity within our larger Christian heritage. The 1984 General Conference decided it was time to take up that discussion again and attempt to update the Discipline's theological statement.

The document presented to the legislative process of this General Conference was a result of broad consultation, intense debate, and a growing awareness of lines of convergence among the various theological perspectives within our church. In the end, the document was presented by the Study Committee with a unanimous recommendation.

The Legislative Committee on Faith and Mission represented the church engaged in serious theological discussion, impressively modeling how United Methodists do theology and reflecting in some ways Wesley's conviction that Christian conference might be a means of grace. By the end of the week our group voted concurrence on a revised document with a more than 90 percent positive vote on each of the four petitions. This is a remarkable accomplishment.

The document presented to you by the legislative committee maintains a significant degree of continuity with the present statement in the Discipline, while making major changes to reflect the church's desire for further clarification and continued development.

As to continuity—Scripture, tradition, experience, and reason are reaffirmed as sources and criteria of our theological endeavors. Second, Scripture is affirmed as the primary authority among these sources while pointing out that our theological inquiry might start from any of them. Third, Wesley's *Sermons* and *Notes*, along with the Articles of Religion and Confession of Faith, are recognized as the established doctrinal standards of United Methodism. Fourth, commitment as a church to ecumenical engagement is affirmed.

By way of clarification—the proposal first reorganizes the material in Part 2 into four clear sections: Our Doctrinal Heritage, Our Doctrinal History, Our Doctrinal Standards, and Our Theological Task. Second, the document submitted to you makes a crucial distinction between doctrinal affirmation and theological exploration. Doctrinal affirmations provide an identifiable anchor for our denomination. Theological reflection entails critical and constructive inquiry from a wide variety of perspectives. Third, the document you have before you incorporates into the substance of the statement itself a variety of viewpoints that display our unity in diversity.

By way of development and enrichment—the proposal expresses increased recognition of the centrality of our encounter with God's love in Jesus Christ. And second, it highlights themes such as God's work in creation, our responsibilities for evangelism, and our historic recognition of the problem of systemic evil.

That our committee could draw this together was an unusual achievement. Among other things, it means that our church has the possibility of leaving this General Conference with a voice that is common among us while also recognizing that there are differences among us.

A young minister was an observer of our committee. He came up after one session to comment, 'Since seminary,' he said, 'I have heard of conciliar theology. Today I have witnessed it.' We covet this experience for the entire conference. For in our committee there was honest argument, intense goodwill, and, withal, gracious encounter over issues of fundamental importance.

The result of that process has not, of course, issued in a perfect document. While the statement exhibits a certain carefully developed balance, it also maintains some tensions that characterize our Wesleyan and United Methodist heritage. As such, this is not a statement simply to comfort the church. It is also a challenge to our church. The intent is not to offer a final consensus, but rather to call the church to continuing theological exploration within a context of doctrinal identity.[3]

No textual changes were made from the floor. Trust of the Committee and its work seemed a strong factor. The question was put and the statement was supported by ninety-five percent of the delegates. The church had found a common voice. It was, as one person on the floor said, "A miracle."

It was further moved that new paragraphing be provided to make the document more readable and that the Legislative Committee on Faith and Mission became a standing committee of General Conference so that continuing theological work would be a part of General Conference activity.

An expressed hope was that this statement will allow the church to be more confident about the things it holds in common and more free about what it needs to explore.

Our theological effort continues. The United Methodist Church as a whole is encouraged to study the statement in the Discipline and to participate with a whole heart in theological discussion.

Reflections upon the 1988 Disciplinary Statement

Introduction

The papers in this section represent subsequent reflections upon and evaluations of both the process and the final document as approved by the General Conference. Russell Richey reflects upon the historical nature of our theological self-understanding. Geoffrey Wainwright presents an analysis of the doctrinal statement in the context of his analysis of the General Conference as a whole. Mary Elizabeth Moore provides a critical evaluation of the document approved in 1988 in the light of the 1972 doctrinal statement, with an attempt to evaluate the state of theological reflection in United Methodism. Thomas Langford's first article outlines a careful distinction between doctrine and theology as found in the new statement; the concluding essay provides an agenda for continuing examination of several issues related to the "quadrilateral."

The selections in this section present a sampling of diverse responses to the new doctrinal statement found in Part II of the 1988 Book of Discipline (and the students' pamphlet entitled "Doctrinal Standards and Our Theological Task" published by Graded Press). These essays are representative of some typical United Methodist theological interests. A serious discussion on these and other issues is continuing. We hope that these papers will contribute to that ongoing discussion.

Chapter 15

HISTORY IN THE DISCIPLINE

Russell E. Richey[1]

The Book of Discipline of The United Methodist Church (1988) provides two historical accounts of Methodism, one in the prefatory "Historical Statement," another in the section entitled "Doctrinal Standards and Our Theological Task." One introduces the Discipline as a whole. The other frames the theological statement, the concern of this volume.

Why are they there?
Why do Methodists introduce themselves historically?
Why do they explain their doctrine historically?
What are we to make of this appeal to history?[2]

I shall endeavor to render several answers:

(1) In turning the *Large Minutes* into a Discipline, American Methodists found they needed to begin with a narrative of the movement.

(2) Ever since, American Methodists have prefaced the Discipline with history.

(3) Such a narrative introduction or self-declaration has been and continued to be a Methodist practice, taking a great variety of forms.

(4) The Disciplinary appeal to history, both in 1972 and again in 1988, to frame Methodist doctrine, makes sense against this long-standing "use" of history.

(5) This "use" of history, though immediately plausible when seen in Methodist context, is by no means an obvious or standard prolegomenon, as comparison with the practice of other denominations will show.

(6) By such comparisons, we can see the 1988 theological statement and the longer Methodist Disciplinary appeal to history as a peculiar and important Methodist trait—doing theology with history and expecting theological value from history.

Early Methodist Disciplines

Almost from the beginning, American Methodists have made Disciplinary appeal to history.[3] The first word they have said about themselves has been an historical one. The exceptions to this pattern were the first two Disciplines. That initial version followed in style, substance and order the loosely constructed, question-and-answer document derived from John Wesley's conferences with his preachers, and known as "The Large Minutes."[4] The Discipline began where the Large Minutes began, with the Question "How may we best improve the Time of our Conferences?" It was, even a Methodist might concede, a curious way to begin, a curious introductory statement. So American Methodists found it.

Two years later, in 1787, the church restructured the volume, announcing it to be "Arranged under proper HEADS, and METHODIZED in a more acceptable and easy MANNER." In this new format, the first statement the church made—before it said anything about what it believed, about Scripture, about sacraments, about authority, about polity—was historical. Still honoring Wesley's question-and-answer style, the church asked first, "What was the Rise of Methodism, so called in Europe?"; second, "What was the Rise of Methodism, so called in America?"; and third, "What may we reasonably believe to be God's design in raising up the Preachers called Methodists?"

The answers to these three questions provided a short history of American Methodism. The first two answers sketched the very beginning of Methodism in Britain and America. The third answer, which Americanized Wesley's original formulation, placed a most significant construction on the first two. It was continuously cited and is still cited as the central definition of Methodist purpose. It epitomized Methodism. God's design was

> To reform the Continent, and spread scripture Holiness over these Lands. As a Proof hereof, we have seen in the Course of fifteen Years a great and glorious Work of God, from New York through the Jersies, Pennsylvania, Delaware, Maryland, Virginia, North and South Carolina, even to Georgia.[5]

Thus, the Discipline gathered the entire Methodist movement into Providence, turned mundane into sacred history, conceived of history in redemptive terms. History rendered the work of God. History made a statement of Methodist belief. History said what no other part of the Discipline could quite so directly affirm—God worked through and God works through the Methodists.

Although Methodists do not seem to have drawn out its implications, they carefully preserved both the precise wording and the placement of this formulation. It continued to be their first statement about themselves. Even when they changed the very character of the Discipline, they retained this providential history and its prominent placement.

So when in 1790 they departed from Wesley's question-and-answer format, Bishops Thomas Coke and Francis Asbury recast this historical-providential self-understanding into a prefatory episcopal address. Two years later in further recognition of history's priority, the church added a new section, placed it immediately after the episcopal address, entitled it "Of the Origin of the Methodist Episcopal Church," and brought the account of Methodist beginnings up to 1784.

This historical addition functioned to legitimize the church as an institution, particularly its orders and sacraments. Each statement—the historical episcopal address and the section "Of the Origin of the Methodist Episcopal Address"—amounted to only one page of text.[6] These two pages sufficed. By them, Methodism introduced itself, said what it was, defined itself.

This self-definition proved to be concise and sufficient. So for the rest of the nineteenth century, the church left these formulations intact and in place. History said the first word about Methodism. History sufficed. History declared Methodist meaning and purpose. History functioned appropriately to introduce Methodism's constituting documents. History provided the definition of Methodism, or to be more precise, The Methodist Episcopal Church [MEC].

History Justifies Methodist Division

When the movement fragmented, the new Methodist bodies recognized their divergence from the MEC, but preserved its sense of historical self-identification. They did so in the way that Methodists claim legitimacy. They also began their disciplines with history. So the Disciplines of the various Methodist bodies—the AME Church, the AME Zion Church, the Evangelical Association, the United Brethren in Christ, the Methodist Protestant Church, the Wesleyan Methodist Connection, the Methodist Episcopal Church, South, the Free Methodist Church, and the Colored Methodist Episcopal Church—all feature some sort of historical preface.[7] Each Methodist movement defined itself, introduced itself, by way of an account of how it had come into being. Like the MEC, each focused on beginnings. These later movements were less prone to discern Providence in events connected with their founding, but they clearly recognized the value of history as a self-definition. For them also, the first word had to be historical.

Comparative Polity

A comparison underscores the distinctive character of Methodism's appeal to history. Two sister denominations, the Episcopalians and Presbyterians, make interesting comparative case studies. Both produced constitutions in the 1780s. Both did so, I would argue, with a clearer sense than the Methodists of what goes into a constitution. Presbyterians and Anglicans possessed then and continued to possess a keen sense, even a theology, of polity (though they differ sharply on its nature, source and limits).[8] For them, as for the Methodists, the American Revolution called for new constitutional arrangements: American independence put them in a situation calling for clarity about the nature of authority; their status in the new nation required a new orientation to the British authorities upon which they had depended; they could no longer depend upon the Bishop of London or the Scottish Kirk for legitimacy, the adjudication of disputes, ordination and the like; they needed to make provision for their own authority, and furthermore through a national rather than just a colonial, provincial or state authority structure; hence each required a formal constitution carrying its own warranty of authenticity. Constitutionally, then, their situations resembled that of the Methodists. In the 1780s then, Presbyterians, Anglicans and Methodists shared in a constitutional crisis.

The documents that resulted were entitled *Constitution and Canons for the Government of the Protestant Episcopal Church* and *The Constitution of the Presbyterian Church*. Both have, like the Methodist Discipline, persisted to this day, serving as the root stock for two centuries of growth and successive grafts and pruning.

Neither the Episcopal or Presbyterian constitution, either initially or in later years, made significant appeal to history.[9] Neither introduces itself historically. Neither prefaces polity with narrative. Neither legitimates the new church by recounting its story. That could scarcely constitute an oversight. Both Presbyterian and Anglican traditions are quite self-conscious about the nature and bases of authority. Neither accorded or would accord history such a place of privilege.

The Episcopalians prize tradition. But tradition for them does not mean the recent saga of God's work in their midst. Instead, it means patristics. History is no companion to tradition in the warranting of a constitution. Instead, tradition apparently expresses itself immediately in canon and liturgy. It is apparently unnecessary, perhaps unthinkable, to render an historical account of that which the church has accepted.

Similarly, Presbyterians put too high a premium on Scripture and its perspicuity to suffer any mediation or dilution of its authority. To explain themselves or what they believe historically would be unthinkable. If a warrant be needed for Presbyterian practice, to Scripture and Scripture alone would they look. The Book of Order translates Scripture directly into structure and procedure. Creeds put Scripture into the mouth of the people. Here, too, a historical preface to either Confessions or Order would be unthinkable.

A Methodist Experience

There is something very Methodist, then, about a constitutional appeal to history, an initial historical statement of legitimacy. At any rate, Methodists, children of Providence by their own estimation, turned to history for the frame for their church, the Discipline. Why? Why? Why did Methodists turn to history in this fashion?

It would be too much to argue that these prefaces represent self-conscious exercises in theological prolegomena. I think and am trying to show that they performed that function. But intentionally so? Probably not. Rather, they seem to be more spontaneous, instinctive movements of the Methodist spirit. Methodists seem drawn to tell how it is with their spirit, collective or individual. Such statements take journal, confessional, conversionist, autobiographical, biographical or historical shape. The root form seems to be the conversion narrative, a powerful account that warrants its own authenticity and has the power to induce a similar experience in others. Each of the other accounts is also self-authenticating, but typically less so and with less capacity to induce religious experience. The early Methodist histories clearly betray their origins in these outpourings of the Methodist spirit. At their root, then, lie the conversion narratives, the dramatic encounters with God that must be related as a personal story. The first histories were little more than a string of accounts of conversions and revivals, the gathering of religious experiences into the narrative of God at work, the church's story as conversion writ large.[10] History attests that God works through the Methodists.[11]

Despite their brevity, then the historical prefaces render existence as story, a narrative construction of the Methodist reality. They share the Methodist religious experience. Hence the appropriateness of their placement and their function as introduction. Just as the individual

Methodists formally began their sojourn in the movement by telling their story, by relating their conversion, by recounting God's saving work in their lives, so also Methodism as a movement began by narrating the salvation story—God at work in its midst. The shared individual experience—in class meeting, love feast, quarterly meeting, camp meeting—quite literally constituted the movement. What better way to constitute the movement formally than with the shared corporate experience! An historical or narrative genre of discourse constituted the movement. Appropriately, an historical reflective maneuver shaped the prefaces. It also expressed itself in the writing of Methodist history generally. Methodists paid tremendous attention over the years to historical endeavor. They did so, in part, because of history's power to define the movement. History represents a kind of proto-theology for Methodism, a lay theology, a witness of Methodism to and for itself.

Experience and not the Quadrilateral?

So, although the Methodists were not as self-conscious as the Presbyterians or Episcopalians about how their 'Book' should be constructed, they had, in fact, discovered an appropriate methodological starting point. History belongs at the beginning because the shared religious experience belongs first. The Discipline appeals to experience.

Yet, the lack of self-consciousness about this appeal—the instinctive rather than reflective use of history—would over the long haul prove troubling for at least two reasons, one having to do with other sources of Methodist authority, the second having to do with the capacity of this historical genre to sustain its richer theological and experiential meaning.

First, early and nineteenth century Methodists would have been greatly troubled had it been suggested to them that their appeal to history and experience implied that Scripture did not take first place. Had the framers of these Disciplines been pressed with a query, "Why history and not Scripture," they would doubtless have quickly asserted the primacy of Scripture. Indeed, when Coke and Asbury produced an annotated version of the Discipline in 1798,[12] they made that the primary appeal. And one can find there and indeed in these historical prefaces themselves, the other elements of what we know as the quadrilateral.[13]

To recognize the appropriateness of a historical, and therefore experiential starting point, is not to suggest that Methodists would not have profited from a more self-conscious theological prolegomenon. They would have. It would have been helpful for Methodists to have been more theologically self-conscious in these prefaces.[14] The fact is that early American Methodism could call upon few persons with formal theological training, and its most eminent resource, Bishop Coke, was not regarded as fully committed to the American movement. The church made do with the intellectual leadership it could trust. In retrospect one could argue that it would have been preferable for Methodism and for the Discipline to have had greater theological clarity about the warrant for doctrine and polity.

Second, had the church been more self-conscious about these historical prefaces, it might have chosen to deal with them in a different way in later years, particularly in the twentieth century. The church, as we shall see momentarily, has sustained the genre, the historical preface, but lost the sense of it as mediating the work of God. The form is there. But it no longer evokes the conversion experience, the recounting of God's work amongst us. The preface had lost its ability to bear its richer theological and experiential meaning.

History Justifies Methodist Union

Prior to the 1939 union, the Discipline of the MEC began in a fashion that Bishops Coke and Asbury would have easily recognized. A very short episcopal address was immediately followed by a four page "Historical Statement." That statement spoke of the rise of Methodism so called in Europe and the rise of Methodism so called in America. To be sure, the quaint language of the early disciplines had long since disappeared. But the gist of the early disciplines was there. Quite striking is the fact the account came no farther than 1784. The statement legitimated the church that had been formed that year (i.e. 1784).[15]

The next discipline, that of 1940, had to make sense of a new church, The Methodist Church formed by the union of the Methodist Episcopal Church [MEC], the Methodist Episcopal Church, South [MECS] and the Methodist Protestant Church [MP]. And for that where else would the church turn, but to the "Historical Statement?" The prior MEC statement gave structure and bulk to the text. The MP and MECS contributed two paragraphs each.[16] The resultant account devoted attention primarily to the origins of the three churches but referenced the stages towards union and its consummation.

This continued to be history in the spare, gospel-like mode, nothing more than what was needed to establish the legitimacy of The Methodist Church. So each church contributed a brief sketch of its origin, the origin of the new Methodist Church was added, and the mix constituted the new history. The new history was in the old mode. Why? One would be hard pressed to argue that the appeal to history at this late stage in the church's life partook of the experiential immediacy and instinctiveness of the early prefaces. General Conferences gathered the theologically trained, included the best theological minds of the denomination. Why history first? If the church still believed its history to be providential, it was reluctant in an ecumenical age to be so self-congratulatory. History's placement here doubtless had more to do with precedent than anything else. And yet that very habit is not unimportant. Narrative had become an established pattern for Methodist reflection.

And Union Again

The 1968 union of The Methodist Church and The Evangelical United Brethren required yet another effort at self-definition. Here, too, the new church found no more appropriate a self-declaration than through history. The statement took up the old task afresh. It established the new entity, The United Methodist Church, as in legitimate continuity with its predecessors.[17]

In regards to the 1968 Discipline, three points are in order. First, that Discipline gave almost equal treatment to The Methodist Church and The Evangelical United Brethren Church—four full pages to the former and slightly less than four to the latter. The separate sagas of the MEC, MECS and MP and the earlier union consumed one small paragraph. The distinct history of the United Brethren and of the Evangelical Church each loomed larger than that of the MECS. The 1968 account established the legitimacy of The United Methodist Church; it was no longer burdened with legitimating the prior union of 1939.

Second, this discipline also carried a list of United Methodist Bishops.[18] That, too, functioned to integrate the separate traditions. After Asbury and Coke came Martin Boehm and Philip William Otterbein; after Whatcoat came Jacob Albright; after McKendree came Christian Newcomer. Here, too, the endeavor to legitimate the 1968 union obscured the prior union and the sensibilities of the Methodist Protestants who did not think so highly of bishops.

Third, this Discipline prefaced "Doctrinal Statements and General Rules" with a terse two-page discussion of standards. Its primary function seemed to be to establish the congruence of the Methodist "Articles of Religion" and the EUB "Confession of Faith" (which followed immediately). It did not yet press history into the service that the 1972 Discipline would.

All three sections—Historical Statement, list of bishops and doctrinal preface—seemed to serve the same general purpose. They functioned, as had earlier statements, to confer legitimacy on the new creation, The United Methodist Church.

Thus, for almost two hundred years, from 1787 to 1968, there persisted a rather striking continuity in the Church's appeal to history. The "Historical Statements" conferred legitimacy on the church

(1) by connecting the church of the present with its origins and Mr. Wesley;
(2) by locating its purposes in those that had animated the church from the start; and
(3) by construing Methodism as a design of Providence.

And yet, as we have seen, the last purpose and the theological force of the prefaces collapsed. The form remained but the content eroded. The 1972 Discipline represents a dramatic addition to that tradition. In continuity with the tradition, an important new appeal is made to history. In enrichment of that tradition, it brings to self-consciousness the theological force and value of historical prefaces.

History and Doctrine

The disciplines up to and including that of 1988 retain the historical statement of 1968.[19] In the Disciplines of 1972 and later, there appear also very substantial interpretive sections both before and after the doctrinal statements and general rules. The authoritative "Landmark" documents are sandwiched between a fourteen-page "Historical Background" and a fifteen-page section entitled "Our Theological Task." Here, for the first time really, something akin to the constitutional self-consciousness of the Presbyterians and Episcopalians is at work. After two hundred years of relatively instinctive or habitual appeal to history as the warrant for its Discipline, Methodism gives deliberate attention, but surprisingly also historical attention, and substantial attention to what is constitutive. These sections should be viewed against the backdrop of what has been here described but also assessed as an important new venture for Methodism, an innovation in the tradition of disciplinary historical reflection. That sense of both continuity and innovation is well symbolized in the fact that these Disciplines carry both a "Historical Statement" prefatory to the Discipline as a whole and historical segments which frame the important and long doctrinal section.

The questions initially posed and the issues of concern they raise invite reflection on this venture. For the most part, they apply to the 1972

Discipline as well as that of 1988. It will be most useful to bring them to bear upon the 1988 Discipline, particularly paragraph 66 beginning with "Our Distinctive Heritage as United Methodists" and continuing through paragraph 67. Several points are in order, each of which draws out the implications of the inclusion within the Discipline of an historical treatment of doctrine.

(1) In assessing this section, readers should keep in view its several possible functions and uses, including some that may have not been anticipated by its drafters or General Conference. It may be seen as

(a) An exercise of General Conference's teaching office;
(b) Midrash or commentary on United Methodist texts;
(c) An effort at doctrinal restoration and conservation;
(d) A judicial finding on the Landmark Documents, as though rendered by the Judicial Council;
(e) Instruction in the reception of Methodist teaching;
(f) Constitutional history in the tradition of Buckley, Neely, or Tigert;
(g) An essay on the evolution of Methodist doctrine;
(h) And insofar as it has been written over against the 1972 statement, a revisionist recasting of the history of doctrine.

This section has purely historical utility, as the last three items suggest. But its value extends beyond mere history, as have the prefatory historical statements over the years. History has consistently played an important legitimating role for Methodist polity. Here it is pressed into a similar service for Methodist doctrine. So though this use capitalizes upon an established Methodist habit of mind, its full implications may not be clear.

(2) The reader who compares this 1988 section with that of 1972 version cannot help but be struck by the differences in shape, tone, structure and emphasis of the two. A detailed accounting and evaluation of those differences might better be left to another hand, perhaps to someone closer to the process.[20] However, a comment on change itself would be in order. As the discussion above should indicate, such a pronounced recasting of its historical self-understanding has not been the church's way. On the contrary, Methodism left the historical prefaces largely unaltered until changed circumstances dictated a new account, i.e. after a division or union. Furthermore, change to a narrative explanatory of Methodist doctrine would seem to be of greater moment than change to the historical prefaces. That, after all, was the point of the Restrictive Rules, to inhibit change that touched those things most precious to Methodism. There is at least an irony or incongruity, if not a

problem, in such a thoroughly revised narrative whose purpose is the preservation of Methodist doctrine. Ends and means, intent and vehicle, are mismatched.

(3) Another impression is of the overwhelmingly Wesleyan character of this Methodist history.[21] To be sure, it locates United Methodist teaching within "Our Common Heritage as Christians" and honors the Reformation's contribution, notably in the Anglican Articles (through the MEC) and the Heidelberg Catechism (through the EUB). However, in the decisive transitional section—"Our Distinctive Heritage as United Methodists"—Wesley figures, implicitly or explicitly, in every paragraph. And Wesley's spirit hovers over the remainder of the Methodist discussion and even that of the EUBs. Here, also, the contrast with the prefatory historical statements is instructive. In those, the American developments claim center stage and Wesley figures primarily as a point of departure. The accent falls on the American character of Methodism. In the 1968 prefatory account (for United Methodism), Wesley looms larger than he had in previous prefaces, but even there the combined Methodist and Evangelical United Brethren sagas yield a very American story. So the strongly Wesleyan motif of the doctrinal historical statement contrasts sharply with the more American theme of the prefatory account. One must wonder about the appropriateness of two such variant constructions within the Discipline.

(4) That contrast serves also to underscore the fact that there are less "Wesleyan" ways of construing Methodist doctrinal history. What does the church intend to say by such an exclusively "Wesleyan" interpretation? Furthermore, one can ask whether the heritage should be envisioned as a self-contained Wesleyan stream and whether its theological purity at any point in time should be assessed by its proximity to the source? There are, after all, other historical readings of the development of Methodist doctrine.[22] Should not the Discipline take account of other factors that impinge upon the formation of doctrine and acknowledge alternative ways of construing its development?[23]

(5) The governing metaphor of this account, declension, would strike many historians as suspect and certainly bears scrutiny.[24] The notion of an original Wesleyan purity, its dissipation and the gradual resultant declension of Methodism doubtless serves what such jeremiadic history typically serves, namely, to build a case for reform through recovery. It is a strategy of primitivism, a prophetic call to return to the covenant. This may be exactly the note that the church wishes to sound. Clearly, some within the denomination have struck this note repeatedly. A challenge at this point serves more than as a reminder that this is not the only way of explaining historical and doctrinal change. A challenge is also a

way of asking whether the church really has committed itself to jeremiadic politics and to the dynamics and implications that jeremiads unleash.

(6) The historical discussion clearly evidences Richard Heitzenrater's interpretation of the Restrictive Rules.[25] Such a textual nuance (and the Albert Outlerian tone of the prior Discipline) may be the consequences of employing top-flight Wesley scholars in the drafting process. Drafters will inevitably put their own stamp on the text. Clearly, the church has been blessed by the services of such qualified scholars. Still, there may be some problems in according disciplinary status to what remains a controversial historical argument.[26] In this last question as in those preceding, the premise is that the historical account functions as a claim of the church about itself. As such, then, this is not mere history but in some sense ecclesiology. It may well be that the historical discussion in the doctrinal section will have more value to the church than the documents it purports to introduce. Certainly one could argue that case for the 1972 historical/interpretive statement. Thus the controversy around it. That statement, its affirmation of pluralism and the notion of a quadrilateral, claimed attention as United Methodist belief, so much attention that the present revision was demanded. "Pluralism was made almost creedal. The quadrilateral slighted the unique witness of Scripture." And so on. The interpretation of the doctrinal statements had become the doctrine. And so now the historical/interpretive statement of 1988 may well be read and critiqued as a faith statement. If so, United Methodists will (1) sustain a long tradition of employing history for self-definition; but (2) become far more self-conscious about the doctrinal implications of that appeal.

The History in the Discipline and the Doctrine in that History

This essay first examined the Discipline's historical prefaces. A rather spontaneous effort to introduce the new church, drawing on an established pattern of Methodist narrative reflection, not developed as self-conscious prolegomenon, nor ever mined for its theological implications, the preface nevertheless functioned successfully to locate Methodism in the economy of providence. History made a statement of Methodist belief, belief about God at work, belief about Methodism itself. For Methodist history was sacred history. At least it was so initially. And even as the nineteenth century wore on and historiography became more objective and scientific, the prefatory histories continued to recall that God works in and through the Methodists. Without ever discussing the matter formally, Methodists of various stripes seemed to know that a historical preface appropriately opened their disciplines. So at every point when new forms of Methodism emerged, history served as prolegomenon.

Since 1972, United Methodist Disciplines have also put history to work in introducing the church's doctrine. On the assumption that here, too, the church's act may speak and may, perhaps, say more than the church has self-consciously willed, this essay has endeavored to begin the process of exploring what this new historical statement means. Clearly, the history has been written to explain the doctrine. What, it may be asked, are the doctrinal implications of undertaking such history? Why, in a doctrinal section, would a church, its highest authority and its theologians, appeal to history at all?

Chapter 16

DOCTRINAL AFFIRMATION
AND THEOLOGICAL EXPLORATION

Thomas A. Langford

A distinction between doctrine and theology is explicitly made, and more thoroughly assumed, in the new theological statement.[1] Because this distinction plays such an important role it needs to be further explicated. To this end, I want to look at each of these dimensions of church life and thought.

Doctrine and Theology as Part of the Church's Existence

The attempt to express and explore the Christian faith within the life of the church has a comprehensive character. Within its modes of expression we can distinguish "doctrine" and "theology." As the affirmations of and reflections upon faith are shaped by and shape the living tradition of the church, they find expression in two particular roles: on the one hand, doctrinal statements speak the consensus of the mind of the church at a given time about its faith; on the other hand, theological reflection leads in the exploration of fresh interpretations of faith on the basis of its basic convictions and through the propulsion of its doctrine.

Doctrine and theology comprise faith reflecting upon itself, upon its source, and upon the new life which that source evokes. They represent faith in both its self-affirming and its self-critical stances: doctrine is the faith of the church coming to rational expression, theology is faith reflecting upon its origination, its preservation, and its future. If understood in this way, doctrine and theology are a part of the service of the church which is offered both to God and to the world.

Doctrinal affirmation and theological reflection are essential dimensions of faith insofar as one worships God as a whole person—with mind as well as with affections and actions. They are the rational aspects of human response to God, and these dimensions of response can be denied only at the peril of diminished discipleship. Doctrinal statements and theological explorations, as they affirm and criticize, help to nurture the faithful life of the Christian community. To pursue this matter I want to suggest some understandings and interpretations.

Doctrine reflects the grasp of the church; theology reflects the reach of the church. To use another analogy: doctrine is the part of the cathedral already completed, exploratory theology is creative architectural vision and preliminary drawings for possible new construction.

The relation of doctrine and theology is complex, each requires the other. In our present context, reflection and exploration follow doctrine in the temporal order of the life of the church, yet doctrine can follow from exploration and reflection. Each can give rise to the other as the church lives off of its inheritance and attempts to serve in its present arena. We shall look at each of these dimensions of the life of the Christian community.

Doctrine

Doctrine may be described as the church's grasp, the consensus of the church at a given time. An illustration of doctrine is a creed or the creeds of a given church.

The gospel of God's grace is a far weightier matter than can be made explicit in any statement, however elaborate. Nevertheless, explication is a primary responsibility of the church as it is guided by the Holy Spirit; hence, theological elaboration through doctrinal affirmation is a basic activity of the church. The faith of the church has infinite implications, and the church's continuing theological task is to attempt to explicate some of these implications. But in the end, no doctrinal statements are final, no system is closed.

Doctrine is essential to the church's existence. Without ongoing doctrinal formulation the church ceases to understand itself as a community; it loses corporate agreement and becomes a group of self-contained, self-isolated mystics. Or the church is at the mercy of every individual person with his or her own peculiar conception of things, tentative speculations, even devout fancies. To speak of collective decision on the part of the church does not mean simply taking majority votes; it does mean the consent of the church through conciliar counsel over time under the guidance of the Holy Spirit.

Doctrine is the declaration of the collective understanding of the church expressed in agreed-upon formulations. The church, responsive to the leadership of the Holy Spirit, makes and the church may amend doctrine; but until it is amended by the church a doctrinal statement is the historical property of the church. This points to an unfortunate aspect of United Methodist doctrine, namely, the Articles of Religion have been made nearly irreformable—as a consequence, they tend to lose their place in the formative and maturing life of the church. They do reflect a consensus of the church at a previous time (and may very well do so today), but being made static by constitutional declaration, they do not remain as vital as they should be in the Church's ongoing intellectual growth. But the Articles of Religion are held together with other inheritances which add dynamic possibility. There is the Evangelical United Brethren Confession of Faith, John Wesley's *Sermons* and *Explanatory Notes upon the New Testament*, the classical ecumenical creeds, and the distinctive emphases of the Wesleyan theological tradition. These provide our doctrinal standards. At this point, the Book of Discipline statement of our doctrinal history and our theological task takes on special importance for continuing intellectual vitality in the life of the church.

The development of doctrine is a primary obligation of the church. The church, by its doctrine, protects itself from the fantastic, the erroneous, the superstitious, and the idiosyncratic. Doctrine provides for the well-being of the church, and it is a special privilege of the church to develop its doctrinal standards.

Theology

There is a second dimension of the church's attempt to express its faith—its exploratory work. Theological exploration is doctrine in the making; it is doctrine stretched in new directions. Exploration is theology expressing the church's reach. Before the church can make new corporate confession of doctrines, there must be long periods of theological reflection, of exploration, of speculation, of freedom and maturation. Speculation and reexamination produce tentative doctrine. This is theology as trial and error. Theological exploration is built upon and nurtured by doctrine, but it utilizes its freedom in Christ through the Holy Spirit to critique doctrine and search for new ways of expressing the Christian faith.

Exploratory theology is an authentic expression of the church's life. If the church's life is full and free, its theology will be rich and growing, fresh and freshly invigorating. Doctrine is the corporate property of the church; reflection, criticism, and exploration are usually individual or sectional pursuits. Exploratory theology is always tentative as compared with doctrine. Combining these elements is precarious, but a tradition which does not allow for serious self-criticism and the freedom of exploration atrophies the growth of faith. At the same time, a tradition which does not allow for the corporate dimension of faith in doctrinal fashion atrophies the living foundation of creative community.

Theological reflection and exploration exists for the sake of doctrine. Doctrine produces exploratory theology, but exploration enriches its parent. Blueprints for possible new construction must keep the present structure in mind, but they can add significant new dimensions. Exploration enriches doctrine. The church restricts exploration only at the expense of maturation. United Methodism encourages critical and creative theological reflection and exploration, and this feature is one of its virtues.

Exploratory theology is usually an individual act, but it has its validity as the individual theologian feeds off of and returns his or her thought to the community of the church. Innovative insight lives off of tradition and is a part of tradition, for tradition is kept alive by the innovations of its continuators. Yet, finally, exploration must be considered by the church. New findings may not be accepted; or they may be utilized for further exploration; or they may be affirmed and assimilated by the church as it develops new doctrinal statements.

Conclusion

Doctrine and theology are two significant ways of expressing Christian faith in the life of the church. Only as they are given their proper place does the church live freely. To confuse the roles or the status of these different forms of expression loosens the anchor or truncates the freedom of faith.

Doctrine and theology, we have claimed, are necessary for the church. People will not respond in any profound way to an institution whose message they do not believe and whose proclamation they find irrelevant or nonsensical. Doctrinal affirmation and theological reflection are both necessary to the church in order to renew and replenish its total life.

Doctrine and theology are both crucial to the health and life of the church; their most vibrant expressions are found within the community of faith. Hence the call of our disciplinary statement for the entire Body of Christ—explicitly laity and clergy (the conciliar reality)—to be engaged in the theological task is not merely an act of politeness, not condescension to a lesser order, not a romantic expression of an ideal (but unrealizeable) vision. To call the church to be engaged in theological reflection is to support that which is necessary for the continuing vitality of faith within the church.

Theological reflection and doctrinal affirmation belong in the church. They are the church's offering of its mind—along with its will, its affections, and its service—to God. The task of expressing and exploring faith within the church is not a simple, straightforward enterprise; it is a complex, multilayered interaction of doctrine and theology. The community of faith, must be theologically engaged in order to nourish its life and mission.

Chapter 17

THE STYLE AND SUBSTANCE OF UNITED METHODIST THEOLOGY IN TRANSITION

Mary Elizabeth Moore[1]

How do United Methodists do theology? Our denomination's style is a little like riding a mule down into the Grand Canyon. A few years ago, my daughter and I made our first mule journey into the canyon, fulfilling a dream that I had held for more than twenty years. We had made an effort a few years earlier, but the rides were already booked. When we arrived at the Grand Canyon this particular year, we learned that visitors could put their names on a waiting list in case of last minute cancellations. We gathered the necessary information on the run; we registered, gathered the recommended supplies, and arose very early to wait by the mule stalls. Sure enough, our names were called, and we were soon on our way.

As we rode down the steep canyon trail, I looked over the chasm and wondered whose idea this had been anyway. Unfortunately, it was too late to turn back. Our situation looked something like this. My mule was an edge-walker, moving along the border of the steep trail. We had a guide in the front of us, but he was far away. We also had a guide at the end of the line, but he was taking a new mule down for the first time. Before we reached our destination, this guide's mule charged the other mules four times, and when we finally reached the level land below, she threw the guide onto a prickly pear cactus and ran away. The guide stood, trembling, visibly, and when he and his partner finally did round up the wandering mule many minutes later, he begged the more seasoned guide to trade mules. The seasoned guide insisted that the wary young man stay with his nervous mule friend because it would be good for both of them.

In the meantime, I was making friends with Frog (my jumping mule) and with the other people in the group. And I was pondering the vastness of God's world, the indescribable beauty of the moment, my own fears, and the craziness of sending this new mule down with greenhorns like us. I felt daring and grateful to be so close to the wonders of millions of years and the awesome movements that had made the Grand Canyon.

This, I believe, is the way that United Methodists do theology—on the run! United Methodists dream of ideas which would be good for the church, ideas for action or belief or structures. The denomination then makes some efforts to put the ideas into practice. Often the efforts are not effective because they are begun too late to win the church's support and get the vote. Sometimes the church leaders intensify and rush the efforts when the conditions seem right. Frequently, the efforts do finally succeed.

Then when the new ideas are being implemented, the church begins to think about what it has done, sometimes wondering, "Whose idea was this anyway?" But, by that time, it is too late to turn back. The situation is like this. The church folk are walking down the edge of a steep path with an even steeper drop-off two inches from their feet. The guide, if there is one, is in the front, far away. The guide in the rear of the line is taking a new mule down for the first time. This person is no help as a guide, and furthermore, has no idea how to deal with the movement. The rear guide is actually a threat to everyone because he or she keeps charging ahead and starting an avalanche of uncontrolled movement. This frightens everyone, even allowing the movement to run away at times.

In the meantime, the United Methodist folk are making friends with one another as they journey. They are pondering the vastness of God's world, the indescribable beauty of the moment, their own fears, and the craziness of this new movement. They feel daring and grateful to be so close to the wonders of life and the historical movements that have led them to this place.

The metaphor of mule-riding calls attention to certain features of the United Methodist practices of theological reflection. First, *theology is continually being done*. It is usually done while the church is moving, rather than before a movement begins. One vivid example is the 1972 doctrinal statement, which was written as an outgrowth of the 1968 merger between the former Methodist and Evangelical United Brethren Churches. Another example in recent history is the extensive number of theological studies on ministry which have followed the 1976 decision by the General Conference to introduce diaconal ministry into the church's ministerial structures. Four theological study commissions (one each quadrennium) have been named since that time, and the number of pages discussing the theology of ministry has multiplied in all ministry sections of the Book of Discipline every quadrennium since.

Another feature of United Methodist theological practice is that *theology is sometimes motivated by wonder, sometimes by fear, and sometimes by the need to analyze the craziness of the present situation.* An analysis of the roots of the 1988 doctrinal statement reveals these various motivations. The 1984 General Conference mandated the Council of Bishops to appoint a committee to write a new theological statement to be presented at the 1988 General Conference. The motivation was a mixture of wonder-filled hope that the United Methodist denomination would give serious attention to its theology, fear of pluralism, and a need to analyze existing theological currents, however differently they were named and argued by different factions within the denomination.

A third feature of the United Methodist approach to theological reflection is that *theology filled with moments of celebration when the people stop to express gratitude for living on the cutting edge and daring to walk down the precipice, moving so close to the wonders of life.* Last year we witnessed this celebration as delegates returned from General Conference pleased that the theological and mission statements adopted represented a compromise that satisfied everyone on some points. A pastor who had supported the Houston Declaration and its attempt to preserve certain traditional doctrines and language wrote to his parishioners after General Conference, saying that they would be pleased to know that conservative Christian principles had not been compromised in the new statements. A pastor who had been an open critic of the Houston Declaration said to his parishioners that the discussions and revisions of the statements were open and conciliatory and the statements themselves were good; he was proud of them. There was celebration not only for the statements, but for the conciliar process that led to their adoption.

Marks of United Methodist Theology

The metaphor of the mule ride may be playful, but the theological enterprise should be taken very seriously. United Methodist theology can be identified by marks that continually appear in the church's theological reflection, quadrennium after quadrennium.

The first mark of United Methodist theology is that it is *practical.* I mention this again because practicality is an enduring part of the style of United Methodist theology. The 1988 General Conference adopted a new ¶ 66 for the Book of Discipline entitled "Our Doctrinal Heritage." Its prologue emphasizes the practical divinity of John Wesley: "The underlying energy of the Wesley theological heritage stems from an emphasis upon practical divinity, the implementation of genuine Christianity in the lives of believers."[2] The characteristic Wesleyan doctrines actually grew from these concerns for practical divinity, for Wesley "considered doctrinal matters primarily in terms of their significance for Christian discipleship."[3] Both the life of the individual Christian and the organization of the church were concerns that affected theological formulations, and these formulations in turn influenced Christian living and church polity. The relationship was interactive.

A second mark of United Methodist theology is *discipline*. Theology is done in a disciplined manner for the sake of discipline; that is, to order life toward the fullness of salvation. The discipline includes an organization for doing theology. In eighteenth-century Britain the organization was based largely in the Methodist societies, and it was based in similar societies in the United Brethren Church and Evangelical Association. All of these societies were designed to edify believers and spread scriptural holiness. Discipline can be observed in the church of today, in that local churches, annual conferences, and general boards and agencies are clearly organized and mandated to foster theological proclamation and teaching. The roles of each are put forth in the Book of Discipline.

By definition, the work of the church takes place under the discipline of the Holy Spirit. The Preamble of the Constitution states: "Under the discipline of the Holy Spirit the Church seeks to provide for the maintenance of worship, the edification of believers, and the redemption of the world."[4] The theme of discipline applies not only to organizational structures, but also to guidance from the Holy Spirit for the whole theological enterprise.

The third mark of United Methodist theology is a tension between *fluidity and constancy*. This is a factor in all formal theological discussions in the denomination, including the discussions that produced the 1988 theological statement entitled "Doctrinal Standards and Our Theological Task." This theme hearkens back to John Wesley himself, who read and reproduced historical treatises widely, but who also critiqued and offered alternatives to historical positions. Wesley maintained the Anglican Articles of Religion for his movement but he made some changes and selections from them.

The United Methodist Church has frequently debated the issue of fluidity and constancy in relation to the first Restrictive Rule in The Constitution: "The General Conference shall not revoke, alter, or change our Articles of Religion or establish any new standards or rules of doctrine contrary to our present existing and established standards of doctrine."[5] This rule led to considerable discussion as to whether the Confession of Faith of the Evangelical United Brethren could be placed side-by-side with the Articles of Religion after the merger in 1968. The theological statement that was adopted by the denomination in 1972 included both doctrinal statements, and it spoke forthrightly about the desire of the denomination to avoid giving final authority to any doctrinal statement. Furthermore, the 1972 document stated that the first two Restrictive Rules are not to be interpreted literally, but that the people are encouraged to "free inquiry within the boundaries defined by four main sources and guidelines for Christian theology: Scripture, tradition, experience, reason."[6] Fluidity and constancy have been a source of contention in the denomination, as well as a clear mark of the United Methodist style of theology.

A fourth mark of United Methodist theology is *connection*. The importance of connection to the organization of the church is obvious. The emphasis on connection goes back to the early roots of the Methodist movement. John Wesley established circuits for the sake of itinerating preachers and implementing ministry across all of the local churches. He established societies, classes, and bands as structures of inspiration, nurture, and accountability. Furthermore, the theological work in the early Methodist movement was done in the connection, primarily in the Conference. The minutes of early Wesleyan conferences are filled with theological discourse, especially Wesley's presentation of answers to frequently asked questions. After the time of Wesley, the theological discourse continued in Conference and other connectional settings, but without such reliance on one central person.

This process of communal theologizing within the connection has been referred to as a conciliar process. In the 1972 theological statement, the pioneers of the United Methodist traditions are described as operating by a conciliar rather than a confessional principle. Thus, they did not function from a "claim that the essence of Christian truth can, and ought to be, stated in precisely defined propositions, legally enforceable by ecclesiastical authority."[7] These early leaders "turned to a unique version of the ancient 'conciliar principle,' in which the collective wisdom of living Christian pastors, teachers, and people was relied upon to guard and guide their ongoing communal life."[8]

References to the communal process do indeed carry over into the 1988 theological statement. It affirms that "our theological task is communal," including all United Methodist constituencies, every congregation, laity and clergy, bishops, boards, agencies, and theological schools.[9] In practice, the doctrinal guidelines are sponsored and adopted by the connection in General Conference, and doctrinal disputes are referred to Annual and General Conferences. The question of the status and function of doctrinal standards has been left somewhat ambiguous, but the answer presented in the 1972 theological statement is that "for the determination of otherwise irreconcilable doctrinal disputes, the Annual and General Conferences are the appropriate courts of appeal, under the guidance of the first two Restrictive Rules (which is to say, the Articles and Confession, the *Sermons* and the *Notes*)."[10]

A fifth mark of United Methodist theological discourse is *breadth*. The theological reflections of the church have been far-reaching and inclusive of many different kinds of concerns. Considerable attention has been given to theological method by the denomination; this emphasis is represented most vividly in the 1972 and 1988 theological statements in which the guidelines (1972) or criteria (1988) for theological reflection are put forth. These are Scripture, tradition, experience, and reason, all of which serve both as source for and as guide to theological deliberation.[11] Besides theological method, theological reflection has also attended to historical doctrines, rules for disciplined living, and principles for social responsibility. These are evidenced in minutes of Annual and General Conferences, in Parts II and III of the Book of Discipline (dealing with doctrine and social principles), and in the newly adopted study document, "The Mission of The United Methodist Church."

The final mark of United Methodist theology to be mentioned here, though this list is by no means exhaustive, is the *universally-minded* nature of the denomination's theological reflections. John Wesley was himself concerned with the whole globe in the sense that he wanted to spread scriptural holiness as broadly as possible, stating at one point that "the world is my parish." Wesley also drew broadly from resources of the larger Christian tradition, including Orthodox, Roman Catholic, Moravian and other sources present in his Anglican and pietistic British background. In addition, Wesley was always aware of the broad social context and social mission of the church, speaking and writing eloquently on the concerns of British miners and on slavery in Britain and other parts of the world. Wesley was also concerned with church unity, the most profound example of which his insistence on keeping the early Methodist movement within the Anglican Church. Such a spirit of opening to the larger world and joining with other Christians has persisted in the various Methodist traditions. The early cooperation and eventual merger among the Methodist, United Brethren, and Evangelical Association communions is one such example.

This universal orientation is still evidenced in the life and documents of The United Methodist Church. The Preamble of the Constitution includes these words: "The Church of Jesus Christ exists in and for the world, and its very dividedness is a hindrance to its mission in that world."[12] The theological statements of 1972 and 1988 affirm the richness of the whole Christian tradition and the importance of the whole tradition to the theological task of The United Methodist Church. Similarly, both affirm the theological contributions that come from various cultures and communities around the globe. The denomination has been more ambiguous about relating with other religious traditions, but both of the recent theological statements call for explorations and understanding of other traditions.

This introduction to the practices and marks of United Methodist theology will provide background for analyzing the most recent theological movements in the denomination.

Formation of the 1988 Theological Statement

Lively theological discussions have characterized the 1980s. The 1984 General Conference acted to recommend three new study commissions for The United Methodist Church. Their respective tasks were to prepare a revision of the 1972 theological statement, to create a new statement on the mission of the church, and to study ministry. All were to be appointed by the Council of Bishops and were to offer guidance to the church. The commissions included laity and clergy, theological scholars and bishops, women and men, and persons of different ethnic communities. The theological commission was specifically asked to consider the problems of pluralism and doctrinal identity in the denomination.

I will focus here on the work of the theological commission. The commission's work took place in a context of considerable ecumenical reflection on theology. The Faith and Order Commission of the World Council of Churches of Christ has been working to define and describe apostolic faith, a term that has found its way into the United Methodist theological statement. The Faith and Order Commission has centered on as a summary of apostolic faith, the Nicene-Constantinopolitan Creed, the last official creed of the church before it divided between east and west. Faith and Order has described this creed as a test of the faith expressions of later Christian bodies. Ecumenical statements and United Methodist theological constructions share the effort to base theological norms on the early church.

We should also note the considerable theological diversity within the United Methodist denomination in the 1970s and 1980s. Several groups have formed to express their theological convictions and to influence the directions of the church. The largest on-going group is the Good News. The largest special group called together to influence General Conference decisions was the group that produced the "Houston Declaration." Other groups also formed, however, and produced statements before the 1988 General Conference, such as the "Chicago Declaration" and "Perfect Love Casts Out Fear." These diverse groups within the church probably influenced the shape of the theological document that was produced, revised, and finally adopted.

The earliest drafts of the theological statement were not discussed widely in the general church, and no mechanism for broad-based discussion was implemented. The drafts did undergo considerable discussion and revision within the commission, however, in dialogue with the Council of Bishops and in a joint meeting with the mission commission. Later drafts were also discussed in the Oxford Institute of Methodist Studies and with several leaders of general boards and agencies and theological schools. Considerable communication was addressed to the commission through informal networks, and considerable debate took place regarding the statements in such public church arenas as *Circuit Rider* and *The Christian Century*. The commission took the responses very seriously and did revisions until the final deadlines.

Then the documents were circulated to General Conference delegates, who began to discuss them in their respective delegations. The discussions were again very active, resulting in further response through formal and informal channels. These responses contributed to further revisions by the legislative committee on Faith and Mission during the General Conference deliberations. The process of the committee was described as collegial and frank, leading to a growing consensus. The document that was finally presented to the General Conference received ninety-four percent concurrence.[13]

The theological document underwent considerable revision from the first drafting to the last. The revisions included: a greater emphasis on the interaction among Scripture, tradition, experience, and reason and the possibility that theological reflection may begin in any of the four; a modification of normative language; an expansion of the meanings of experience and reason to include the breadth of human experience and reason (rather than experience and reason related only to the biblical witness); and an expanded statement of the church's ecumenical and interfaith commitments. Such revisions obviated some of the sharp differences between the 1972 and 1988 theological statements without obliterating them. The revisions reflected a dynamic process of dialogue in the denomination, not necessarily pre-planned to continue the communal and conciliar processes described above, but certainly reflecting that those processes are alive and well.

Theological Shifts from 1972 to 1988

A comparative study of the theological statements of 1972 and 1988 reveals many continuities. The continuities are considerably greater with the final version of the 1988 document than with the earlier versions. In fact, some language from the 1972 statement was reintroduced into the new statement. My focus, however, will be on what I think are potentially the most influential changes made in the new statement.

The first and most profound shift in the 1988 theological statement is the *move to be more normative in the approach to doctrine.* This appears even in the new title of Part II in the Book of Discipline; the title is changed from "Doctrine, Doctrinal Statements, and the General Rules" to "Doctrinal Standards and Our Theological Task." The language of standards, criteria, and validity dominates the new theological statement, whereas the language of guidelines held sway in the earlier one.

The 1972 statement acknowledged more theological diversity and the dynamic of critique within the Christian tradition itself. One example of this is the 1988 statement's introduction to the heritage that United Methodists share with Christians of all times and places: "This heritage is grounded in the apostolic witness to Jesus Christ as Savior and Lord, which is the source and measure of all valid Christian teaching."[14] The earlier statement read, instead: "There is a core of doctrine which informs in greater or less degree our widely divergent interpretations. From our response in faith to the wondrous mystery of God's love in Jesus Christ as recorded in Scripture, all valid Christian doctrine is born. This is the touchstone by which all Christian teaching may be tested."[15] This is one of the few places where the word valid is used in the earlier statement, and it refers back to "our response in faith," leaving room for divergent interpretations and appealing to scriptural and doctrinal guidelines for testing interpretations. The new statement not only eliminates the rejoinder about different interpretations, it refers to the apostolic witness as "the source and measure of all valid Christian teaching."

This, of course, is only one example of the shift toward a normative status of doctrine, and it is subtle. Several other examples exist, but these will only be summarized here. One example is the removal of language recognizing and affirming pluralism.[16] The word pluralism is not used at all in the new document, and the word diversity is used sparingly. Scripture is now the primary source and *criterion* for doctrine, rather than the primary source and guideline.[17] Finally, the new document gives a more normative interpretation to the work of our theological forebears by concentrating on the history of doctrinal authority. The earlier statement maintained instead that our forebears followed a conciliar principle rather than a confessional principle.[18] Also, the earlier statement gave far less attention to the status of doctrine in general.

The degree of this shift to normativity can be overemphasized, however. In its final version, the new statement does recognize theological diversity and the critical and communal nature of the theological enterprise. In fact the theological task is described in one section as critical, constructive, conciliar, and a matter of individual responsibility, reminding the reader that the Christian truth is not a complete and unequivocal given.

One might say that the two statements were written to answer very different questions. In the 1972 statement, the dominant question seemed to be, "How do we do theology faithfully in the context of a rich tradition and a pluralistic church and world?" In the 1988 statement, the dominant question seems to be, "How do we do theology that clearly defines our Christian identity in relationship to our doctrinal tradition, and offers standards for judging the adequacy of theological formulations?"

The second shift in the new theological statement is *an appeal to history for answers to questions of faith.*[19] The expansion of the historical material is the most vivid evidence of this trend. Another example of the shift is the frequent appeal to the Wesleyan heritage as the rationale for a particular belief or practice. The frequent appeals to Wesley and other forebears are somewhat ironic in that more weight is being placed on tradition (even appealing to it as a starting point) than the description of tradition in the statement would warrant.

A third shift relates to the first two, namely, that *the theological method moves from a critical and constructive theology to an applied theology.* Both the normative status given to doctrine and the dominant appeal to history for answers to questions of faith suggest a theological method that is less critical of the tradition itself, less constructive in response to new revelation, and less open to new interpretations in light of faith experience in the contemporary world. Appeals to the conciliar principle, flexibility, doctrinal development, loyalty and freedom, pilgrim people, and non-literalism have been removed from the earlier statement.[20] Both fluidity and mystery are deemphasized. The history of practice is elaborated much less than the history of doctrine.

Again, the differences are subtle, but they are real. For example, the new statement reveals a fluid perspective on the Wesleyan tradition: "The heart of our task is to reclaim and renew the distinctive United Methodist doctrinal heritage."[21] The statement also has a fluid perspective on the theological task: "Our theological task includes the testing, renewal, elaboration, and application of our doctrinal perspective in carrying out our calling 'to spread scriptural holiness over these lands.'"[22] Such statements do not call for theological rigidity, but the tone is different from the 1972 statement which addressed the "pressing need of renewed effort both to repossess our legacy from the churches we have been and to re-mint this for the church we aspire to be."[23]

A fourth change in the 1988 document is closely connected to the different perspectives on theological method. This is the *shift in the approach to Scripture in relation to tradition, experience, and reason*. Both documents affirm the primacy of Scripture, but the relationship between Scripture and the other sources is shifted in the new document. In earlier drafts of the 1988 document, a complete organizational and descriptive separation of Scripture was offered. This is greatly modified in the final 1988 document, but the Bible is still separated from tradition, experience, and reason in much of the language. One example is found in the description of Scripture in relation to the rest of the quadrilateral: "The Wesleyan heritage . . . directs us to a self-conscious use of these three sources in interpreting Scripture and in formulating faith statements based on the biblical witness."[24]

Another example is the tendency to relativize tradition, but not Scripture: "But the history of Christianity includes a mixture of ignorance, misguided zeal, and sin. Scripture remains the norm by which all traditions are judged."[25] Such statements about Scripture and tradition separate them in a way that moves counter to the recent work in the World Council of Churches of Christ, which affirmed the unity of Scripture and tradition. It also runs counter to much recent biblical criticism which recognizes the ignorance and misguided zeal that often helped shape the biblical witness as well.

Furthermore, the 1988 theological statement clearly describes tradition, experience, and reason as subservient to Scripture, in that each is described largely in relation to Scripture, with frequent reference to scriptural truth and norms.[26] Despite the examples given here, the picture is somewhat ambiguous because some credence *is* given in the 1988 statement to the mediation of God's grace that is possible through all four elements of the quadrilateral. Perhaps the best summary of the position of the document is found in the conclusion of the section on doctrinal guidelines:

> In theological reflection, the resources of tradition, experience, and reason are integral to our study of Scripture without displacing its primacy for faith and practice. These four sources—making distinctive contributions, yet all finally working together—guide our quest as United Methodists for a vital and appropriate Christian witness.[27]

A fifth shift between the 1972 and 1988 theological statements is the *shift toward Christocentrism*. Less attention is given to the triune God, and more to God revealed in Christ. The frequent references to Jesus Christ, as well as some subtle changes of wording, are evidence of this shift. For example, the 1972 statement describes the complex texture of the biblical witness as "memories, images, and hopes." In the 1988 statements, the biblical witness is that which reveals Jesus Christ, or the way by which "the living Christ meets us" and we "are convinced that Jesus Christ is the living Word of God."[28]

Another subtle change is in both documents' concluding words discussing the purpose of the theological task. The 1972 statement spoke of the task "to understand our faith in God's love, *known* in Jesus Christ," whereas the 1988 statement speaks of the task "to understand the love of God *given* in Jesus Christ" (italics mine).[29] The subtle difference between the words "known" and "given" suggests a shift to the idea that God is revealed *only* in Jesus Christ. Although the new statement does not deny other forms of revelation, it deemphasizes these considerably. Such a shift has considerable implications for the Christian relationship with other religious traditions, particularly Judaism.

A sixth shift with the 1988 theological statement is a *self-conscious attempt to be more holistic in the approach to theology*. Examples abound. The document speaks of both personal and corporate experience, love of God and neighbor, the critical and constructive roles of theology, the individual and communal dimensions of the task, the multiplicity of traditions, the concern of theology with the poor and oppressed and with justice and peace.[30] These accents are not missing from the 1972 statement, but they are not featured so vividly.

The 1988 document does sometimes contradict such thinking, however. The most obvious example is the tendency to affirm insights from the multiplicity of traditions on the one hand, but to relativize them greatly in relation to scriptural norms on the other. In fact, some of the critical insights that have emerged from feminist and liberation traditions have been ignored in the formulation of the document, particularly the insights regarding scriptural interpretation and critique. The contradictions, however, do not take away the power of the holistic thinking in the new document.

The 1988 theological statement represents another *shift toward slightly less emphasis on ecumenical and interfaith commitments*. More attention is given to John Wesley and other pioneers of the United Methodist movement, and a particular accent is placed on sharing *our* heritage in the ecumenical arena. Less emphasis is given to the ferment that comes from the ecumenical arena into United Methodism or to the critiques and challenges that come from the search for unity. The 1972 statement spoke of tough decisions that are required in the quest for agreement, decisions whether "something truly essential is in jeopardy, something belonging not only to our own heritage but to the Christian tradition at large."[31]

Even more evident is a shift in the understanding of interfaith commitments. The 1988 statement includes the idea that God is "the Creator of all humankind," but no longer includes the idea that "God has been and is now working among all people."[32] The idea that God is actually working within non-Christian peoples has been eliminated. Likewise, the idea has been removed that people of different traditions need to work with God and one another for the "salvation, health, healing, and peace" of the planet.[33] The interfaith work described, instead, is "to be both neighbors and witnesses to all peoples."[34] These alterations should be pointed out, despite the strong overall similarities in the documents regarding ecumenical and interfaith attitudes.

Finally, there is a *shift away from acknowledging problems and critiques that emerge in theological dialogue.* The impetus to reflect critically on the faith tradition and to respond to contradictions is not featured. But problems often do emerge in interpreting Scripture, adjudicating contradictions among the four sources of the quadrilateral, responding to critiques that come from the multiplicity of traditions, responding to the challenges of persons from different cultural and gender communities, and dealing with issues that surface in ecumenical and interfaith dialogue.

One particular example of the shift to deemphasize such problems is found in the description of the Bible in the 1988 theological statement; the Bible is said to express "the fundamental unity of God's revelation as received and experienced by people in the diversity of their own lives."[35] This statement of unity is made without acknowledging the major tensions and debates within the canon itself, as well as in the interpretations of the canon. Perhaps the 1988 statement presents a simpler picture of our theological task than is possible if we are to take seriously the challenges that are before us.

And so, The United Methodist Church has a new statement for theological reflection, continuing the tradition that *United Methodist people are continually doing theology.* One can even argue that the document is *practical,* arising in response to practical issues. Certainly, two issues influencing the statement were the conflicts that had emerged from differences in the church, together with the Christian struggle for identity in a rapidly changing and pluralistic world. The statement also continues the United Methodist tradition of *discipline,* rising out of the organizational structures of the church and offering a disciplined statement to guide the church. It represents both the *fluidity and constancy* of the United Methodist theological tradition, although the document itself appeals more to constancy. The statement represents the *connection*. It was commissioned by General Conference, appointed by the Council of Bishops, written by a committee, responded to by numerous groups within the church, reformed by legislative committee, and adopted by General Conference. The process of communal theologizing seems to be alive and well. And finally, the move toward holism reinforces the *breadth and universal-mindedness* of the denomination's theology. The question now is where do the United Methodist traditions and the recent developments in those traditions lead the church in its future theological reflection?

The Future of Theological Reflection in United Methodist Tradition

The future awaits us, but many questions remain to be answered. How will we respond to the new theological statement—as a fixed statement of United Methodist doctrine or as a dynamic statement of the church's faith and practice? Will we attend only to the words of the statement or also to the process that gave it birth? What challenges arise before us?

One set of challenges comes from the practices of theological reflection within the United Methodist tradition. Though theological reflection may seem less dramatic than riding a mule into the Grand Canyon, it is no less adventuresome or frightening. The first challenge is to *do theology continually even while the church is moving*. This is the challenge to continue to reflect theologically on issues even after decisions are made. It is the challenge to see theology as a dynamic movement which is never finished, but belongs to all times and places of the church. The second challenge that comes from the tradition of theological practice is to *welcome various motivations for doing theology and for teaching*. The motivations may be wonder or fear or frustration, but all are occasions for thinking seriously about our faith. In fact, the ambiguities of diversity and the search for identity will continue to be important motivations for doing theology. Listening to minority voices will also be important. The third challenge is to *recognize that celebration is part of the process*. Creating opportunities for genuine celebration is an important part of the theological enterprise.

The new theological statement, taken alone, supports a transmissive mode of theological reflection grounded in doctrine and biblical interpretation. Critical reflection and reformation of the tradition would be limited, as would be theological reflection on the contemporary world itself. Less attention would be given to the pilgrimage quality of Christian life, and more to the quest for truth and its application. Less passion would be invested in ecumenical and interfaith relationships, and more would be invested in the United Methodist Christian identity. A strong Christian identity would be passed on, respecting differences but trying to avoid the possibility that these differences might lead to radical transformation of the identity itself.

The same document, when seen within the communal and dynamic contexts in which it was formed, can reinforce and enlarge on the marks of United Methodist theology. It reminds us that United Methodists need to seek ways to understand and proclaim their faith and to find their identity in the midst of a rapidly changing and pluralistic world. It also reminds us of the many resources that guide us in that faith, resources that we can offer to the larger church and to the world. It reminds us of the diversity inside the Christian tradition and the possibility of seeking unity in diversity. It reminds us of the multiplicity of traditions which can contribute to our fullness and enrich our unity.

These various reminders could lead to Christian exclusiveness, historical literalism, denial of diversity, and refusal to take seriously those people who raise radical critiques of the emerging consensus. On the other hand, these reminders can enrich our theological reflection to be more self-conscious of who we are, more aware of the dynamic quality of any theological statement, more humble and open in relation to our own theological affirmations, and more eager to participate in the ongoing formulation and reformulation of our theological task. As we look back on our theological witness, we can genuinely celebrate, and we can move from that witness into the future.

Chapter 18

From Pluralism Towards Catholicity? The United Methodist Church After the General Conference of 1988

Geoffrey Wainwright[1]

The United Methodist Church is the most widespread Protestant denomination in the United States. It is also perhaps the most accommodating. Statistically, it is in decline, both in absolute membership figures and as a proportion of the population. While the flexibility of Methodism helped it to grow, overstretching appears to have led to such a loss of contour that there no longer exists a sufficiently coherent identity to attract and retain many new adherents. In recent decades, "inclusivism" and "pluralism" have become formal ideological substitutes for a true catholicity which is always both substantive and qualitative. At the General Conference of 1988, there were a few signs —no bigger maybe than a man's hand—that the Church is coming to that awareness of its own predicament which is the human precondition for acceptance of a divine renewal.

It is a matter of the faith, which comes to expression in the teaching of a church and its worship. The two most important documents before the General Conference in St. Louis were therefore the Report of the Hymnal Revision Committee and the Report from the Committee on Our Theological Task. That the proposal of a new hymnbook should have aroused popular interest is no surprise, for the Christian people have always maintained at least a lingering sense that the liturgy is the place where the faith is signified. Less expected, given the reputation and modern self-understanding of Methodism, was the attention shown before and at the Conference to the revision of the statement on doctrine and theology in the Book of Discipline of The United Methodist Church. In both matters, this represented not only formally but (as we shall see) substantially, something of a return to Methodist origins. The early Methodist Conferences of Mr. Wesley with his preachers were much occupied with "what to teach." And Methodism "was born in song"; John Wesley considered that his definitive *Collection of Hymns for the Use of the People called Methodists* of 1780 contained "all the important truths of our most holy religion, whether speculative or practical . . . a distinct and full account of Scriptural Christianity."[2] We need perhaps to see what happened in the intervening years in order to make a recovery of identity desirable.

Liberal Methodists like to cite Wesley's dictum that "we think and let think." They forget that this magnanimity was confined to "opinions which do not strike at the root of Christianity."[3] Wesley distinguished between opinions and *doctrines*. The doctrines *essential* to Christianity included "the Three-One God," the deity and redeeming work of Christ, original sin, repentance, justification by faith, and sanctification. When, in his *Letter to a Roman Catholic* of 1749, Wesley set out "the faith of a true Protestant," he followed the Nicene Creed for its content ("the faith which is believed"), and he showed the attitude and act of faith ("the faith which believes") to consist in trust and obedience towards the God who is so confessed. In his generous sermon "Catholic Spirit" (on the text, "If thy heart is right with my heart, give me thy hand") Wesley made clear, as in other writings, that Deists, Arians, and Socinians did not meet the conditions. Wesley explicitly rejected "latitudinarianism," whether of a doctrinal or a practical kind. How, then, did Methodism fall into the indifferentism which has increasingly marked its later history?

Robert E. Chiles offered a perceptive interpretation in *Theological Transition in American Methodism 1790–1935*.[4] He traced a shift "from revelation to reason," "from sinful man to moral man," "from free grace to free will." I would put it briefly this way: What had been secondary poles in a Wesleyan ellipse—"reason," "the moral character," "free will"—took over from the primary poles, in subordinate relation to which alone they find their proper place in a Christian understanding of the human condition and divine salvation—"revelation," "the sinful condition," "free grace." Methodism thus both helped to shape and, even more important, allowed itself to be shaped by an American culture that was already subject to the strong humanistic influences of an (at best deistic) Enlightenment. The distinctive Christian message was being lost.

Constitutionally, Methodism retained as its "doctrinal standards" the first four volumes of Wesley's Sermons, his *Explanatory Notes Upon the New Testament*, and the Twenty-Five Articles of Religion adapted from the Anglican Thirty-Nine. At the union of the Methodist Episcopal Church and the Evangelical United Brethren in 1968, the Confession of Faith of the latter and the Wesleyan standards were judged "congruent" within the new United Methodist Church. Methodist academic and bureaucratic theology, however, had come to bear a more and more tenuous relation to the official standards. Prompted in part by the self-examination that the 1968 union had made necessary, the Church undertook to clarify the continuing status and function of its doctrinal standards as well as what was to be expected of theology.

Following the work of the Study Commission on Doctrine and Doctrinal Standards, the result is seen in ¶¶ 68–70 of the 1972 Book of Discipline. First, the "historical background" of the official standards is described, with an admission of "the fading force of doctrinal discipline": "By the end of the nineteenth century, and thereafter increasingly in the twentieth, Methodist theology had become decidedly eclectic, with less and less specific attention paid to its Wesleyan sources as such."[5] Then the "landmark documents" were laid out. Finally, "our theological task" was set forth. It was this third section which became, in the 1980s, the object of most controversy.

The 1972 text spoke of "four main sources and guidelines for Christian theology: Scripture, tradition, experience, reason." Although the term is not used there, these four became known (fleetingly, one hopes) as the "Methodist" or "Wesleyan Quadrilateral." Scripture is said to be "primary," and the functions of the four are differentiated: there is a "living core" of "Christian truth" which—the 1972 text apparently wishes to affirm in continuity with the United Methodist "pioneers"—"stands revealed in Scripture, illumined by tradition, vivified in personal experience, and confirmed by reason." But there is such a stress of the "interdependence" and "interaction" of the four that—as the popular image of the quadrilateral both expresses and encourages—they have been perceived as placed by the 1972 text all four on an equal footing.

There arose from the "evangelicals," but not from them alone, a call for a clearer recognition of the normativity of Scripture. Thus the fifty pastors—by no means all conservatives but rather most of them traditional Methodists—who in December 1987 issued the Houston Declaration, spoke of "the confusion and conflict resulting from the ambiguity of the present doctrinal statement" and "reaffirmed the Wesleyan principle of the primacy of Scripture." The "primacy of Scripture" is doubtless to be understood analogously to Wesley's designation of himself as "a man of one book": his being *homo unius libri* makes Scripture not so much the "boundary of his reading" as "the center of gravity in his thinking."[6]

Meanwhile, the Committee on Our Theological Task, appointed from the General Conference of 1984, was hard at work in preparation for the General Conference of 1988. Its report made a structural move to emphasize the special place of Scripture; a section on "The Primacy of Scripture" was followed by one which took "Tradition, Experience, and

Reason" all together, without dignifying each by a heading that might appear to rank them severally with the Scriptures. A strong direct statement was made on the Scriptures as norm and nourishment of the Church:

> United Methodists share with other Christians the conviction that Scripture is the primary source and criterion for authentic Christian truth and witness. The Bible bears authoritative testimony to God's self-disclosure in the pilgrimage of Israel, in the life, death, and resurrection of Jesus Christ, and in the Holy Spirit's constant activity in human history, especially in the mission of early Christianity. As we open our minds and hearts to the Word of God through the words of human beings inspired by the Holy Spirit, faith is born and nourished, our understanding is deepened, and the possibilities for transforming the world become apparent to us. The Bible is sacred canon for Christian people, formally acknowledged as such by historic ecumenical councils of the church. . . . Our standards affirm the Bible as the source of all that is "necessary and sufficient unto salvation" (Articles of Religion) and "the true rule and guide for faith and practice" (Confession of Faith). We properly read Scripture within the believing community informed by the tradition of that community. We interpret individual texts in light of their place in the Bible as a whole. . . .

With only a little retouching, that text was to stand in the version finally adopted by the General Conference. The most notable change was the insertion, after the first sentence, of this: "Through Scripture the living Christ meets us in the experience of redeeming grace. We are convinced that Jesus Christ is the living Word of God in our midst whom we trust in life and death. The biblical authors, illumined by the Holy Spirit, bear witness that in Christ the world is reconciled to God."

As successive drafts of the report of the Committee on Our Theological Task had become available, there was some attempt in the press to align the controversy with that among Southern Baptists on the inerrancy of Scripture; but it is clear that that was not at all the issue for United Methodists. Much more important was the fear expressed by some that the new statement would place unnecessary and unacceptable constraints upon theological work. Thus John Cobb of the Claremont School of Theology, in an article for *Circuit Rider* in May 1987, wanted to "keep the quadrilateral"; and the faculties of the Wesley Theological Seminary in Washington, D.C. and of the Iliff School of Theology in Denver signed like memoranda.

At the General Conference, treatment of the report was entrusted to the Legislative Committee on Faith and Mission under the chairmanship of Dr. Thomas Langford of Duke University. As we have seen, the strong statement of the normativity of Scripture is maintained; but sensitivity is also shown to the concerns expressed by those theologians who were most anxious that fixity[7] be avoided:

> In [the theological] task Scripture, as the constitutive witness to the well-springs of our faith, occupies a place of primary authority among these theological sources. In practice, theological reflection may also find its point of departure in tradition, experience, or rational analysis.

The last sentence quoted there was in fact reintroduced from the 1972 text. Further, the description of the differences allowed by the "catholic spirit" of Wesley and Methodism was extended to read "forms of worship, structures of church government, modes of baptism, *or theological explorations*" (though the Wesleyan distinction as to "all opinions *which do not strike at the root of Christianity*" is retained).

Apart from one or two promethean touches about creativity, the final text has managed to state the "critical," "constructive," and "contextual" nature of theology in a way that acknowledges the properly active human role in redemption without on the whole falling into the Pelagian temptation which perpetually besets Methodists:

> Our theological task is both critical and constructive. It is *critical* in that we test various expressions of faith by asking. Are they true? Appropriate? Clear? Cogent? Credible? Are they based on love? Do they provide the church and its members with a witness that is faithful to the gospel as reflected in our living heritage and that is authentic and convincing in the light of human experience and the present state of human knowledge?
>
> Our theological task is *constructive* in that every generation must appropriate creatively the wisdom of the past and seek God in their midst in order to think afresh about God, revelation, sin, redemption, worship, the church, freedom, justice, moral responsibility, and other significant theological concerns. Our summons is to understand and receive the gospel promises in our troubled and uncertain times. . . .
>
> Our theological task is *contextual* and *incarnational*. It is grounded upon God's supreme mode of self-revelation—the incarnation in Jesus Christ. God's eternal Word comes to us in flesh and blood in a given time and place, and in full identification with humanity.[8] Therefore, theological reflection is energized by our incarnational involvement in the daily life of the church and the world, as we participate in God's liberating and saving action.

Tradition, experience, and reason are each given their own heading in the final text. Tradition is viewed in a preponderantly positive way, though with a recognition that "the history of Christianity includes a mixture of ignorance, misguided zeal, and sin. Scripture remains the norm by which all traditions are judged." Experience is given a largely confirmatory role; the authors claim that we should be following Wesley in looking for confirmations of the biblical witness in human experience, especially the experiences of regeneration and sanctification, but also in the "common sense knowledge of everyday experience." My own greatest worry concerns the uncritical confidence which, after a nod towards the mystery of grace, the text places in "reason":

> By reason we read and interpret Scripture. By reason we determine whether our Christian witness is clear. By reason we ask questions of faith and seek to understand God's action and will. By reason we organize the understandings that compose our witness and render them internally coherent. By reason we test the congruence of our witness to the biblical testimony and to the traditions which mediate that testimony to us. By reason we relate our witness to the full range of human knowledge, experience, and service.

There follows a further brief concession, this time to "the limits and distortions characteristic of human knowledge." But I cannot help recalling how much the modern sociology of knowledge has shown us to be governed by our "interests"—and remembering the insistence of the Christian tradition upon the human will as the perpetrator and victim of our fall.

Although the 1988 text recognizes that "all Christians are called to theological reflection," it clearly sets the individual effort within the churchly community. Gone, certainly, is the glorification of "pluralism" in which the 1972 text indulged itself. Gone, too, is the most unfortunate confusion made by the 1972 text between doctrine and theology. The new document makes abundantly clear that the theological endeavors of individuals and schools are to take place upon the solid base, and within the stable framework, of "our doctrines." The constitutionally protected texts are no longer labelled mere "landmarks" as they had been since the Discipline of 1972. Whereas "pluralism" risks having no center and no edges, true catholicity has a firm substantive center which makes the edges both rather easier, and yet perhaps also slightly less important, to define.[9]

One major doctrine that had appeared under threat in the Report of the Committee on Our Theological Task as it came to the General Conference was that of the Trinity. This is not the place to establish systematically how utterly vital the doctrine and reality of the Trinity is to Christian faith. That was already done by the councils of the fourth century and the theological labors of Athanasius and Hilary and the Cappadocians. Here there is, in principle, ecumenical agreement. Wesley shared in it, amid all the questionings and debates of the eighteenth century. In what may have been a concession to the liberals or progressives in return for a stronger emphasis on the primacy of Scripture, the report nowhere used the allegedly sexist trinitarian name of Father, Son and Holy Spirit. (The advocates of pluralism usually follow the axiom familiar in liberal and progressive politics: *pas d'ennemis à gauche!* For their part, orthodox trinitarians cannot treat the doctrine as merely optional.) The cited "Standards of Doctrine" did of course use the trinitarian name, dating as they did from earlier times; but as to *what the committee itself wrote*, it would *almost* have been possible to read it in a Sabellian sense. That is the inadequacy of the "Creator, Redeemer, Sustainer" formula, which an early draft had seemed to countenance alongside the traditional formula. When the Houston Declaration stated that "God's richly personal being cannot be defined merely in functional terms," it was echoing the perception of John Wesley that "the quaint device of styling them three offices rather than persons gives up the whole doctrine."[10] In what may prove to have been its most significant single gesture, the Legislative Committee on Faith and Mission reintroduced the scriptural and traditional Name: "With Christians of other communions we confess belief in the triune God—*Father, Son, and Holy Spirit.*" The formulation found the approval of the General Conference. This leaves room for the document to make proper use of the verbs of creating, redeeming, and sanctifying, without their exclusive appropriation to particular trinitarian persons. In a similar move, the General Conference has now made the Discipline specify that candidates for ordination "are ordained by the bishop, who will use the historic language of the Holy Trinity: Father, Son, and Holy Spirit" (¶ 432).

In a related area, the General Conference rejected a proposal to reword the Preamble to the "Social Principles" in the Discipline—"We, the people called United Methodists, affirm our faith in God our *Father,* in Jesus Christ our Savior, and in the Holy Spirit, our Guide and Guard"—so as to read "Creator." It was no doubt the progressive reluctance to call God "our Father" which, perhaps subliminally, caused the Committee on Our Theological Task to downplay, when stating "distinctive Wesleyan emphases," the category of adoption, which is a major soteriological figure for Wesley. In strictly trinitarian terms (where the Father is the Father of the Son), the substitute formula favored by some—"Creator, Christ, and Spirit"—has neo-Arian implications. As the Houston Declaration succinctly points out, "Christ and the Spirit are not mere creatures."

[*Wainwright's original article here contained a section welcoming the new Hymnal for its scriptural and traditional content, for its patterning after the creeds, redemptive history, and the ordo salutis, and for its inclusion of material from the Wesleys and other cultures. —Editor*]

Another report that came to the General Conference of 1988 was entitled "Grace upon Grace: God's Mission and Ours." Here evangelism is consistently expounded before service. Albeit under the slogan of "inclusiveness," one aspect of catholicity is well captured in ¶ 51: "As a gracious community, a church in mission embraces those whose appearance, behavior, mental or physical conditions mark them as different. People who represent race, ethnic, class, age, and gender differences become one in the Body of Christ. The reach of grace is unlimited, the binding of grace is firm." This is wedded to the qualitative aspect of catholicity by being placed under a rubric that structures the report: "As United Methodists, we envision lives changed by grace, a church formed by grace, and a world transformed by grace." The substantive content of catholicity is stated epigrammatically: "Jesus Christ defines grace: Immanuel, God with us as a person." On two occasions, the report cites the great commission of Matthew 28:18–20 in its full trinitarian form. . . .

Now what are we to conclude about this General Conference overall? At the outset I suggested that the signs in favor of a return to catholicity were no bigger than a human hand. Some pluralists have expressed the view that the perceptible shift in United Methodism may simply be the following of a conservative mood in the country at large—a mood which they expect will change. What is there to stop the General Conference of 1988 from turning out to be yet one more example of Methodist accommodationism—this time, for once, in a conservative direction? The answer must reside in the signs of qualitative and substantial renewal throughout "the connection" (as Methodists like to designate their form of church life). We may look, for example, to the growth of "covenant discipleship groups" and to the very modest revival in sacramental observance.

Bishop Richard B. Wilke gave a fresh twist to the Wesleyan hymn by which Methodist Conferences traditionally begin. "And are we yet alive?" Will Willimon and Robert Wilson spoke of "rekindling the flame."[11] The 1984 General Conference had set the implausible target of doubling the Church's membership to twenty million by the year 1992. It is not at all certain that such a growth of United Methodism in its present form is desirable. My argument would be that significant growth and renewal are impossible, or at least undesirable, without a prior or concomitant recovery of substantive catholicity—a reentry into that scriptural and creedal Christianity which undergirded and motivated the Wesleys' evangelism and social action. Sound doctrine is not a sufficient condition for the revitalization of a church, but it is a necessary one. The General Conference of 1988 will have made a lasting contribution if it has promoted that cause in the seminaries, the bureaucracy, the pastorate, and the episcopate—so that through preaching, teaching, and singing, the Methodist people may be shaped throughout its whole life of worship, witness, and service for the glory of God and the salvation of the world. We shall see what emerges from the mandated study of the revised statement on "Doctrinal Standards and Our Theological Task" and from the reception given to the new Hymnal.

Chapter 19

THE UNITED METHODIST QUADRILATERAL: A THEOLOGICAL TASK

Thomas A. Langford

One of the most accepted, praised and utilized aspects of United Methodist theology is the so-called "Wesleyan Quadrilateral." The quadrilateral underwrites theological construction by placing in relation to one another Scripture, tradition, experience, and reason.

The comprehensive range which these ingredients suggest, the dynamics and variety of interaction allowed, and the ability to relate inheritance to new modes of theological construction help the quadrilateral to give special character to United Methodist theology. Consequently, the quadrilateral is commonly and enthusiastically endorsed by United Methodists. This wide, thorough and appreciative acceptance gives the impression that the quadrilateral represents a long-standing self-understanding. Yet, this is not the case.

Formal shaping and presentation of the quadrilateral was first articulated in the 1972 theological statement prepared for the Book of Discipline. The formulation itself was the work of Albert C. Outler who distilled these elements from John Wesley's writings. The formulation—although not explicitly found in John Wesley—is generally true to Wesley's intention and mode of theological work. Albert Outler made a lasting contribution by distilling this essence, and this achievement remains one of his creative contributions to United Methodism.

Appeal to and use of the quadrilateral has become characteristic of this theological tradition and if anything can be said to provide an identity to United Methodist theological method it is conscious employment of the quadrilateral.

Deceptive Simplicity

Nevertheless there is a deceptive simplicity about this formula. The basic deception is the assumption that each of the categories is clear and all that is needed is to work out a proper relationship among them. So the evident struggle among Methodists is over the primacy of Scripture and/or an equality among the four elements. Does the quadrilateral rest upon one specific side or is it an equilateral without priority?

This issue has been debated since 1972. In that document, Scripture was affirmed as primary, yet the further development of the statement itself, and in its subsequent use, this primacy was not maintained with sharpness.

In the new theological statement for the 1988 Book of Discipline, the primacy of Scripture is more consistently affirmed. Yet it is significant that in the legislative committee discussion at the 1988 General Conference, the quadrilateral was never questioned as a foundation for United Methodist theology; debate was over the interaction of the elements, and the conclusion was an affirmation of the primacy of Scripture while continuing to assert the value of tradition, experience, and reason as media for interpreting Scripture and as beginning points for theological exploration. There was a clear desire to utilize the quadrilateral and this intention characterizes much United Methodist theology.

The deception, however, is the general assumption that each of the four elements is clear in itself and that the only issue is how to relate them. So, it has been commonly assumed, when we say "Scripture" or "tradition" or "experience" or "reason" the reference is clearly established and agreed upon. It is this assumption which must be challenged.

Objections

There are two direct objections to this dominant understanding of the quadrilateral and one argument for change which should be noted.

The most radical objection would come from those contemporary philosophers and theologians who oppose all *a priori*, ahistorical, universal categories (a position called nonfoundationalism). From this perspective, all general categories derived *a priori* or ahistorically, such as reason or experience, are abstract and vacuous and carry no clear denotative quality. In contrast, only understandings of reason, experience, tradition, or Scripture which are historically and communally developed have legitimate and usable meaning.

A less radical objection is to maintain that even if the categories do possess some legitimate status, there are such varieties of understanding of each category that greater clarity is needed before the formula can be helpfully utilized. On this ground, the argument is that the general agreement about the value and usefulness of the formula is due to the multiple understandings of each term—so persons agree, for instance, that experience is a source of theology although they may have divergent or contradictory understandings of the term.

Another possible objection is to argue that the present terms can be clarified in an adequate manner but, even so, there is an essential dimension missing, namely that of activity or *praxis* (in this paper practice is understood as the application of a previously formed theory; *praxis* is the setting in which theory is developed and utilized). That is, the present quadrilateral remains too cognitive, too theoretical, too separated from any specific historical context or social location. This argument maintains that for John Wesley the categories do not possess abstract truth. Rather it is only as they serve to transform concrete human life and only as this transformative expression in *praxis* is ingredient in the theoretical (theological) interpretation that Christian truth can be found.

We shall discuss each of these objections. It is possible, of course, to see the lack of precision or stability of meaning as a strength of the quadrilateral. Differing interpretations within a community may generate mutual enrichment. But we shall take sharper clarity to be desirable and discuss the mentioned objections.

Nonfoundationalism

The more radical argument accuses the Enlightenment (especially as expressed in Descartes and Kant) of perpetuating a false understanding of human beings as individual, autonomous, rational persons who possess *a priori* categories of thought and uniquely represented universal forms of experience. Both the radical individualism (the independent ego) and the possession of universal characteristics (*a priori* categories of reason and experience) separate the understanding of human beings from their historical setting and process, from concrete traditions of development, and from the multiple forms of human existence and diverse modes of reason and experience. Since these concepts do not have universal meaning, they must each and together be understood in terms of the tradition out of which they have grown and in terms of their interpretation within their specific tradition. For United Methodists to use these categories constructively they must explore their tradition and find the dominant specifications of these categories.

Varieties of Meaning

A second and different objection to the present common understanding of the quadrilateral is that each of the four central terms is open to a variety of interpretations even within the United Methodist tradition. Consequently, there is no stability or consistency in the use of these elements in discussions among Methodists. For purposes of illustration, we shall look briefly at each of the elements.

Scripture

To affirm the primacy of Scripture is significant and for United Methodism it represents a clarification of priorities, but to make this affirmation does not conclude an argument; rather, it constitutes the beginning point of a long and adventurous process.

To affirm the primacy of Scripture is to commit oneself to the study of Scripture utilizing all available tools (linguistic, historical, sociological, literary, etc.) under the guidance of the Holy Spirit.

To affirm the primacy of Scripture is to commit oneself to the authority of Scripture. But the nature of authority is itself subject to various interpretations and the character of the authority acknowledged will determine the manner in which Scripture is viewed and used in terms of itself and in its relation to the other elements. To refer to the Bible as "Scripture" is to recognize the special place which the Bible holds in the United Methodist tradition, but the exact nature of the "special place" is in need of careful elaboration.

It was significant that in the discussion of the primacy of Scripture at the 1988 General Conference, no one argued for the plenary inspiration of infallibility of Scripture and no one argued for a subordination of Scripture to other elements of the quadrilateral. But it is also significant that there was no effort to reach consensus on how Scripture functions authoritatively or how it would concretely serve as a "criterion" for theological statements.

What was affirmed was Scripture's primacy. What was left open was the explicit character of that primacy.

To affirm the primacy of Scripture is significant, for such an affirmation makes the use and interpretation of Scripture our basic responsibility. Such primacy is expressed in the church's worship and ministry. This affirmation means that however Scripture is interpreted it must be in terms of its uniquely basic position in the quadrilateral and in ways which maintain its base position in ordering life and in theological activity. But, given this primacy, there are multiple ways of expressing Scripture's meaning and significance.

The current understanding and use of Scripture represents no unified agreement; the discussion remains open ended and requires greater clarification among United Methodists.

Tradition

In recent decades, the precise definition of "tradition" has been a recognized problem; and the historical delineation of a specific tradition has proven to be notoriously difficult. For philosophy, tradition identity has been as difficult to gain consensus about as has personal identity.

The 1988 disciplinary statement makes clear that tradition refers to the variety of historical ways the Christian tradition has interpreted Scripture and understood its faith—as this was inspired by the Holy Spirit—and this represents United Methodism's ecumenical awareness. Tradition also refers to the ways in which the traditions which reach confluence in United Methodism have interpreted and understood their faith. Tradition in addition, refers to the ways in which contemporary interpreters utilize these developments for present interpretations of faith.

Tradition is clearly taken to be a formative context for the conveyance and reception of faith and sets the framework in which ongoing interpretation must occur. Yet there is imprecision about the explicit ligaments of the traditions referred to.

Tradition in the disciplinary statement expressly refers to church tradition but also emphasizes the actual historical context in which interpretations of faith occur. Consequently, to think of tradition is to look for the ways in which interpretations are developed within and in response to particular church location and to concrete social, political, and economic conditions. Tradition does not come as a transhistorical reality but rather places theological activity in specific historical contexts and social locations.

If one asks, Is there a Wesleyan tradition? there must be careful indication of where historical lines are being drawn, who appropriate representatives are. What are the historical and social conditions in which its mission and witness have been shaped? What, if any, are enduring emphases which, even with their changes, persist as identifying elements in the formation of United Methodism? And what mission understanding and tasks have shaped and should shape our current theological activity? These issues remain important elements in our critical task.[1]

Once again, to say that tradition constitutes one of the elements of the quadrilateral is not to conclude an argument, rather it is to set an agenda for the further work of delineating and specifying the understanding of tradition which one will utilize.

Experience

Again, to pursue our chief point, experience is a constantly changing category and presents special problems for clear utilization. Michael Oakeshott says, experience is "of all the words in the philosophic vocabulary . . . the most difficult to manage; and it must be the ambition of every writer reckless enough to use the word to escape the ambiguities it contains."[2]

For instance, when John Wesley spoke of Christian experience, he primarily meant the experience *of* Jesus Christ or experience as determined *by* the Holy Spirit. The reference was to the agent who creates and shapes experience. By the late nineteenth century, Methodism had moved to more subjective interpretations, so experience became *my* experience of Jesus Christ or the Holy Spirit and then, more vaguely, my experience of God. A further move reinforced subjectivity by speaking of "religious" experience with no definite external reference. It was this "religious experience" that psychology of religion studied in the first half of the twentieth century.

With the rise of black and feminist theology, the understanding of experience shifted from isolated individuals to specific corporate groups. The attention was still focused on human experience, though now understood in corporate and not in exclusively individual terms. Liberation theology shifted attention to class considerations where, once again (but now with a sociologically defined group) there was exploration of the experience of these groups as in part defined in reference to external political, economic, and social impingements.

To some extent all of these varieties (and others) of understanding remain among people who speak of experience as one element of the quadrilateral. But the differences are so pronounced that before one can relate experience to the other elements, one needs to make clear what understanding she or he is employing.

Our chief point is reemphasized, to say that experience is one of the acknowledged and honored elements of the quadrilateral is not to conclude an argument, rather it is to accept the task of specifying one's understanding of experience and how that understanding will be utilized.

Reason

Reason, in spite of some interpreters, is not a generic term. Since the Enlightenment, and especially under the influence of Immanuel Kant, there has been a dominant assumption that human beings are autonomous possessors of innate rationality. In this tradition the understanding of reason is that it represents a native human capacity which functions in every person (given normal human capability) in the same way—that is, it is universal and necessary.

This view is currently being radically challenged, as we saw in the discussion of nonfoundationalism. But even if one does not go so far, there is need for clarity about reason, how it is understood and how it is employed, for reason is variously used in different traditions and does not have a single meaning. Canons of rationality need to be specified so that the relation of cognitive activity to practical activity or to emotion can be sorted out with care.[3]

Consequently, as with the other elements, the affirmation that reason is a part of the quadrilateral concludes nothing, but it does set important tasks.

With each element in the quadrilateral we have found that the bold statement that it is an essential part of the base of theological construction is to make an important originative affirmation, but rather than achieving closure it only sets the agenda for United Methodist theological effort.[4]

A New Dimension

A third unease about the quadrilateral is of another kind. Even if it is possible to be clear about each of the elements, something essential may be left out. Namely, for John Wesley all of these elements—Scripture, tradition, experience and reason—are integrally related to *praxis*.

Stephen Toulmin has argued that philosophy since the seventeenth century has been dominated by a "theory-centered" style, which poses philosophical problems, and frames solutions to them, in timeless and universal terms."[5] By doing this, Toulmin claims, these philosophers left half of the subject "languishing." That is, the practical dimensions of thought-life were unattended to and what was lost were spheres of thought such as the "oral," the "particular," the "local," and the "timely." Certainty rather than wisdom was the goal. But this understanding of reason must be challenged. The recovery of practical philosophy is a paramount task and theologically this means that a firm sense of social location and change-effective wisdom is fundamentally important.

In important and interesting ways, John Wesley did not forsake the practical sphere of theology and in this he cut across the grain of his own and subsequent times. Wesley's position was not one which he gained from a consideration of the history of philosophy but from his own life story of movement from intense ethical struggle to empowered Christian living. Life, action, embodiment were fundamental. It is significant, for instance, that Wesley's *Christian Library* has decidedly more biography than any other literary genre. The transformation of life became not only the end (the application, practice) of correct theory, rather the events of transformation were ingredient to any valid understanding of Scripture, tradition, experience, or reason. Wesley's primary interest in the formation of Christian character shapes his discussion of theological issues and provides his theological emphases.

The present statement of the quadrilateral does not make this practical (*praxis*) dimension a necessary and indispensable part of the quadrilateral dynamic and is to that extent a misrepresentation of Wesley's basic theological intention. For Wesley, doctrines are not ends in themselves but are guidelines which help us know how to tell the story of God's grace rightly and live it with integrity. Hence, this argument maintains that the present formula requires clarity about this fundamental issue. For instance, in the present statement (and I speak as one who worked on and supported the statement) it would be better if the commentary subsequent to the statement of the quadrilateral—commentary which sets the context and mission of theological effort—were placed prior to the quadrilateral statement. This was the loss—unavoidable in terms of time and energy—of not providing a clear mission statement prior to the statement of "Our Theological Task". The quadrilateral is not situation neutral; it functions within the arena of our concrete context of mission and serves the goals of that mission with the spirit of that mission.

Modes of Interaction: A Proposal

After mentioning these objections and the resulting challenge for reconsideration, it must also be noted that in every case, whether the present statement or some altered form is considered, there is the further work of nuancing the interrelationships of these elements. The issues of what primacy means as dynamic interaction, what impingements and balances are to be sought, how each element conditions the others—all of this awaits clear delineation.

As a suggestion of a way to utilize the quadrilateral, a brief sketch of understanding might be provocative.

Setting

The setting or social-location in which my particular church community undertakes the theological task is in rich, powerful, "Christian" North America. We exist as a privileged, confident, assertive people who are thankful for personal freedom, political enfranchisement, economic strength, and the fruits of cultured existence. In the midst of this general abundance we also experience traumas of broken relationships, loneliness, psychological privation, economic greed and insecurity, and persistent unease about the marginal people in our society, international relations, and nuclear threat. How can one be a Christian in a "Christian" nation which possesses this character?

The mission of God sets our mission; God's way of being in the world challenges, judges, and encourages our way of being in the world. We are people of God who are called to be people for God in our place and time. We are called to embody God's grace; we are called to use our resources for the sake of the hungry and homeless, for issues of peace and concrete expressions of justice, for empowerment of others to assert their freedom and hope. We are called to recognize and confront sin in its most concrete manifestations in personal and social life; we are called to serve God's reign in our place and in our world.

How does the quadrilateral serve us in our particular theological effort? Let's look again at the four elements in the formula.

Scripture

In this setting Scripture comes as a dynamic, formative influence through interaction with interpretive reception; by this dialectic our way of being with God and in the world is authorized.

The primacy of Scripture (not *sola scriptura*) is a way of acknowledging the Bible as the basic presentation of God's activity in human history especially as this culminates in Jesus Christ. But Scripture always stands in inseparable dialectic with an interpretive tradition. The Scripture is a recorded dialogue between God and human beings, a dialogue in which God takes gracious initiative and in which human beings respond with faith and with unfaithfulness. The dialogue continues through creative interaction and freshly authorizes an historical community. Scripture, as the record of God's self-presenting in the history of Israel, in Jesus Christ and dialectically through the interpretive inspiration of the Holy Spirit, functions to create and sustain God's community.

As scriptural dialectic is the medium for the genesis and nurturing of community life, theology is the critical attempt at communal self-understanding and critical assessment of communal endeavor to live out its identity. Hence, scriptural authority functions in a variety of ways to constitute and empower communal life, such as in liturgy, preaching, theological reflection, education, and polity. Through these uses, the vocation of the community is discerned, and in these multiple ways of reception and use, Scripture functions to authorize Christian existence.

The Bible is authoritative in that it is the witness-through-dialogue by which church life is formed, informed, and empowered. The first authority of Scripture is that of the medium of interpretive dialogue by which a new existence is established and a way of life is guided. The Bible does not stand alone, separate from interpretation; it is not an ahistorical dogmatic textbook; it is not a criterion in the sense of a set of propositions by which other propositions may be judged. On the contrary, the Bible is the word of God as it conveys the living Word who is Jesus Christ and as it becomes alive through the Holy Spirit. The Scripture is authoritative as it encounters us within our particular social location as we struggle to enact life as God's people in our historical setting. Hence, participation in God's mission in a concrete location provides a vantage point for unlocking scriptural meaning for us. The dialectic between the biblical text and human reception always occurs in specific situations and only interpretation from within concrete historical contexts produces scriptural authority.

Scripture becomes Scripture as we (through the agency of the Holy Spirit) are drawn into its orbit and as our situation (through the agency of the Holy Spirit) shapes our reception of the Bible's meaning. The dialogue with God is specific; it occurs in our historical situation. We are addressed by God who has, through Scripture and our setting in life, acted in concrete expressions of grace, judgment, redemption and hope.

Tradition

The Christian tradition is tradition as it mediates the past to our present historical setting. Tradition is not an accumulation of past heroes or informative events. Tradition and Scripture are inseparably connected, for tradition is the record of the reception and interpretation of Scripture and its implications for the concrete life of the church. Tradition is the historical conveyance of found meaning and explicit actions of the past to the particularities of our present. As such, tradition transmits not only the internal life of Christian communities but also awareness of the contexts in which Christian communities have lived.

Tradition becomes alive as there is mutual interdependence of previous settings and our setting. Tradition and its appropriation occurs in dialectical exchange. Interactive conditioning shapes what we receive from the Christian past in our particular place in the present.

The Wesleyan tradition comes to bear upon the situation of my concrete church setting in explicit ways. The theme of prevenient grace affirms God's concrete presence, judgment, and redemption. Justification speaks to the new being which we possess in Jesus Christ and the implications of that new existence in sanctification (wholeness of life with God and neighbors). The notion and the reality of tradition are dynamic. As actualized in a concrete situation tradition challenges the situation even as its meaning is interpreted from within the situation. It is also evident that the Wesleyan tradition requires supplementation and correction by resources found in other Christian traditions. Our Wesleyan tradition insists that we ask how we can witness in our setting; for instance, through our prayerful caring, through the use of our political power, and our economic well-being. It calls us to ask how we feed those in spiritual need and those who are hungry, give home to the homeless, sanctuary to the oppressed. It challenges us to witness to God's gift of new being and to incorporate that new being into our mode of existence.

Tradition identifies us; it brings to focus the witness of the past and the present; it gives us the courage of company in our proclamation and struggle; it sets a hope for the ongoingness of God's mission in our world, of which our own mission is a small part.

Experience

We need to begin by saying what experience in this context is not. Experience is not an abstract, universal notion of how human beings may react. Experience is not cultivation of aesthetic attitudes or titillation of our emotions or developing good vibes within a self-defined circle, experience is not an isolated, privatized set of emotions. Rather, experience is God's engagement with us in such a way that we are redeemed, given tasks, and called to be faithful. Experience is God's encounter with us through the concrete elements of Scripture, our actual social, personal, economic, political situation. Experience is engagement by God which places us firmly where we are and sets us in engagement with the people and place where we are.

Experience, as utilized in the quadrilateral, helps to tie Scripture and tradition inseparably to our place of life and arena of mission. Our experience situates us in our place in the sequence of the scriptural account of God's dialogue with human beings; our experience establishes our place in the sequence of Christian tradition. In the Wesleyan tradition, personal/social redemption and holiness are always bound together so that we receive as we share through word and life the grace of God given in Jesus Christ and conveyed to us by the Holy Spirit.

Reason

Reason, in this specific social location, functions to clarify our mission (its ground, its meaning, its imperative) and to clarify how mission is to be enacted (how choices and commitments are to be made) in our particular situation. At times this may take the form of clarifying these matters for those within the Christian community. At times this may take the form of presenting this self-understanding to communities outside of our community (unbelievers or different believers). At times our rational responsibility may be exploration of the relation of Christian mission to newly discovered or freshly recognized sociological or ecological conditions.

Reason is not context free; it does not function in some abstract, transcendent dimension which is equidistant from all special historical settings. Faith and character direct reason, and concrete faith and explicit character development which are always historically specific direct reason to faithful understanding. Faith and reason, tradition and rationality are complicates: each requires the other for wholeness of Christian life and mission.

In the Wesleyan tradition, reason is dominantly understood as practical reason, reason must serve the transformation of life. The function of practical reason is to gain wisdom about how to live as a Christian community. Hence rationality is not so much a theoretical and theory-building activity as it is a means for ordering and reordering life within a community of commitment and a tradition which seeks to build personal and communal character.

Our Theological Task

In this outline proposal there has been an effort to suggest a way of utilizing the quadrilateral for theological construction. It is intended that this effort reflect the special nature of our Wesleyan theological tradition and, even more emphatically, that it demonstrate the necessity in our tradition of undertaking the theological task in a particular social location. Theology is never written for all people in all places and it is never written for all time. Rather, theology is the effort to respond to God's engaging grace where we are through faithful and concrete participation in God's mission.

Whether or not this model is convincing, it should indicate that clear and explicit interpretation and use of the quadrilateral is an ongoing task in United Methodist theology.

Afterword

The Wesleyan theological tradition continues. The positions represented in the articles in this collection indicate both the rich diversity and the intensity of recent and current discussion among United Methodists. Theological work in this tradition has two foci: reception and fresh activity. Historical perspective keeps the theological inheritance of this tradition in mind while explorations in terms of our theological task today make evident the vitality and growing edges of current theological activity.

Study of these documents is intended both to make the developing tradition a part of present discussion and to make present discussion accountable to the Wesleyan tradition. Each of these dimensions is important for the vitality of contemporary United Methodism. This tradition does not seek simple unity or general agreement on all points of theological interest. Rather, as is evident in its total development, while sharing common interests found in the grace of God as expressed in the gospel of Jesus Christ and the enlivening activity of the Holy Spirit, there is also encouragement to apply its received understandings and practices to present issues and the shaping of faithful discipleship.

To serve these goals in the contemporary life of The United Methodist Church, these selections are drawn together and made available for ongoing theological discussion.

Notes

Introduction

1. Thomas A. Langford is the William Kellon Quick Professor of Theology and Methodist Studies at the Divinity School, Duke University.

2. Quoted by John H. Leith in *Introduction to the Reformed Tradition* (Atlanta: John Knox Press, 1977), pp. 21–22; as found quoted by Jacques de Senarclens, "Karl Barth and the Reformed Tradition," *Reformed World* 30 (March, 1969):206, from an interview in *Realité* (February 1963):25.

3. *Practical Divinity* (Nashville: Abingdon Press, 1983), p. 263.

Chapter 1

1. Albert C. Outler was a distinguished church historian and student of John Wesley. He was the chief author of the 1972 theological statement. This selection is the introductory statement made by Albert C. Outler to the General Conference of 1972 as he presented the report of the study commission that prepared "Doctrine and Doctrinal Statements and the General Rules." These comments appeared in the *Daily Christian Advocate* (April 19, 1972):218–22. The report was adopted and appeared in the 1972 Book of Discipline of The United Methodist Church.

2. *Journal of the 1968 General Conference of The United Methodist Church* (n.p.), p. 1419.

Chapter 2

1. Frederick Herzog is Professor of Systematic Theology at The Divinity School, Duke University. This article appeared in the *Perkins Journal* 28 (Fall 1974):1–10, and is used with permission.

2. C. Eric Lincoln, Atlanta, Ga., December 12, 1973, speaking to some 500 United Methodist blacks on the relationship of the 400,000 United Methodist blacks to the black masses. *The United Methodist Newscope* 1 (December 21, 1973):1.

3. "Doctrine and Doctrinal Statements," Part II of the Book of Discipline (Nashville, 1972), p. 29 (hereafter Part II).

4. Ibid., p. 32.

5. It is clear to me that various concerns went into the making of Part II. Besides doctrinal emphasis, there is also acknowledgement of pluralism. The most obvious manifestation of the latter is of course the juxtaposition of "The Articles of Religion of the Methodist Church" (1784) and "The Confession of Faith of the Evangelical United Brethren Church" (1962).

6. *The Bishops' Call for Peace and the Self-Development of Peoples.* Adopted by the General Conference of The United Methodist Church in Atlanta, Ga., April 1972 (hereafter *Bishops' Call*).

7. As indicated by C. Eric Lincoln quote; see fn. 2 above.

8. Martin E. Marty, *The Fire We Can Light* (Garden City, 1973), p. 20.

9. James L. McCord, *Princeton Theological Seminary Alumni News* 14 (Autumn 1973). "The President's Letter," inside front cover.

10. Marty, p. 24.

11. Ibid., pp. 75, 136, 147, *passim*.

12. Ibid., p. 24.

13. Part II, pp. 39ff.

14. Ibid., p. 31.

15. Ibid.

16. Ibid., p. 32.

17. This should at least be seriously discussed in regard to such a region as the South or the "Bible Belt." The most challenging statement in this regard thus far is Samuel S. Hill, Jr. (ed.), *Religion and the Solid South* (Nashville: Abingdon Press, 1972). See especially pp. 41ff.

18. Part II, p. 34.

19. Ibid.

20. Ibid.

21. Ibid., p. 30.

22. *Bishops' Call*, p. 9.

23. Ibid., p. 8.

24. Part II, p. 29.

25. Ibid., p. 34.

26. Ibid., p. 32.

27. Ibid., p. 34.

28. Part II, p. 37. In Southern culture-religion the corporateness of the life in Christ is often misrepresented to apply to one's own group. Cf. Samuel S. Hill, pp. 52 ff.

29. Ibid., p. 38. We dare not forget that in many areas of the world liberation is a very costly thing for Christians. When we use it in our affluent setting fellow Christians in other parts of the world are easily puzzled unless they see concrete applications. Cf. the comment by the Latin American theologian Hugo Assmann in *Risk* 9:2 (1973): "In Europe the word *liberation* covers anything you like to think of whereas in reality throughout history it has been the instrument of a struggle" (p. 9).

30. *Bishops' Call*, p. 9.

31. See fn. 2.

32. John Dewey, *Individualism Old and New* (New York, 1962), p. 14.

33. Max Weber, *The Protestant Ethic and the Spirit of Capitalism* (New York: Charles Scribner and Sons, 1958), p. 172.

34. Part II, p. 30. The *Leaders' Guide* asks: "What role do these theologies have in the process of theological debate and development in The United Methodist Church?" (p. 16). My essay is in part an attempt to answer this question.

35. *Leaders' Guide*, p. 15.

36. *Leaders' Guide*, p. 14.

37. Part II, p. 32.

38. H. Richard Niebuhr, *The Social Sources of Denominationalism* (New York, 1957), p. 86.

39. Ibid., p. 89.

40. Ibid., p. 71. Cf. footnote 32.

41. Ibid.

42. Ibid., p. 65.

43. Ibid., p. 66.

44. Ibid., pp. 69–71. The whole issue of ideology that is involved in Niebuhr's analysis needs careful reflection. Obviously, no one can escape ideology entirely. But it makes for

a considerable difference whether one is aware of the ideological factor or not. Cf. Louis Althusser, *For Marx* (New York, 1970), pp. 232 ff.

45. *Leaders' Guide*, p. 2.

46. Our theologies are still very much modeled on the sciences which work with methodologies; a methodology deals with an object. For the debate of hermeneutic vs. methodology see Richard E. Palmer, *Hermeneutics* (Evanston, 1969). The focus of the European debate of this issue is Hans-Georg Gadamer, *Wahrheit und Methode* (Tübingen, 1960).

47. *Leaders Guide*, p. 5.

48. This of course implies a significant reorientation in theology. Dietrich Ritschl, in *Memory and Hope* (New York and London, 1967), tried to classify contemporary theology also in regard to Methodist schools. Among other trends, he noted "the postwar personalistic-existentialistic systematization of historical critical exegesis, fighting the 'subject-object split,' searching for thought and language forms to 'make relevant' the ancient message (represented exegetically and systematically in Europe, systematically and practically in America, especially in the sphere of influence of Methodist theological schools, perhaps as a stopgap for obsolete conversion-theology) " (p. 7).

49. Part II, p. 33.

50. In regard to social transformation an older volume is still quite pertinent: S. Paul Schilling, *Methodism and Society in Theological Perspective* (Nashville: Abingdon Press, 1960). It is only that today we are much less challenged to work out a theology of society as primary objective. What we have been stressing is primarily a praxiology of the church that puts the liberation of the *church* first. Cf. pp. 215–21.

51. In regard to praxiology as a theory of action see Tadeusz Kotarbinski, *Praxiology: An Introduction to the Sciences of Efficient Action* (Warszawa, 1965). The emphasis lies here on "formulating standards of effective action" (p. 8). The theological task is much more specific. It becomes a matter of working out a framework of action within the context of the church. For theology, the important thing is that here the praxis of man is considered as belonging integrally to ratiocination. Every local situation affords opportunities for developing a praxiology pertinent to the concrete context. See my article "Let Us Still Praise Famous Men," *Hannavee* 1 (April, 1970):4–6.

Chapter 3

1. Schubert M. Ogden is University Professor of Theology at the Perkins School of Theology, Southern Methodist University. This article appeared in the *Perkins Journal* 28 (Fall 1974):19–27, and is used with permission.

2. See my essay, "What Is Theology?" *Perkins Journal* 26 (Winter 1973), pp. 1–13.

3. Trans. John Drury (Maryknoll, N.Y.: Orbis Books, 1973).

4. Ibid., p. 81.

5. Ibid., p. 82.

6. Ibid., pp. 84, 82.

Chapter 4

1. Leroy T. Howe is Professor of Pastoral Theology at Perkins School of Theology, Southern Methodist University. This article appeared in the *Perkins Journal* 28 (Fall 1974):11–18, and is used with permission.

Chapter 5

1. Robert E. Cushman is Research Professor Emeritus of Systematic Theology at The Divinity School, Duke University. This article appeared in *Religion in Life* 44 (Winter, 1975):401–11, and is used with permission.

[Original editor's note: The discussion of the doctrinal statements in the Discipline is an ongoing opportunity for and responsibility of United Methodists. Consideration of the theological process outlined in the disciplinary statement is in an initial stage, but this stage of the discussion has set forth a challenge that can issue in renewal in the life of this church. Among those who have participated in the discussion and have helped set some agenda items is Robert E. Cushman.

In view of critique by this essay of "theological pluralism" as a "principle" for doctrinal formulation, it may be noted that, by action of the General Conference of 1980, the following sentence of ¶69 (p. 72) of the Discipline was replaced: "In this task of reappraising and applying the Gospel, theological pluralism should be recognized as a principle" by "In this task of reappraising and applying the Gospel according to the conciliar principle, we recognize the presence of theological pluralism." By this action, "theological pluralism" was dethroned as a norm for doctrinal reformulation and accepted simply as a fact of life.]

Chapter 6

1. Albert C. Outler's article appeared in the *Wesleyan Theological Journal* 20 (Spring 1985):7–18, and is used with permission.

2. See his *Journal*, Nov. 11, 1738.

3. It was not in the first edition of volume 3 of the *Sermons* (1750) but appeared in the subsequent edition of 1763.

4. *Ecclesiastical Polity*, I, xvi, 8.

5. Ibid., III, ix, 2.

6. "To the Reader," *Works* (Bristol: Pine, 1771), ¶ 4.

7. *Explanatory Notes upon the New Testament*, on Romans 12:6, on "the analogy of faith."

8. Second Letter to Bishop Lavington, Preface, ¶ 5, in *The Works of John Wesley* (Oxford: Oxford University Press, 1975), 11:381.

9. See *The Principles of a Methodist Farther Explained*, VI.4, in *Works* (1989), 9:227.

10. Sermon 63, "The General Spread of the Gospel" (1783) ¶ 13, in *The Works of John Wesley* (Nashville: Abingdon Press, 1985), 2:490–91. These are the truths to which, he says, the Oxford Methodists began testifying fifty years earlier.

11. See J. J. Pelikan's recent essay, *The Vindication of Tradition* (New Haven: Yale University Press, 1986).

12. *Locke, Wesley and the Method of English Romanticism* (Gainesville: University Press of Florida, 1984).

13. Sermon 10, "The Witness of the Spirit I," I.7, in *Works* (1984), 1:274.

Chapter 7

1. Richard P. Heitzenrater is Albert C. Outler Professor of Wesley Studies at Perkins School of Theology, Southern Methodist University. He was Vice Chairman of the Committee on Our Theological Task and chaired the writing sub-committee that produced the proposed revision of the doctrinal statement for the 1988 Book of Discipline.

2. *Daily Christian Advocate* (1984), pp. 412, 614.

3. *DCA* (1984), pp. 613–14.

4. See especially Robert E. Cushman, "Church Doctrinal Standards Today," in *Religion in Life* 44 (Winter 1975):401–11 (see above, chapter 5); Schubert M. Ogden, "Doctrinal

Standards in The United Methodist Church," in *Perkins Journal* 28 (Fall 1974):19–27 (see above, chapter 3); Jerry L. Walls, "What is Theological Pluralism," in *Quarterly Review* 5 (Fall 1985):44–62; Frederick Herzog, "Methodism in Agony," in *Perkins Journal* 28 (Fall 1974):1–10 (see above, chapter 2); Richard P. Heitzenrater, "At Full Liberty: Doctrinal Standards in Early American Methodism," in *Quarterly Review* 5 (Fall 1985):6–27 (see below, chapter 8).

5. One of the clearest diagnoses of United Methodism's "identity crisis" was presented in an address to the Council of Bishops in Boston in 1978 by Professor Albert C. Outler, who challenged the bishops to exercise their pastoral and spiritual leadership within the church.

6. In 1980, the phrase, "theological pluralism should be recognized as a principle," was replaced by "we recognize the presence of theological pluralism," changing the concept from normative to descriptive (1972 Book of Discipline, p. 69; 1980, p. 72). In 1984, the latter phrase was expanded to read, "we recognize under the guidance of our doctrinal standards (¶¶ 67–68) the presence of theological pluralism" (1984 BOD, p. 72). In neither conference was the phrasing in the next few sentences changed, so that they continued to "acknowledge the positive virtues of doctrinal pluralism" (apparently using the terms "theological" and "doctrinal" as synonymous).

7. This term refers to the fourfold doctrinal guidelines outlined in the 1972 statement: "Scripture, tradition, Christian experience, and reason," seen by the chairman of the 1968–72 study commission, Albert C. Outler, as "perhaps the most crucial (certainly the most innovative) proposal" in their report. See Introduction to the pamphlet edition of *Doctrine and Doctrinal Statements: Part II of The Book of Discipline* (Nashville. Graded Press, 1972), p. 1.

8. *DCA* (1984), p. 614.

9. "We idealized our heritage. . . . We waffled on the fact and import of the general thinness of doctrinal concern in our pulpits. . . . We may have fudged a bit by insisting that these other standards included Wesley's *Notes* and *Sermons*, 'by plain historical inference.'" Outler also provided a summary critique of the "quadrilateral" as found in the 1972 statement: "The primacy of Scripture as the primary and final source of Christian doctrine is not adequately expounded. Tradition is not credibly explained. Experience is defined in an overly subjective fashion, and reason is so sadly underestimated as to appear almost as a caricature. The ease with which this fourfold metaphor has been accepted and then largely misconstrued has been one of the major dejections of my old age." Tape of Dr. Outler's presentation, Bridwell Library Center for Methodist Studies, November 15, 1985.

10. Paul A. Mickey, "Confession without Confessionalism: Living up to Our Theological Task," 9 pp.

11. Riley B. Case, "United Methodism and the Doctrinal Statement," 9 pp.

12. Thomas A. Langford, "Theology as a Part of the Church's Existence," 12 pp.; cf. Cushman, "Church Doctrinal Standards Today," reprinted in Langford, *Wesleyan Theology: A Sourcebook* (Durham: Labyrinth, 1984), esp. pp. 283, 285, 289.

13. "An Invitation to Discover . . . Reaffirm," subsequently revised and adopted by the World Methodist Council meeting in Nairobi, Kenya, July 28, 1986, as "An Invitation for Christians in the Methodist tradition to claim and reaffirm the essential Apostolic and universal teachings of the historic Christian Faith."

14. The third section, "Our Doctrinal Standards," was comparable to ¶ 68 in the then current Book of Discipline and contained the text of the Articles of Religion, the Confession of Faith, and the General Rules. The text of these documents, deemed by the Judicial Council to be protected by the First Restrictive Rule of the church's Constitution, are not subject to simple legislative revision by the General Conference, and the COTT (as with its predecessor body in 1972) decided not to change or revise these standards, which would have entailed a specific and difficult process of constitutional amendment.

15. The finer distinction between doctrinal standards and doctrinal statements was dropped and did not play a significant role in the discussions of the committee.

16. The report of the monitor from the Commission on the Status and Role of Women concluded that the committee was "substantively dealing with this issue" and that "the committee's struggle with this issue is an excellent indication that an attempt is being made toward ['inclusiveness in concept and language']." Overseas members of the committee, however, cautioned the group to be sensitive to non-North American perspectives.

17. Although suggestions on these topics were received from several persons, the most pointed observations and proposals came from Schubert Ogden, John Cobb, and Albert Outler. The chair of the writing committee was also doing the final editorial work on the last volume of Professor Outler's edition of Wesley's *Sermons*; the regular contact allowed for occasional candid conversations on the developing doctrinal statement.

18. As an example, the inclination to list all the new and emerging theological emphases evolved into the following two sentences: "Of crucial importance in the present are concerns generated by great human struggles for dignity, liberation, and fulfillment. These concerns are borne by theologies that express the heart cries of the downtrodden and the aroused indignation of the compassionate." Draft of October, 1986, pp. 30–31; cf. BOD (1988), p. 87.

19. This list included clergy and lay readers, about thirty theologians, all the members of the Council of Bishops, executives of the general boards and agencies, faculties of the theological schools, and anyone else who had requested a copy of the document.

20. Three examples of this can be seen in these sentences that were added to the sections on "Tradition," "Experience," and "Reason":

"Christian tradition precedes Scripture, and yet Scripture comes to be the focal expression of the tradition."
... "Our experience interacts with Scripture since we read Scripture in the light of the conditions and events that help shape who we are."
"By reason we relate our witness to the full range of human knowledge and experience."

See also note 21 below.

21. Two very similar sequences of phrases were retained in the document in two different contexts. The familiar formula from the 1972 statement was retained in ¶ 69: "... the living core of the Christian faith stands revealed in Scripture, illumined by tradition, vivified in personal experience, and confirmed by reason." This was only slightly modified for inclusion in ¶ 66: [our forebears'] preaching and teaching were grounded in Scripture, informed by Christian tradition, enlivened in experience, and tested by reason." Undaunted by this repetition, the legislative committee at General Conference added the 1972 phrasing again in ¶ 67 (with two words added): "this living core stands revealed in Scripture, illumined by tradition, vivified in personal and corporate experience, and confirmed by reason."

22. See note 20 above.

23. E.g., "Scripture remains the decisive test of the validity of appropriateness of our Christian witness" becomes "Scripture remains central in our efforts to be faithful in making our Christian witness."

24. The new wording corrected errors in the previous statement and updated bibliographical references to available editions of Wesley's *Sermons* and *Notes*. The preface (within brackets in a constitutionally-protected paragraph of the Discipline) was deemed "editorial matter" by the editorial committee of the Book of Discipline, and was therefore not included as part of the legislative proposals from the COTT.

25. The Report briefly outlined the process followed by the committee and summarized the main concerns of the new document that was being proposed. Unfortunately, suggested rewording of the portion on "Ecumenical Commitment" in ¶ 69 was received from

the General Commission on Christian Unity and Interreligious Affairs too late to incorporate into the proposed document. The executive committee of COTT agreed to support it as a substitute text during the legislative deliberations at General Conference.

26. The interim report of the previous commission in 1970, when talking about the fourfold guidelines, uses the comment that "Scripture stands foremost without a rival." The 1972 statement says, "there is a primacy that goes with Scripture as the constitutive witness to the biblical well-springs of our faith."

27. *Circuit Rider* 12 (April 1988):18.

28. Thomas Oden, "Here I Stand: Keep Wesley's 'Sermons,' 'Notes' in Theology Report," *United Methodist Reporter* 134 (January 8, 1988):2. The article by John B. Cobb, Jr., appeared in *Christian Century* 105 (April 6, 1988):343–47 (see below, chapter 12), and that by Thomas W. Ogletree in *Quarterly Review* 8 (Spring 1988):43–53 (see below, chapter 13).

29. Some other candidates for the chair had been openly hostile to the proposed COTT document, at least one of them hoping to retain the 1972 statement as the basis for Legislative Committee revision.

30. "Conciliar Theology: A Report," *Quarterly Review* 9 (Summer 1989):7 (see below, chapter 14).

31. *Doctrinal Standards and Our Theological Task* (Nashville: Graded Press, 1989), p. 44.

32. The executive committee of the COTT had accepted this as a suitable substitute wording, recognizing no substantive differences in the texts.

33. *Doctrinal Standards*, p. 35.

34. Ibid., p. 36.

35. Ibid., p. 37.

36. Ibid., p. 39.

37. Ibid., p. 42; also a suggestion from the COTT representatives.

38. Ibid., p. 43.

39. This has led me to think that any major revisions or re-writings of such important documents in the future should not be liable for quick revision and vote at any given General Conference, but should be presented, read, debated, then voted on whole as to whether or not to study the document for a quadrennium before final revisions and a final vote is taken.

Chapter 8

1. Richard P. Heitzenrater's article is published in *Quarterly Review* 5 (Fall 1985):6–27; it is republished in *Mirror and Memory* (Nashville: Abingdon Press, 1989), and is used with permission.

2. *Journals of the General Conference of the Methodist Episcopal Church* (New York: Carlton & Lanahan, n.d.), vol. 1, 1796–1836, p. 89, hereafter cited as *Journal*. Curiously, only the first volume has a number; others bear only dates. The 1984 Book of Discipline (¶ 16) contains only slight revisions: "nor" has been changed to "or"; "articles of religion" has been capitalized; most commas have been omitted.

3. The terms *doctrine* and *doctrinal standards* are used in this paper with the specific connotation that their role is distinctly different from the task of *theology* or *theological reflection*. *Doctrinal standards*, established by and for the church, provide criteria for measuring the doctrinal adequacy of the witness of clergy and laity in the church, whereas *theological reflection*, based on norms such as Scripture, tradition, reason, and experience, necessarily is not subject to such standards and in fact is intentionally and appropriately critical in its task of examining such standards. See Schubert M. Ogden's essay, chapter 3 above. Doctrinal *standards* can also be distinguished from other doctrinal writings in that the standards are carefully formulated documents that provide established norms for measuring the adequacy of various other doctrinal writings ("our doctrines" and "our

doctrinal *standards*" are not the same thing, a distinction which Professor Oden totally misses in his discussion of the question; see chapter 9 below).

4. Preface to Part II, *The Plan of Union, as Adopted by the General Conferences* (the "Blue Book", copyright 1967 by Donald A. Theuer for the Joint Commissions on Church Union of the Methodist Church and the Evangelical United Brethren Church), p. 22 (subsequently contained in the 1968 Book of Discipline, p. 35).

5. 1984 Book of Discipline, ¶ 67, p. 49. This section of the Discipline, which is not a part of the constitution, was adopted in 1972 from the report of the Theological Study Commission on Doctrine and Doctrinal Standards. The line of interpretation contained in the statement reflects in large part the opinions of the last generation of Methodist constitutional historians, who were writing at the turn of the twentieth century. See note 38, following. I began this research in order to *support* that claim with historical evidence, not just historical inferences; the task has concluded just the opposite. As of the republication of this article in 1990, no one has yet provided *any* actual reference (1785–1840) or other solid historical evidence to back up the claim of the 1972 Discipline, and even the author of that sentence has admitted that he may have "fudged a bit" in making that claim (see above, chapter 7, note 9).

6. *Minutes of the Methodist Conferences, Annually Held in America from 1773 to 1794* (Philadelphia: Henry Tuckniss, 1795), p. 77.

7. Benson's proposal to organize Methodism into a distinct denomination separate from the Church of England was passed on to Wesley by Fletcher with some alterations and additions. Two items are of particular note:

> 4. That a pamphlet be published containing the 39 articles of the Church of England rectified according to the purity of the gospel, together with some needful alterations in the liturgy and homilies. . . .
> 10. That the most spiritual part of the Common Prayer shall be extracted and published with the 39 rectified articles, and the minutes of the conferences (or the Methodist canons) which (together with such regulations as may be made at the time of this establishment) shall be, next to the Bible, the *vade mecum* ["constant companion" or "handbook"] of the Methodist preachers. (*The Journal of the Rev. John Wesley* [London: Epworth Press, 1960], 8:332–33.)

Frank Baker comments that this proposal "was almost certainly present in Wesley's mind, and possibly before his eyes" in 1784 when he put together his scheme for American Methodism. *John Wesley and the Church of England* (Nashville: Abingdon Press, 1970), p. 212.

8. This assumption is clearly alluded to in an account of a private interview held during the Christmas Conference, at which Coke, Asbury, William West, and John Andrews (the latter two Protestant Episcopal priests in Baltimore County) discussed the possibility of merging the two emerging episcopal churches in America. Andrews's account of the conversation, in a letter to William Smith, notes that *The Sunday Service of the Methodists* makes plain that "the people called Methodists were hereafter to use the same Liturgy that we make use of, to adhere to the same Articles, and to keep up the same three orders of the Clergy" (interesting that he notes no basic difference between the Wesleyan version of these documents and their English counterparts). Andrews also points out that, "as to Articles of faith and forms of worship, they already agreed with us." Emora T. Brannan, "Episcopal Overtures to Coke and Asbury during the Christmas Conference, 1784," *Methodist History* 14 (April 1976): 209.

9. In fact, the interview mentioned above failed to produce a working agreement in part because West and Andrews perceived that Coke and Asbury considered it "indispensably necessary that Mr. Wesley be the first link of the Chain upon which their Church is suspended." The "binding minute" makes it clear that the American preachers at the Christmas Conference were willing to acknowledge themselves as Wesley's "Sons in the Gospel, ready in matters belonging to church government, to obey his Commands," a very

polite and precise acknowledgment of Wesley's relationship to them in matters of polity. This approbation of Wesley's personal leadership disappeared from the Discipline after 1786, and Wesley's name was omitted from the published minutes of the American annual conferences from 1786 to 1788.

10. James Everett (who was present at Baltimore in 1785), in his autobiographical reflections written to Asbury in 1788, makes a reference to "the Christmas conference, when Dr. Coke came from England, and the Methodist church separated from all connection or dependence on the church of England, *or any other body or society of people*" (italics mine). "An Account of the Most Remarkable Occurrences of the Life of Joseph Everett," *Arminian Magazine* 2 (Philadelphia, 1790):607.

11. *Minutes of Several Conversations between the Rev. Thomas Coke, the Rev. Francis Asbury, and Others . . . Composing a Form of Discipline* (Philadelphia: Charles Cist, 1785), p. 3.

12. This point is not taken seriously by Professor Oden, who spends a great deal of time discussing pre-1785 American Methodism (still a part of British Methodism) in his arguments; all of the "evidence" he quotes concerning the *Sermons* and *Notes* is from documents prior to 1785, which he wrongly assumes continued in effect into the new church (see chapter 9 below). The references to "Minutes" in the 1785 Discipline clearly refer to that document itself, as can be seen in the answer to Question 3, cited above. Also in Question 69, "Questions for a New Helper," where the prospective preacher is asked, "Have you read the *Minutes of the Conference?*," the reference is clearly to the American document, and not to the British *Minutes*, because in 1787, when the third edition of the disciplinary *Minutes* changed its title to *A Form of Discipline*, the question was changed to read, "Have you read the Form of Discipline?"

13. *Minutes of Several Conversations between the Rev. Mr. John and Charles Wesley and Others* (London: Paramore, 1780), p. 43. This edition of the "Large Minutes" was in effect at the time of the Christmas Conference; the "model deed" had been included in the three previous editions of the "Large Minutes": 1763, 1770, 1772.

14. The first conference in 1773 agreed that the doctrine and discipline of the British Methodist *Minutes* should be "the sole rule of our conduct who labour, in the connection with Mr. Wesley, in America." The conference in 1781 noted that the preachers were determined "to preach the old Methodist doctrine, and strictly enforce the discipline, as contained in the notes, sermons, and minutes, as published by Mr. Wesley." At the conference of 1784, held the spring previous to the specially called Christmas Conference, the preachers agreed to accept among them only those European preachers who would, among other things, "preach the doctrine taught in the four volumes of Sermons, and Notes on the New Testament . . . [and] follow the directions of the London and American minutes." *Minutes of the Methodist Conferences* (1795), pp. 5, 41, 72.

15. Question 64 in the "Large Minutes." Part of the answer to Question 65 was retained (as Question 74 in the Discipline): "Let all our Chapels be built plain and decent; but not more expensively than is absolutely avoidable: Otherwise the Necessity of raising Money will make rich men necessary to us. But if so, we must be dependent upon them, yea, and governed by them. And then farewell to the Methodist-Discipline, if not Doctrine too." *Minutes . . . Composing a Form of Discipline* (1785), p. 32. A parallel comparison of the "Large Minutes" with the first American Discipline is published in Appendix VII of John M. Tigert's *Constitutional History of American Episcopal Methodism*, 4th ed. (Nashville: Publishing House of the Methodist Episcopal Church, South, 1911), pp. 532–602. The fact that the Americans did not include the Model Deed in their constitutive documents does not mean that they "rescinded" or "rejected" the British document—starting anew, they simply never implemented it in their new church structure. No evidence of any use in America after 1785 of the British model deed (containing the reference to Wesley's *Sermons* and *Notes*) has turned up.

16. The wording in the American deed follows very closely the wording of the British document before and after the omitted section, indicating that the doctrinal stipulation ("preach no other doctrine than is contained in . . .") was consciously dropped from the American form, or more precisely, never implemented in the new American church. Documents previously authoritative in America (before 1785, such as the British *Minutes*) had no constitutional standing in the new church.

17. The "fifth edition" of the Discipline (New York: William Ross, 1789), section XXXIII.

18. This wording is on the title page of the Discipline; the "useful pieces" have separate title pages but are paged continuously in the volume. Some are written by Wesley, whose doctrines and writings still provided the basic shape of American Methodist doctrine (in addition to the "standards" he also had provided in the form of Articles). In 1790, the Articles of Religion became section XXXV of the *Form of Discipline*; in 1791, section XXXVI.

19. The answer stipulates that the preacher of such "erroneous doctrines" shall confront the same process as is observed "in cases of gross immorality" which had just been spelled out.

20. This wording, not only used in 1808 in the Restrictive Rules but also still in effect today in the section on trials, implies a method of measure quite different from the early British rule that allowed preaching of "*no other doctrine* than is contained in Mr. Wesley's Notes upon the New Testament and four volumes of Sermons," which is strictly delimiting in its intention (my italics). The "contrary to" concept and language was adopted by the British Conference in 1832.

21. The explanatory notes of Asbury and Coke, included in the 1796 Discipline, for the section on trial of a minister for erroneous doctrines, point out that "the heretical doctrines are as dangerous, at least to the hearers, as the immoral life of a preacher." The heresies mentioned specifically were "arian, socianian, and universalian." *The Doctrines and Discipline of the Methodist Episcopal Church in America* (Philadelphia: Tuckniss, 1798), p. 113.

22. E.g., Wesley's *Works, Notes, Christian Library, Primitive Physick*, Fletcher's tracts, Richard Baxter's *Gildas Salvianus*, Kempis, and the *Instructions for Children*. These were all carried over from the British *Minutes*; the American Discipline omitted some, such as the reference to Wesley's fourth volume of *Sermons* in Question 33 (Question 51 in the Discipline). The bishops' notes in the 1798 Discipline say nothing after the two doctrinal sections, simply referring the reader to "Mr. Wesley's excellent treatise" after the section "Of Christian Perfection," and to "that great writer, Mr. Fletcher" after the section "against Antinomianism." A footnote in Bishop Roberts's address to the conference at Baltimore in 1807, in a section headed "take heed unto the doctrine," refers the reader to several guides to understanding the Bible, including works by Stackhouse, Doddridge, Bonnett, Watson, Addison and Beattie, Jenny, Wilberforce, Leland, and Ogden, but no mention is made of Wesley's *Notes*. These references (or the wide availability or scarcity of particular publications), however, do not speak to the question of officially "established standards" of doctrine.

23. In 1790 when the doctrinal treatises were introduced into the body of the Discipline (with section numbers), the title was altered to read, *A Form of Discipline* . . . (*now comprehending the Principles and Doctrines*) *of the Methodist Episcopal Church in America*. Two years later, the sacramental services were added and the title became *The Doctrines and Discipline of the Methodist Episcopal Church in America* as we noted above. The doctrinal treatises were by and large "Wesleyan" tracts, though only half of them were by John Wesley: *Scripture Doctrine of Predestination, Election, and Reprobation*, by Henry Haggar, abridged by Wesley (inserted beginning in 1788); *Serious Thoughts on the Infallible, Unconditional Perseverance of All That Have Once Experienced Faith in Christ* (beginning in 1788); *A Plain Account of Christian Perfection* (beginning in 1789); *An Extract on the Nature and Subjects of Christian Baptism*, by Moses Hemmenway (beginning in 1790). The tracts were omitted from the 1798 Discipline (tenth edition) to make room for the bishops' explanatory notes, but (with the

exception of the treatise on baptism) were restored in the following (eleventh) edition of 1801.

24. These treatises were removed from the Discipline by action of the General Conference of 1812 to be published separately. The directions of the conference were only slowly and inaccurately heeded.

25. One document, by Coke, contained twenty-eight Articles; the other, probably by Clarke and Benson, contained thirty-eight Articles. See *Articles of Religion Prepared by Order of the Conference of 1806*, publication no. 2 of The Wesley Historical Society (London: Kelly, 1897).

26. *Journal*, 1:76, 79.

27. *Journal*, 1:82; compare "A Journal of the Proceedings of the General Conference of the Methodist Episcopal Church, 1800–1828" (MS, Drew University Library), p. 168; referred to hereafter as "manuscript journal" or "MS journal." The last phrase, starting "contrary to," was inadvertently omitted in the printed version. Contrary to Professor Oden's argument, the reference to "Articles of Religion" can surely be seen as plural, referring to the several articles contained therein as standards of doctrine.

28. *Journal*, 1:89.

29. MS journal, p. 68; this page also contains the Restrictive Rules.

30. *Journal*, 1:128–29. The committee that had determined the necessity for such a committee of safety, based on the episcopal address, consisted of one member from each conference and included Philip Bruce and Nelson Reed, two members of the 1808 "committee of fourteen" that had drawn up the Restrictive Rules.

31. Horace M. Du Bose, *Life of Joshua Soule* (Nashville: Publishing House of the Methodist Episcopal Church, South, 1916), p. 110.

32. *Journal*, 1:155. The Committee of Safety ended its report with eight resolutions which were passed by the conference, including, "1. That the General Conference do earnestly recommend the superintendents to make the most careful inquiry to all the annual conferences, in order to ascertain whether any doctrines are embraced or preached contrary to our established articles of faith, and to use their influence to prevent the existence and circulation of all such doctrines" (*Journal* 1:57). It might also be noted that the following day, the conference adopted the report of the Committee on Ways and Means which included a proposal that the section of the Discipline on "The Method of Receiving Preachers" include the stipulation, "It shall be the duty of the bishops, or of a committee which they may appoint at each annual conference, to point out a course of reading and study proper to be pursued by candidates for the ministry. . . ." (*Journal*, 1:160–61).

33. *Journal*, 1:348.

34. *Journal*, 1:350–51.

35. *Guide-Book in the Administration of the Discipline* (New York: Carlton & Phillips, 1855), p. 152.

36. *A Manual of the Discipline of the Methodist Episcopal Church, South* (Nashville: Publishing House of the Methodist Episcopal Church, South, 1870), p. 131.

37. Discipline (1880), ¶ 213; see also *Journal* (1880, no vol. no.), p. 323.

38. *Constitutional and Parliamentary History of the Methodist Episcopal Church* (New York: Methodist Book Concern, 1912), pp. 157–69. See also John M. Tigert, *A Constitutional History of American Episcopal Methodism* (Nashville: Publishing House of the Methodist Episcopal Church, South, 1894), pp. 113, 139–48, and Thomas B. Neely, *Doctrinal Standards of Methodism* (New York: Revell, 1918), pp. 225–37.

39. At about the same time, the southern church received a report by the College of Bishops to the General Conference of 1914, stating that Wesley's *Notes* and *Sermons* "have never been adopted by organized Episcopal Methodism" and therefore "it is not clear that [they] are standards of doctrine." See the eighteenth edition of Bishop McTyeire's *Manual of the Discipline* (1924; edited by Bishop Collins Denny), pp. 147–48.

Chapter 9

1. Thomas C. Oden is Henry Anson Butts Professor of Theology and Ethics at the Theological School, Drew University. This article appeared in *Quarterly Review* 7 (Spring 1987):42–62, and is used with permission.

2. For the full text of the deed, see Robert Emory, *History of the Discipline of the Methodist Episcopal Church* (New York: Lane & Sanford, 1844), pp. 70, 71.

3. Although technically disputed as to number according to various editions, whether forty-three, forty-four, fifty-two, or fifty-three, at least forty-three are undisputed.

4. "At Full Liberty: Doctrinal Standards in Early American Methodism," *Quarterly Review* 5 (Fall, 1985):6–27 (hereafter Heitzenrater; see above, chapter 8).

5. *Minutes of the Annual Conferences of the Methodist Episcopal Church for the Years 1773–1828* (New York: Mason & Lane, 1840), vol. 1, Qns. 1, 2, p. 5. Hereafter this source is referred to as MAC.

6. 1780 Journal of the General Conference, Qn. 7. Compare analyses by J. Tigert, *Constitutional History of American Episcopal Methodism*, 4th ed. (Nashville: Publishing House of the Methodist Episcopal Church, South, 1904), p. 113; and J. M. Buckley, *Constitutional and Parliamentary History of the Methodist Episcopal Church* (New York: Eaton and Mains, 1912), pp. 162, 163.

7. *MAC*, p. 13.

8. Buckley, p. 163.

9. *Minutes of Several Conversations . . . Composing a Form of Discipline, 1784* (Philadelphia: Charles Cist, 1785), Qn. 73, p. 27.

10. Heitzenrater, p. 11.

11. Tigert, pp. 544, 548, 540, and 545, resp.

12. Heitzenrater, p. 12.

13. 1785 Discipline; full text in Tigert, pp. 562, 567, 576, 585, and 535, resp.

14. Heitzenrater, pp. 10 ff.

15. *Doctrines and Discipline of the Methodist Episcopal Church 1792* (Philadelphia: Perry Hall, 1792), preface, p. iv.

16. Heitzenrater, p. 12.

17. See *Journal of General Conference, 1792. Reconstructed by T. B. Neely* (New York: Eaton and Mains, 1899), pp. 40, 41.

18. Heitzenrater, pp. 9–12.

19. Heitzenrater, p. 10.

20. Jesse Lee, *History of the Methodists* (Baltimore: Magill and Clime, 1810), p. 86.

21. Tigert, pp. 142 ff.

22. Heitzenrater, p. 10.

23. 1796 *Journal of the General Conference*, p. 13.

24. Letter from John Wesley, received by the conference of 1783; text in Lee, *History*, p. 85.

25. Heitzenrater, pp. 12, 13.

26. Heitzenrater, p. 12.

27. Buckley, pp. 105, 106.

28. The phrase "duplex norm" comes from Albert Outler's 1958 *Handbook of Selected Creeds and Confessions*, a mimeographed document used in classes at Perkins School of Theology, Dallas, Tex., pt. 4, p. 6.

29. Buckley, p. 168.

30. Heitzenrater, p. 21.

31. Heitzenrater, p. 19. The phrase "established articles of faith" comes from the Committee of Safety, 1816 *Journal of the General Conference*, p. 155.

32. 1816 *Journal of the General Conference*, p. 156.

33. See *A Union Catalogue for the Publications of John and Charles Wesley*, ed. Frank Baker (Durham, NC: Duke Divinity School, 1966).

34. Heitzenrater, p. 11.

35. 1824 *Journal of the General Conference*, Address to the General Conference, in *Journal of the General Conference, 1796–1836* (New York: Carlton & Phillips, 1855); for further references see Nathan Bangs, History of the Methodist Episcopal Church, 4 vols. (New York: Mason & Lane, 1840), 3:115 ff., 259 ff.

36. Bangs, 3:131.

37. Heitzenrater, p. 18.

38. Manuscript of the 1808 General Conference Journal, p. 68.

39. Heitzenrater, p. 17.

40. *Journal of the General Conference*, p. 75.

41. *Journal of the General Conference*, May 17, 1808, p. 83.

42. Letter to Tho. Roberts of May 27, 1808, in Francis Asbury, *Journals and Letters* (London: Epworth, 1958), 3:391, 392.

43. Heitzenrater, p. 7.

44. Heitzenrater, p. 13.

45. The quotations come from Heitzenrater, pp. 20, 21.

46. Heitzenrater, p. 21.

47. Heitzenrater, pp. 21–23. The interpreters I have in mind are Baker, McTyeire, Neely, Buckley, and Outler, as well as the writers of the Plan of Union and the 1972–84 *Disciplines*.

Chapter 10

1. At the October 1986 meeting of the General Commission on Christian Unity and Interreligious Concerns (GCCUIC), it was determined that the work of the Committee on Our Theological Task would prove to be of crucial importance to the shaping of The United Methodist Church of the future. Therefore, in March 1987, two staff persons of GCCUIC, Jeanne Audry Powers and Bruce Robbins, presented reports to the Commission analyzing the study committee's draft and comparing it with the material in Part II of the 1984 Book of Discipline. After plenary and small group discussion and feedback from GCCUIC members, this report was drafted by the previous authors under the direction of Robert Huston, General Secretary, reviewed once again by GCCUIC members, and was formally submitted in August 1987 to the Committee on Our Theological Task by GCCUIC for their consideration.

2. *Consensus*, p. 30

3. Ibid.

Chapter 11

1. Ted A. Campbell is Assistant Professor of Church History at The Divinity School, Duke University. This paper was presented as the Stover Lecture at St. Paul School of Theology, Kansas City, Mo., on September 23, 1987, and has been revised for this volume.

2. *The Book of Discipline of The United Methodist Church, 1972* (Nashville: United Methodist Publishing House, 1972; hereafter cited as "1972 Discipline"), ¶ 70, p. 75–79.

3. An example of the fourfold pattern used as a tool for theological and ethical analysis is found in Dennis M. Campbell, *Doctors, Lawyers, Ministers: Christian Ethics in Professional Practice* (Nashville: Abingdon Press, 1982). United Methodist confirmation materials have also stressed the "quadrilateral."

4. *The Book of Discipline of The United Methodist Church, 1988* (Nashville: United Methodist Publishing House, 1988; hereafter cited as "1988 Discipline"), ¶ 69, p. 80–86.

5. See, for instance, R. Denny Urlin's works, *John Wesley's Place in Church History* (London: Rivington's, 1870), and *Churchman's Life of Wesley* (London: SPCK, revised edition, 1880), or David Baines-Griffiths, *Wesley the Anglican* (London: MacMillan and Co., 1919).

6. George Croft Cell, *The Rediscovery of John Wesley* (Lanham, New York, and London: University Press of America, 1984; reprint of 1935 edition), passim. Cf. William Ragsdale Cannon, *The Theology of John Wesley with Special Reference to the Doctrine of Justification* (Lanham, New York, and London: University Press of America, 1974; reprint of 1946 edition; this work is a revision of Cannon's 1942 dissertation), pp. 20–21, where Cannon argues that Wesley reasserted *sola scriptura* against the Deists.

7. Herbert Brook Workman, *The Place of Methodism in the Catholic Church* (London: Epworth Press, 1921); a similar argument was laid out by the North American Methodist Umphrey Lee, *John Wesley and Modern Religion* (Nashville: Cokesbury Press, 1936).

8. An important exception to this generalization is Stanley B. Frost's Marburg dissertation entitled *Die Autoritätslehre in den Werken John Wesleys* (Munich: Verlag Ernst Reinhardt, 1938), although, unfortunately, Frost's work received very little attention in English-speaking circles.

9. (Nashville: Abingdon Press, 1960), pp. 23–38.

10. Ibid., p. 23.

11. Ibid., pp. 37–38.

12. [Theological Study Commission of The United Methodist Church], "The Theological Study Commission on Doctrine and Doctrinal Standards: An Interim Report to the General Conference," [no place of publication given; date is presumably early 1970].

13. Albert C. Outler, "The Wesleyan Quadrilateral—in John Wesley," *Wesleyan Theological Journal* 20:1 (Spring 1985), p. 16.

14. 1972 Discipline, p. 75.

15. Ibid., pp. 78–79.

16. Leroy T. Howe, "United Methodism in Search of Theology," *Perkins Journal* 28 (Fall 1974):13–16.

17. Robert E. Cushman, "Church Doctrinal Standards Today," *Religion in Life* 44 (1975):409–10.

18. Timothy Smith, an unpublished paper delivered to the Wesley Studies Working Group of the 1982 Oxford Institute of Methodist Theological Studies.

19. [Committee on Our Theological Task of The United Methodist Church,] "Report of the Committee on our Theological Task to the General Conference of The United Methodist Church" [n.d., distributed in 1987], pp. 26 and 27.

20. 1988 Discipline, pp. 80–86.

21. Ibid., p. 80.

22. Outler, pp. 7–18.

23. Ibid., pp. 13–16.

24. Ibid., pp. 9–10.

25. John Wesley, "The Doctrine of Original Sin, according to Scripture, Reason, and Experience" (in Thomas Jackson, ed., *The Works of the Reverend John Wesley, A.M.* [14 volumes; London: Wesleyan Conference Office, 1872], 9:191).

26. Preface to 1771 edition of the *Works*, ¶4 (cited in Jackson, 1:iv).

27. "A Fruitful Exhortation to the Reading of Holy Scripture," Part I; *Certain Sermons or Homilies Appointed to be Read in Churches in the Time of Queen Elizabeth of Famous Memory* (London: SPCK, 1890), p. 2.

28. John Wesley, Sermon 112 "On Laying the Foundation of the New Chapel, near the City-Road, London" II:3, *Works* (1986), 3:586; idem, "Farther Thoughts on Separation from the Church," pars. 1–2, *Works* (1989), 9:538.

29. *Life* (10 November 1947); cited in Walter N. Vernon, *United Methodist Profile* (Nashville: Graded Press, 1959), p. 7, note 1.

Chapter 12

1. John B. Cobb, Jr. is Ingraham Professor of Theology at the School of Theology at Claremont. This article appeared in *The Christian Century* 105 (April 6, 1988):343-7 and is used with permission.
2. *Daily Christian Advocate* Advance Edition C (No. 7, Feb. 25, 1988):C13.

Chapter 13

1. Thomas W. Ogletree is the Dean of the Theological School, Drew University and served on the Committee on Our Theological Task which prepared the statement submitted to the 1988 General Conference. This article appeared in *Quarterly Review* 8 (Spring 1988):43-53, and is used with permission.
2. "The New Doctrinal Statements: A First Draft Proposal," *The Circuit Rider*, 11 (February, 1987):9-15.
3. Richard P. Heitzenrater, "At Full Liberty: Doctrinal Standards in Early American Methodism," *Quarterly Review* 5 (Fall, 1985):6-27.
4. Thomas C. Oden, "Here I Stand: Keep 'Sermons,' 'Notes' in Theology Report," *The United Methodist Reporter*, January 8, 1988.
5. *The Constitution for The United Methodist Church with Enabling Legislation and Other Historical Documents*, p. 24.
6. Ibid., p. v.
7. Cf. Oden, "Here I Stand."
8. Sanctification and Christian perfection are treated in Article XI of the Confession of Faith, and in an article taken from the Methodist Protestant Discipline which is included with the Articles of Religion though never voted on by the three bodies which united in 1939. Cf. Book of Discipline, ¶ 62.

Chapter 14

1. This essay is a recounting of the theological discussion in the Legislative Committee on Faith and Mission at the United Methodist General Conference, April 26-May 6, 1988. It appeared in *Quarterly Review* 9 (Summer 1989):3-15, and is used with permission. The report hopes to promote the Committee's desire that ongoing theological discussion in The United Methodist Church might be stimulated.
2. See essays by Albert Outler and Ted Campbell, chapters 6 and 11 above.
3. *Daily Christian Advocate* (May 5, 1988):520.

Chapter 15

1. Russell E. Richey is Associate Dean for Academic Programs and Research Professor of Church History at the Divinity School, Duke University. This article appeared in *Quarterly Review* 9 (Winter 1989):3-20, and is used with permission.
2. What should one make of the historical self-estimate United Methodists render in their Discipline? A series of questions might sharpen the issue:

Why do Methodists need two such historical accounts, one prefatory to the Discipline as a whole, the other introductory to the section "Doctrinal Standards and Our Theological Task"?

Why would Methodists grant history such a privileged place in their book?

Why do Methodists introduce themselves historically?

Why do they explain their doctrine historically?

Why would they commit such a proportion of the Discipline to history, devoting to it the first eighteen pages of the book (if one counts the chronologically arranged list of bishops), as well as the first twenty pages of "Doctrinal Standards" (twelve pages if one excludes the discursive sections, "Our Common Heritage as Christians," "Basic Christian Affirmations" and "Our Distinctive Heritage as United Methodists")?

Why, in a doctrinal section, would a church, its highest authority, and its theologians appeal to history at all?

Why would they set the doctrinal section within a historical framework?

How is history functioning in the Discipline as a whole? Within the section on "Doctrinal Standards"?

In that discussion, what do the structure of the narrative, the starting point, the topics covered, and the topics omitted indicate about how Methodism understands itself, its doctrine, and its authority?

What does one learn about Methodism by recognizing its dependence upon history, by acknowledging that at critical junctures it turns to history?

What does this use of history suggest about what *really* functions as authority for Methodism?

Why does the church need this historical statement?

And for that matter, why in this whole section does it need anything more than the Standards themselves? Why all the explanation? Do not the history and the explanation infringe upon the Standards?

3. Behind the American Methodist appeal to history lay that of John Wesley. Wesley's apologetical use of the Methodist story, which lies beyond the purview of this essay, obviously informed these early American efforts. Asbury, Coke, and others of the American leadership would have known his "A Plain Account of The People Called Methodists," of 1748; the historical appeals made elsewhere in Wesleyan apologetics; the premium he placed upon his own and his itinerants' diaries and journals and his efforts to publish them; and the place of history in the recently launched *Arminian Magazine*. For Wesley's "A Plain Account," see *The Works of John Wesley*, Jackson edition, 14 vols (Grand Rapids: Zondervan, 1959), VIII, 248–68.

4. The initial version of the American Discipline suggested in its title the loyalty to the Wesleyan format—*Minutes of Several Conversations between The Rev. Thomas Coke LLD. and The Rev. Francis Asbury and others, at a Conference, begun in Baltimore, in the State of Maryland, on Monday, the 27th of December, in the Year 1784. Composing a Form of Discipline for the Ministers, Preachers and other Members of the Methodist Episcopal Church in America* (Philadelphia, 1785). For comparison of the American with the Wesleyan minutes see John James Tigert, *A Constitutional History of American Episcopal Methodism*, 6th rev. and enl. ed. (Nashville: Publishing House of the Methodist Episcopal Church, South, 1916), Appendix VII, which puts the two in parallel columns. Consult this volume and Nolan B. Harmon, *The Organization of The Methodist Church*, 2nd rev. ed. (Nashville: The Methodist Publishing House, 1962), on constitutional matters.

5. *A Form of Discipline, For the Ministers, Preachers, and Members of the Methodist Episcopal Church in America* (New York, 1787), 3–4. For sustained reflection on the import of the changes that the Americans made see the first seven essays in *Reflections Upon Methodism During the Bicentennial* (Dallas: Bridwell Library Center for Methodist Studies, 1985; Papers presented at the 1984 Regional Conference of the World Methodist Historical Society).

6. An accessible version of the early Methodist disciplines is *The Methodist Discipline of 1798, Including the Annotations of Thomas Coke and Francis Asbury*, facsimile edition, edited by Frederick A. Norwood (Rutland, VT: Academy Books, 1979). Designed for apologetic

purposes to address critics from other denominations and critics from within like James O'Kelly, the annotations bear on the argument of this paper. They appeal consistently to Scripture; and, as appropriate, to tradition. And they make a reasoned case for the rubrics of the Discipline. Here, then, in the notes—after the fact, as it were—the bishops become self-conscious about the nature of Methodist authority. Why, one might ask, had they and the church not been more self-conscious in their prefatory statements? Or, perhaps had they?

7. See *The Doctrines and Discipline of the African Methodist Episcopal Church* (Philadelphia, 1817); *The Doctrines and Discipline of the Wesleyan Methodist Episcopal Zion Church in America, Established in the City of New-York, October 25th, 1820*, 2nd ed. (New York, 1840); *The Doctrine and Discipline of the Evangelical Association, Together with the Design of Their Union, translated from the German* (New-Berlin, 1832); *Origin, Constitution, Doctrine and Discipline, of the United Brethren in Christ* (Circleville, Ohio, 1837); *Constitution and Discipline of the Methodist Protestant Church* (Baltimore, 1830); *The Discipline of the Wesleyan Methodist Connection of America*, particularly in the 2nd, New York, 1845, and 3rd, New York, 1849, versions which include a Preface by a committee appointed "to prepare a short account of the Wesleyan Methodist Connection of America, to be inserted in the Discipline" (1845: iii); *The Doctrines and Discipline of the Methodist Episcopal Church, South* (Richmond, 1846); *The Doctrines and Discipline of the Free Methodist Church* (Rochester, 1870); *The Doctrines and Discipline of the Colored Methodist Episcopal Church in America* (Louisville, 1874). All were consulted in The Archives Center, Drew University.

8. For a fascinating study of the contrasts see *Religion, Order, and Law. A Study in Pre-Revolutionary England* by David Little (New York: Harper & Row Publishers, 1969).

9. See, for instance, *The Constitution of the Presbyterian Church (U.S.A.)*, Part I "Book of Confessions," and Part II "Book of Order" (New York: Published by the Office of the General Assembly, 1985), and *Constitution & Canons for the Government of the Protestant Episcopal Church . . . Adopted in General Conventions 1789–1987, Together with the Rules or Order* (Printed for the Convention, 1985).

10. See Jesse Lee, *A Short History of the Methodists* (Baltimore, 1810; reprinted Rutland, Vt: Academy Books, 1974), especially the preface.

11. Why history? Perhaps, the claim must finally be confessional. Our fascination with history has to do with the dynamics and character of our movement—the prominence we allow to both tradition and experience in our epistemology; the premium we (along with other evangelicals/pietists) put on the inward experience of salvation; the place we have given to testimony in class meeting and Sunday school; the emphasis we place (following Wesley) on popular media (magazine, tract, newspaper) which both necessitates and accommodates narrated experience; the confidence we have had that God works providentially in our corporate life as well as savingly in our individual lives; the recognition we consequently gave to Wesley's demand that we record (and share) our stories, our histories; the apologetical use we found for appeals to history and tradition; and the obvious value and impact that we (members and prospective members) discovered in the story of conversion, revival, missionary encounter.

Human interest, Methodists learned, displayed the Divine Interest. Personal testimony discloses the spiritual identity of an individual; history evidences corporate identity. So we Methodists do theology in our own way. And one way we do theology is by telling our story, the narrative of God's work in us and among us. History is a Methodist mode of theologizing. We begin our Discipline with a historical word about ourselves and we publish history because we know we need to tell God's modern story.

12. See note 5.

13. To accent the experiential bases of the prefaces should not imply that other resources of Methodist reflection were wholly absent. Reason functions in any ordering of discourse. It was obviously at play in the conference's re-ordering and

'METHODIZING' of the Discipline, construction of the historical narratives, and decision to place them first. The historical statements expressed Methodism's dependence upon reason. So also they represented an appeal to tradition—in their retention of the Wesleyan queries and answers, in their identification of a tradition that was passed along, in their focus upon the constitutive phases of the movement (in both Britain and America) that had "traditioning" value, in their function as the memory of the church, in their definition of the Discipline as a living past. The appeal to Scripture is less obvious but also operative in the representation of Methodism as a scriptural way of holiness.

For elaboration of the quadrilateral (Scripture, tradition, reason and experience), see 1972 and later versions of *The Book of Discipline of The United Methodist Church*. Also note Thomas A. Langford, "The United Methodist Quadrilateral: A Theological Task" (chapter 19 below).

14. To recognize these historical prefaces as deriving from experience is not quite the same as to posit that the Discipline made experience (rather than Scripture, tradition or reason) normative and its point of theological departure. To reiterate a point made earlier, these prefatory essays were more instinctive than reflective; they indicate the priority of conversion narrative and historical account in Methodist genre. These prefaces do not present themselves as premises of the Discipline as a whole. The present debates concern the shape and internal priorities of those premises and appropriately appeal the legislative record of early Methodism. To identify the premises, one does have to look to those factors, beliefs and commitments that informed the "Book." In that sense, the debates in conference have at least as much theological bearing on the Discipline as the prefaces.

15. These historical statements did not even pretend to carry the church's history toward the present. The function was actually the reverse, to claim that the present remained faithful to the past. By the twentieth century, the MEC Discipline had added an additional page which identified, celebrated and apologized for the Methodist system. It affirmed of the MEC, "While its polity and administrative rules have been modified from time to time to meet changing conditions and opportunities, it remains unchanged in doctrine and ministerial offices" (Discipline, 1932:9). The brief apology and self-conscious attention to doctrine set important precedents for what would follow in 1972.

16. In an interesting reflexive moment, the "Historical Statement" indicated consciousness of its high calling, of its obligation to tell the story, of its function as an authoritative statement about the movement. On mention of the Methodist Protestant Church, it said, "The history of this movement may be read in the last DISCIPLINE of the Methodist Protestant Church..." *Doctrines and Discipline of The Methodist Church, 1940* (New York: The Methodist Publishing House, 1940), 6. The Methodist Protestant disciplines always carried a much fuller and expressive historical account, some 10 pages by the 1930s. Even so it only detailed origins.

17. This particular function is especially interesting since constitutional continuity was formally and legally cared for elsewhere in *The Discipline*.

18. The listing of bishops had actually begun in the 1964 Methodist Discipline and was carried over into United Methodist practice.

19. One significant addition to the initial historical statement of the Discipline was made in 1976 and continues to the present. It is entitled "Black People and Their United Methodist Heritage." It functions, as does the rest of the "Historical Statement" and as have the prefaces over the years, to confer legitimacy. In this case, it symbolizes within the Discipline the end to the segregated Central Jurisdiction, the end to *de jure* marginal status for blacks, the end to *de facto* racism.

20. As an aside, I would concede perplexity at the Church's dramatic revision of the 1972 historical account. I made this point to Heitzenrater when outside comment was invited. It strikes me that radical changes to constitutional and quasi-constitutional documents tend to induce skepticism and doubt. The advocates of change to the 1972 Discipline,

persons wanting greater doctrinal clarity and commitment, may have set in process a self-defeating strategem.

21. Here the 1988 Discipline does not diverge radically from the 1972 version. That account also portrayed Methodist doctrinal development in Wesleyan terms.

22. See, in particular, Thomas A. Langford, *Practical Divinity: Theology in the Wesleyan Tradition* (Nashville: Abingdon Press, 1983), which struggles with the issue of whether such a tradition exists and how it might be conceptualized. Langford devotes an early chapter to "The Americanization of Wesleyan Theology," and there attends to matters raised here.

23. For instance, the focus upon Wesley and upon Methodism's loyalty or disloyalty to his literary corpus obscures the way that other features of the Methodist ethos have affected doctrinal development. A compelling case can be made for rather considerable impact upon Methodist doctrine of Methodist practice, polity, and worship. Camp meetings and revivalism are only the most obvious of a variety of influences that deserve mention. So also the powerful influences of American culture and also of both Pietism and the Enlightenment could readily be acknowledged. This point seems to be conceded in the text but not explicitly developed. Obviously, there are severe limits as to what can be included in such a brief account. Still, can the church afford to depict the heritage as a self-contained Wesleyan stream?

24. A jeremiadic construction of reality comes easily to Americans who have, according to Sacvan Bercovitch, defined their very being, construed their national self-understanding, in such terms. For discussion of the genre and its uses, see his *The American Jeremiad* (Madison: University of Wisconsin Press, 1978).

25. Heitzenrater's argument has been advanced in several places. See, for instance, "At Full Liberty: Doctrinal Standards in Early American Methodism," *Quarterly Review* 5 (Fall 1985), 6–27. Thomas C. Oden responded in "What are 'Established Standards of Doctrine'?: A Response to Richard Heitzenrater," *Quarterly Review* 7 (Spring 1987), 41–62, and more extensively in *Doctrinal Standards in the Wesleyan Tradition* (Grand Rapids: Francis Asbury Press of Zondervan Publishing House, 1988).

26. The issue is raised as a matter of principle. I happen to concur in Heitzenrater's reading. If the church decides that the Discipline can fittingly embrace historical controversy, then one might ask why not acknowledgment of the entanglement of doctrine with slavery, war, opposition to women's lay rights and ordination, anti-Romanism? Obviously, those dimensions to the evolution of doctrine the church would rather forget. Nor is it the place of an official (and brief) history of doctrine to examine, critique and assess in the manner of a scholarly (and massive) survey. Yet, here, as above, one can legitimately ask about the consequences of a selective memory.

Chapter 16

1. "The theological task, though related to the church's doctrinal expressions, serves a different function. Our doctrinal affirmations assist us in the discernment of Christian truth in ever-changing contexts. Our theological task includes the testing, renewal, elaboration, and application of our doctrinal perspective in carrying out our calling 'to spread scriptural holiness over these lands.'" 1988 Book of Discipline, ¶ 69, pp. 77–78.

Chapter 17

1. Mary Elizabeth Moore is Professor of Theology and Christian Education at the School of Theology at Claremont, California. This article appeared in *Quarterly Review* 9 (Fall 1989):44–63, and is used with permission.

2. "Our Doctrinal Heritage," *Book of Discipline of The United Methodist Church* (Nashville: United Methodist Publishing House, 1988), p. 44 (hereafter 1988 Book of Discipline).

3. Ibid.

4. "The Constitution," *Book of Discipline of The United Methodist Church* (Nashville: United Methodist Publishing House, 1984), p. 19 (hereafter 1984 *Book of Discipline*).

5. Ibid., p. 25.

6. "Our Theological Task," 1984 *Book of Discipline*, p. 78.

7. "Historical Background," 1984 *Book of Discipline*, p. 41.

8. Ibid.

9. "Our Theological Task," 1988 *Book of Discipline*, p. 79

10. "Historical Background," 1984 *Book of Discipline*, p. 49.

11. See "Our Theological Task" in both documents: the 1984 *Book of Discipline* 1984, esp. pp. 78–81; 1988 *Book of Discipline*, esp. pp. 80–86.

12. "The Constitution," 1984 *Book of Discipline*, p. 19. The theme of organic union appears on this same page, where the union of The Methodist Church and The Evangelical United Brethren Church is seen as obedience to God's will that the people of God be one.

13. *Daily Christian Advocate* 7 (No. 12, May 7, 1988):7.

14. "Our Doctrinal Heritage," 1988 *Book of Discipline*, p. 41

15. "Our Theological Task," 1984 *Book of Discipline*, p. 73.

16. Ibid., pp. 71–72.

17. Ibid., p. 78; and "Our Theological Task," 1988 *Book of Discipline*, p. 81.

18. "Historical Background," 1984 *Book of Discipline*, p. 41.

19. See the essay by Russell Richey, ch. 15 above.

20. These references in the 1972 theological statement can be found respectively on the following pages of the 1984 *Book of Discipline*: pp. 41, 42, 50, 54, 71, and 78.

21. "Our Doctrinal History," 1988 *Book of Discipline*, p. 56.

22. "Our Theological Task," 1988 *Book of Discipline*, p. 78.

23. "Historical Background," 1984 *Book of Discipline*, p. 50.

24. "Our Theological Task," 1988 *Book of Discipline*, p. 82.

25. Ibid.

26. Ibid., pp. 83–86.

27. Ibid., p. 86.

28. Compare the two statements on Scripture for subtle changes of emphasis, in regard to God's self-disclosures and in regard to the nature and function of the Bible itself. The particular phrases cited here are found in "Our Theological Task," 1984 *Book of Discipline* 1984, p. 78; 1988 *Book of Discipline*, p. 81.

29. "Our Theological Task," 1984 *Book of Discipline*, p. 85; 1988 *Book of Discipline*, p. 89.

30. The particular references to the phrases listed are found respectively in the following passages: 1988 *Book of Discipline*, pp. 51, 78, 83, 84, 85.

31. "Our Theological Task," 1984 *Book of Discipline*, p. 84.

32. "Our Theological Task," in 1988 *Book of Discipline*, p. 89; *Book of Discipline* 1984, p. 84.

33. "Our Theological Task," 1984 *Book of Discipline*, p. 84.

34. "Our Theological Task," 1988 *Book of Discipline*, p. 88.

35. Ibid., p. 82 [255].

Chapter 18

1. Geoffrey Wainwright is Professor of Systematic Theology at the Divinity School, Duke University. This article appeared in *This World: A Journal of Religion and Public Life* 25 (Spring, 1989):109–18, and is used with permission.

2. Preface, §5, in *The Works of John Wesley* (Nashville: Abingdon Press, 1988), 7:74.

3. So in *The Character of a Methodist*, §1, in *Works* (1989), 9:34.

4. New York: Abingdon Press, 1965; reprinted Lanham, MD: University Press of America, 1983.

5. For one view of the history of *doctrinal* standards, see Thomas C. Oden, *Doctrinal Standards in the Wesleyan Tradition* (Grand Rapids: Francis Asbury Press of Zondervan Publishing House, 1988). For an attempt to make the most of what unity there is in the *theological* tradition, see Thomas A. Langford, *Practical Divinity: Theology in the Wesleyan Tradition* (Nashville: Abingdon Press, 1983). The distinction between official *doctrine* and the more individual but still ecclesial task of *theology* was unfortunately lost in the linguistic usage of the 1972 text. It has been respected in the 1988 text that we shall be presenting, and I have tried to observe it throughout this article.

6. A dictum of George Croft Cell, quoted in Oden, *Doctrinal Standards*, p. 82.

7. In Sermon 39, "Catholic Spirit," Wesley says that "a man of truly catholic spirit . . . is fixed as the sun in his judgment concerning the main branches of Christian doctrine." *Works* (1985), 2:93.

8. A printer's proof read "come" rather than the "comes" of the final version in the Discipline. It would have been equally possible to leave "come" and replace the previous period by a comma. I have reason to believe that would have corresponded better to the thought of the Committee. It would probably make better theology.

9. For insistence on the distinction between doctrine and theology, and the normativity of the former, see Schubert Ogden's essay, chapter 3 above; see also Jerry L. Walls, *The Problem of Pluralism: Recovering United Methodist Identity* (Wilmore, KY: Good News Books, 1986; updated 1988).

10. Letter of August 3, 1771 to Ms. Marsh.

11. Richard B. Wilke, *And Are We Yet Alive? The Future of The United Methodist Church* (Nashville: Abingdon Press, 1986); William H. Willimon and Robert L. Wilson, *Rekindling the Flame: Strategies for a Vital United Methodism* (Nashville: Abingdon Press, 1987).

Chapter 19

1. See Thomas A. Langford, "Is There Such A Thing As Wesleyan Theology?" *Epworth Review* (May 1988):67-71.

2. Quoted in Nicholas Lash, *Easter in Ordinary* (Charlottesville: University Press of Virginia, 1988), p. 10.

3. See Alasdair MacIntyre, *Whose Justice? Which Rationality?* (Notre Dame: University of Notre Dame, 1988) for a sustained argument about tradition-shaped rationality.

4. For a suggestive effort at clarification of a use of the quadrilateral, see Frederick Herzog, *God Walk* (Maryknoll, NY: Orbis, 1988), pp. 29-33.

5. "The Recovery of Practical Philosophy," *The American Scholar* (Summer, 1988):338.

INDEX

LaVergne, TN USA
01 September 2009
156546LV00003B/58/A

Made in the USA
Lexington, KY
28 November 2009